Challenges in Health and Development

Sandy A. Johnson

Challenges in Health and Development

From Global to Community Perspectives

Second Edition

Springer

Sandy A. Johnson
Josef Korbel School of International Studies
University of Denver
Denver, CO
USA

ISBN 978-3-319-85089-4 ISBN 978-3-319-53204-2 (eBook)
DOI 10.1007/978-3-319-53204-2

Printed on acid-free paper

This Springer imprint is published by Springer Nature
The registered company is Springer International Publishing AG
The registered company address is: Gewerbestrasse 11, 6330 Cham, Switzerland

This book is dedicated to the community-based health and development workers who believe in positive change, and to my students for their enthusiasm and insight. Continue using your power for good!

Preface

A friend and development practitioner once told me that development is a messy business. It lacks a clear beginning and a clear ending, it often entails unforeseen consequences, and it cannot happen in isolation—multiple people and sectors must be involved to establish the conditions for 'development' to occur. My own experience is more closely tied to community health, where I have seen that one cannot hope to address 'health' without considering livelihoods, conditions within the physical and social environment, and the constraints and opportunities that come with economic development and national policy. Creating the conditions to allow people to live a healthful and content life is also a messy business. I have observed that those who work in economic develoment and those who work in public health often work as though their project occurs in a space devoid of history, culture, or the influence of institutions or policies outside of their particular sphere. Although I believe that such tunnel vision often comes out of necessity, it does not honor the intricacies of the health-development web.

During the past 20 years, international rhetoric began to acknowledge the cyclical interaction of education, health, economic growth, political harmony, and well-being. Recent endeavors such as the Millennium Development Villages give hope that the health and development sectors are becoming more cohesive and adopting holistic, sustainable methods to realize human development. In terms of programming, however, much has yet to change in order to employ a well-rounded approach to human development. Many programs continue to treat health and economic development as separate and somewhat unequal enterprises. The main purpose of this book, therefore, is to discuss how health and development, by various definitions, interact with each other across local, national, and global scales.

This book has three specific learning objectives. The first is to introduce the reader to the idea that there is not one single operational definition of health or of development. The diverse actors who engage in development and/or health programming rarely operate from the same definition. Because of this, they often seek very distinct outcomes, and yet, these outcomes are homogenized under a single, titular goal of 'health' or 'development.' By acknowledging that there are different definitions, one can better understand that there are diverse program choices to make and that there is a multiplicity of outcomes by which to gauge whether or not a program is successful and development is being achieved. In this book, I adopt the position that there is not a single, correct definition, nor can there be given the diversity of cultures, needs, and desires found on a planet of seven billion people. Rather, I look at several of the more common definitions of and approaches to health and development as utilized by the World Health Organization and the World Bank, and attempt to show how the operational definition influences programming efforts by these two agencies. This informs the content of Chaps. 1 and 2. I selected these two institutions because they are recognized as global authorities in health and in development, but they are not the only actors engaged in these fields. A more comprehensive exploration of global actors is well beyond the scope of my abilities to discuss. Further, because my goal herein is to explore how actors and policies interact at global, national, and local levels, I provide only a general summary of these two institutions. There are many good sources that provide more in-depth analysis than do I.

The second goal of this book was to describe how actions that occur in different geographical scales and different institutional domains impact each other. Meso-, macro-, and micro-policy realms, and the impacts of the same, are inextricably linked. In Chap. 3, I look at how global political and economic forces interacted with domestic forces in Chile and Sri Lanka. Prior to the 1970s, both countries had adopted very different domestic policies in regard to social welfare and economic development, and yet by the 1970s, both states were engaged in dramatic policy restructuring in response to domestic and international pressures. The changes in national policy, in turn, impacted local options and outcomes vis-à-vis health and material wealth. I use these examples to show that macro-level policy change affects community-level change, and I ask how much of an impact locally initiated programs can have on national goals and outcomes.

In fields such as development and health, fields that are driven by technocrats and experts, often the expertise of local community and individuals, is overlooked or devalued, and cultural differences are ignored. In Chap. 4, I use examples of community-based health care and micro-enterprise from South Africa and Bangladesh to examine the successes and failures of locally-based innovations and their interactions with national programs and priorities. Even though the trickle-down effects of national policy are frequently more forceful than locally initiated change, the smaller scale enterprises can resonate across the national landscape. This chapter concludes by exploring the Millennium Development Villages— a pilot program that incorporated economic *and* health interventions tailored to local context.

Failed states and countries emerging from conflict are especially challenging contexts for improving human health and development. The political and fiscal situation is such that actors who operate on a more local basis are best able to deliver necessary goods and services but are often resource-poor. In Chap. 5, I look at the difficulties and opportunities of harnessing small-scale operations to realize national gains in failed and conflict-ridden countries using case studies from Haiti and Rwanda. I also examine how state fragility propagates itself and how it contributed to the Ebola epidemic in West Africa.

The final goal of this book is to illustrate how the public and private sectors need each other. Examples from Chaps. 2–5 show how intergovernmental organizations and state institutions work with non-governmental actors. Chapter 6 looks specifically at public–private partnerships that formed to address global healthcare gaps. The goal of Chap 7 is for readers to understand that geopolitical conditions in the twenty-first century necessitate public and private sectors working together. Although these institutions may not have the same explicit goal, both public and private agents stand to gain through strategic alliances and methodological innovation.

In closing, this book is meant to introduce the reader to the interactions that occur across health and development, and across different operational institutions and scales. I hope that the case studies in each chapter help to solidify the more conceptual discussion that occurs through most of Chap. 1, and at the beginning of each chapter. I hope, too, that the reader gains some appreciation for the diversity found in the fields of health and development, and uses this book as a beginning rather than an end to her or his own exploration of the topics.

Denver, CO, USA Sandy A. Johnson

Acknowledgements

A book is never the work of one person. It is the work of the people who gave generously of their time to share thoughts and data. It is a product of the colleagues who agreed to answer one more question, or proof a chapter one more time. It is the product of the friends who gave mental, emotional, and nutritional support, and understood when I turned down a movie in order to write.

Rebecca Roth is quite possibly the best research assistant on the planet. Without her research acumen, critical review, and ability to read my mind, I doubt that I would have been able to finish this book. Andrew Wood picked up where Rebecca left off and provided research and insight that made the second edition of this book possible. Kwame Wireru provided a second set of eyes to review and proof. Della Williams and Susanna Park also helped proof. It is good to see the future of global health is in your hands!

The entire staff of the Office of Academic and Student Affairs deserves thanks for their professionalism, support, and for giving me the space I needed to complete this revision. Deana, Kendra, Frank, Tara and Debbie—you are the best!

Thanks go to Stanley Samarasinghe, friend and mentor, who continues to challenge and inspire. Thanks also to Randall Kuhn for his critical insight, humor, and tremendous knowledge of health. Harald kept me sane when I had too many projects to manage and provided a sounding board for my ideas. Shaki patiently sat on my shoulder during writing and revision.

My research in Sri Lanka would not have been possible without many people, most especially Dr. Samarasinghe. Global Vision—Centre for Knowledge Advancement, and the International Centre for Ethnic Studies were both kind enough to host me on separate trips. The Sri Lankan Ministry of Healthcare and Nutrition granted generous access to data and personnel whose assistance informed much of the work in Chap. 3. Shirley, Ananda, Sumida, and Nilam all proved to be knowledgeable and kind hosts. Thanks also to the front line community health and development workers who shared their experience working in the context of conflict, post-conflict, and disaster recovery. I hope this book does all of these people justice, but I assume full responsibility for any errors.

The WHO, World Bank, UN, and UNDP continue to provide rich, publicly accessible repositories of data online. These organizations espouse the important ideal that knowledge and data should be freely accessible. Without these databases, those of us who work in health or development would not be able to do research.

My sincere gratitude also goes to the University of Denver Faculty Research Fund, without which the research trip for the first edition of this book would not have been possible.

Contents

Abbreviations

AAI	Accelerating Access Initiative
ACT	Artemisinin Combination Therapy
AIDS	Acquired Immune Deficiency Syndrome
AMFm	Affordable Medicines Facility—Malaria
ART	Antiretroviral therapy
BoP	Balance of payments
CAB	Current account balance
CBPR	Community-based participatory research
CMH	Commission on Macroeconomics and Health
COPH	Community-oriented Primary Health care
DALY	Disability-Adjusted Life Year
DRC	Democratic Republic of Congo
DRP	Diagnostic-related payment
EPI	Expanded Program on Immunization
EVD	Ebola Virus Disease
FDI	Foreign direct investment
FONASA	*Fondo Nacional de Salud*
FSLN	Sandinista National Liberation Front
GAVI	Global Alliance for Vaccines and Immunization
GDP	Gross Domestic Product
GK	Gonoshasthaya Kendra
Global Compact	United Nations Global Compact
Global Fund	Global Fund to Fight AIDS, Tuberculosis, and Malaria
GNI	Gross National Income
GNP	Gross National Product
GoR	Government of Rwanda
GoSL	Government of Sri Lanka
GPPPs	Global Public–Private Partnerships
HDI	Human Development Index
HIPC	Highly indebted poor countries

HIV	Human immunodeficiency virus
IDP	Internally Displaced Person
IFIs	International finance institutions
IHR	International Health Regulations
ILO	International Labor Organization
IMR	Infant mortality rate
INGO	International Non-governmental organization
IOs	International Organizations
IRDB *see World Bank*	International Bank for Reconstruction and Development
ISAPRES	*Institutos de Salud Provisional*
ISI	Import Substitution and Industrialization
LNHO	League of Nations Health Organization
MCH	Maternal and child health
MDGs	Millennium Development Goals
MDV	Millennium Development Village
MFI	Microfinance institutions
MMR	Maternal Mortality Ratio
MoH	Ministry of Health
NAFTA	North American Free Trade Agreement
NGO	Non-governmental Organization
NIEO	New International Economic Order
OIHP	Office International d'Hygiéne Publique
PIH	Partners in Health
Plan AUGE	*Plan de Acceso Universal con Grantí Explícitas*
SAPs	Structural adjustment programs
SARS	Severe Acute Respiratory Syndrome
SDGs	Sustainable Development Goals
SERMENA	*Servicio Médico Nacional de Empleados*
SNS	*Servicio Nacional de Salud*
SNSS	*Sistema Nacional de Servicios de Salud*
SSA	sub-Saharan Africa
STIs	Sexually transmitted infections
TFR	Total fertility rate
TRIPS	Trade-Related Aspects of Intellectual Property Rights
UN	United Nations
UNAIDS	Joint United Nations Program on HIV/AIDS
UNDP	United Nations Development Program
UNFPA	United Nations Population Fund
UNGASS	United Nations General Assembly Special Session
UNHCR	United Nations High Commission on Refugees
UNICEF	United Nations Children's Fund
US	United States
USSR	Union of Soviet Socialist Republics
WDI	World Development Indicators

WHO	World Health Organization
WTO	World Trade Organization
ZL	Zanmi Lasante

Chapter 1
Two Hundred Years of Change in Health and Development

Abstract Health and development have a symbiotic relationship that impacts human potential as well as community and national capabilities. Although the relationship between health and development has been discussed for centuries, there is no concrete agreement as to which deserves primacy as a key to improving well-being. A healthy population can contribute to economic growth, and economic growth provides financial resources that can, in turn, be invested in inputs to health and overall well-being. The improvement in the wealth and health of much of the world's population that occurred from the 18th to the 21st century serves as an example of the interaction between the health of a population, the welfare of a state, and overall well-being. Parts of the Americas, Australia, Europe and China realized large improvements in well-being but regions such as Africa and South East Asia lagged behind. Although various theories attempt to explain the outcomes, no single theory has been able to fully explain both the improvement and the divergence. Rather, the theories offer different perspectives in terms of the impact and interaction of the growth in national wealth and human health, and describe how geographic location and political institutions inform national needs and capabilities. These, in turn, inform policy options that direct the development trajectory. This chapter examines the theoretical and empirical roots of the health and development paradigm, and introduces standard measurements used to gauge change in health and development outcomes.

The story of health and development is one of constant change that includes increased global wealth, increased economic activity and exchanges, substantial gains in life expectancy, eradication of diseases once considered intractable, and attendant gains in access to material wealth for many around the world. At the same time, old threats to health and well-being have been replaced by new ones, such as unsustainable national debt, mitigation of and adaptation to climate change, and the emergence of cancer, heart disease, and HIV as major health concerns. Other threats are on-going, such as ensuring basic needs are met, providing for adequate levels of nutrition, controlling diarrheal disease and the spread of tuberculosis, and prioritizing competing needs of human welfare and economic growth in an environment

S.A. Johnson, *Challenges in Health and Development*,
DOI 10.1007/978-3-319-53204-2_1

of finite resources. It is in the context of constant change in the status of health and global development, however, that a consistent pattern begins to emerge. It is a pattern showing that human health and development are intertwined.

As we begin our exploration of health and development, we may ask, "What is health?" "What is development?" There is no single definition of each term. One of the intents of this book is to show the differences and commonalities in how institutions operationalize health and development. But we do need a common base from which to start this exploration. With that in mind, we will define health as the physical well-being of populations and the individuals of which populations are made. We will soon learn that other definitions of health are more expansive and holistic, but all share the common concern with the physical state. Development entails the accumulation of wealth and growth of income at the population level, be it local or national. We will look at how the increase of national wealth may impact household or community wealth. Again, this is a narrow but pervasive definition. Ensuing chapters will introduce you to the broader notion of sustainable human development which entails and expands upon this idea of economic development.

If one accepts the idea that health and development are intertwined, then a central concern for those who work in health or development is how to prioritize policies and programs. If the ultimate goal is to increase the well-being of a people, a nation or a planet, how does one work towards such a goal? Should investment in development, that is economic growth, take precedence, or should resources be focused on the provision of health care? At the macro or state level, should the top priority be with state security, that is ensuring the preservation of state institutions and political power, or should there be greater concern with the welfare of the individuals who make up the constituents of state, that is to say with human security? Some argue that the need for economic development must be prioritized above human security because only economic prosperity can provide the money necessary to pay for the instrumental inputs to human health and build capabilities to improve human well-being. Further, economic growth ensures a nation's ability to pay for institutions and the operations of the state, including providing security for the citizens of the state. Others argue that health is a basic need which demands primacy in policy and action. Without a healthy workforce, there is no industry or economic growth. Without people, there are neither agents of state security nor stakeholders nor beneficiaries of state wealth.

1.1 Industrial Expansion, Globalization and Population Health—the Cases of England and Panama

Perspectives on the primacy of health versus development shift back and forth. Much of the dialogue is rooted in studies of changes in economics and population health associated with the Industrial Revolution (Brunton 2004a; Kunitz 2007; McKeown 1976). In the early years of industrialization, Western powers such as

England and the United States placed a premium on economic growth with concern for health growing out of necessity as the environmental and human tolls of the revolution became known (Brunton 2004b; Jacyna 2004). The result was that industry grew as did national wealth and private wealth. Dehumanizing and unsafe conditions for industrial workers, increased social and economic inequality, social isolation and anomie, and pollution were seen as negative outcomes of economic growth associated with the revolution. Public action was viewed as necessary to remedy these evils, and a wave of social consciousness and campaigns for public reform began in European nations and the United States (Brunton 2004b; Kunitz 2007; McKeown 1976). These reforms targeted environmental and human health, and also targeted workplace regulations. The increased public and private wealth that resulted from the revolution meant that financial resources were available to meet the public demand for change by increasing public goods and implementing new social programs to reduce the negative costs of industrialization. But the emphasis on what public action and policy should be adopted, and agreement as to whether or not any such programs were needed to redress social ills were by no means universal. Some nation-states, like England, placed economic development at the fore of policy focus, whereas others heavily invested in population health. Countries such as Germany and Sweden advanced social welfare programs in the early 1800s/early stages of industrialization, suggesting that they placed a high priority on having a healthy population as a critical aspect of economic growth (Kunitz 2007).

While the Industrial Revolution necessitated urban and workplace health reforms, the idea of creating and maintaining an empire also fueled global investment in health as an offshoot of economic growth (Comaroff 1993; Worboys 2004). During this time period, Western nations were actively colonizing other parts of the world in order to increase their economic and political power. Health was a necessary investment for colonization. After all, empires could not be built upon the back of dead labor. The colonial foothold could only be maintained so long as there were troops to enforce the rule of law, colonizers to populate the area, and an adequately healthy workforce to ensure the function of the colonial administration and its economic activities. The occupying forces had to contend not only with known diseases which they carried with them, but also with new diseases and the problems of alien ecosystems to which the colonizers had no previous exposure. Western nations also confronted tropical diseases in their home territories as infectious diseases such as yellow fever were introduced from distant lands into Europe and North America via migration and trade (Warren 1951). Public and private investment in medical research to understand and control these diseases, particularly those endemic to the tropical empire, came out of necessity and self interest, but ultimately proved beneficial to large populations.

Progress in understanding the causes of and appropriate interventions for infectious diseases during the 19th and 20th centuries often occurred in health posts located in the colonized world. In the 1800s, little was known as to the origins and causes of diseases that today are well understood.[1] For example, the transmission route between mosquitoes and humans, common to numerous illnesses, was a mystery until 1878 when Patrick Manson, a British doctor working in China, demonstrated that mosquitoes transmit filariasis to humans (Gilles and Warrell 1993). Carlos Finlay, a Cuban physician, built upon Manson's work and, in 1881, posited that mosquitoes were responsible for yellow fever transmission (Delaporte 1991). Around the same time, the United States sent a U.S. Army delegation, known as the Yellow Fever Commission, to Cuba. The Commission's primary objective was, "To ascertain the actual sanitary condition of the principal ports in Cuba … and more especially as to what can and should be done to prevent the introduction of the cause of yellow fever into the shipping of these ports." (Chaillé and Sternberg 1879) American physician Walter Reed went to Cuba in 1900 to work with the commission. Building on the work of the Cuban-based researchers, in 1901, the U.S. military undertook wetlands drainage and mosquito eradication in and around Havana in order to eliminate yellow fever. The effort was a success (Warren 1951). Although much about malaria remained unknown, the general in charge of the Havana yellow fever eradication effort, Gen. William Gorgas, noted that malaria decreased following the yellow fever campaign (Warren 1951). This proved to be an important lesson that Gen. Gorgas would carry with him to Panama and employ during the construction of the Panama Canal.

The construction of the Panama Canal successfully merged strategic political, military, economic, and health interests. The opening of an intercontinental canal in the Americas held tremendous implications for regional and global economic and political authority. The isthmus in Panama, identified as the site for this endeavor, presented climatic and geographic advantages over other locations. Unlike previous French-led efforts that focused on a sea level canal, the U.S. effort opted to harness changes in elevation to move waters through a system of locks. The tropical climate and evapotranspiration cycle ensured a renewable water source to recharge the canal flow. Unfortunately, the same tropical climate that promised sustainable water resources also harbored the threat of disease. Malaria and yellow fever were rampant in the area. These diseases killed upward of 22,000 workers in the late 1800s during the failed French effort to construct a Panamanian Canal (Avery and Haskins 1913).

The Americans began construction of the Canal in 1904, determined to achieve success where the French had failed. An important difference in the U.S. plan was the role of health and hygiene. Several project leaders, including John Frank Stevens, Dr. Walter Reed and Gen. William Gorgas, determined that investment in health was critical to successful completion and operation of the Canal (Warren 1951). They ensured that adequate and sanitary housing for the workers was

[1]European nations and the United States are the subject of the discussion of colonization and Empire.

available in order to protect their health. Sanitation programs included monitoring of and efforts to decrease standing water around the worker camps. Where possible, wetlands and other water hazards were drained. Petroleum was also used as a larvicide on the water hazards. A program of health monitoring for fever, and isolation of sick individuals, helped curb the transmission of the mosquito-borne diseases (Warren 1951). The triumph of this health orientation was a decrease in yellow fever and malaria mortality in the Canal Zone, and the successful completion of the Canal in 1914. These sanitation practices were implemented elsewhere and contributed to a taming of yellow fever and malaria. The Canal Zone became operational, providing critical military and commercial transport between the Atlantic and Pacific Oceans, and an access point controlled by the United States. But yellow fever and malaria remained endemic in many areas around the world that continued to be vital to the economic interests of the U.S. and European powers.

The concern for yellow fever, malaria, and other tropical diseases hastened early public-private partnerships. By the completion of the Canal, yellow fever was designated a national priority (for the U.S.) and an international priority. The Rockefeller Foundation, a philanthropic organization created through the New York State legislature and endowed with US$100 million by John D. Rockefeller in 1913–1914, targeted yellow fever for eradiation (The Rockefeller Foundation 2010). It formed the International Health Commission to oversee its health program. In 1915, the International Health Commission adopted a resolution to target yellow fever for eradication because of the health and security threat it posed not only in the Panama Canal, but along the global shipping routes (Warren 1951). The first yellow fever vaccine was tested on humans in 1931.

The examples of the Industrial Revolution and construction of the Panama Canal highlight the point that the primacy of health or development in terms of programs and policy varies according to time, place, and goals. Changes in social welfare and well-being have been and will likely continue to be associated with changes in the economic status and capabilities of individuals and the broader social and physical environment in which they are placed. It is important to understand the possible routes of interaction between the two in order to better inform public and private choice. Such is the intent of this book, which will explore program approaches that alternately prioritize economic development and health. We will look at specific programs of development and health as implemented at global, national, and local scales, and attempt to understand how health programs impact economic development and how economic development impacts health. In order to do this, it will be helpful to understand the current status of global health and development and look at how they have changed in the 20th and early 21st centuries.

1.2 Comparative Measurement of Health and Development

Before we look at global changes in development and human well-being, it will be helpful to understand how different aspects of health and development are measured. If one looks at development databases such as the World Development Indicators published by the World Bank (http://databank.worldbank.org/ddp/home.do) or the Human Development statistics published by the United Nations Development Program (http://hdr.undp.org/en/statistics/), or the Global Health Observatory statistics maintained by the World Health Organization (http://www.who.int/gho/en/) it becomes clear that there are a multiplicity of views as to how best to measure progress in development and health, and therefore multiple measures exist for the purpose of international comparison. If one looks to the smaller geographic or institutional scales found in national or local assessments, the variety of data is even larger. Such diversity is useful when considering an in-depth analysis of a specific country or sectoral issue. The proliferation of indicators does have its downside. When sorting through the data and trying to determine which data are valid for specific questions, which data are comparable across diverse contexts, and whether or not common methodology was employed in data collection, the process of culling appropriate data can be extremely time consuming and datasets may prove to be unwieldy. However, the literature on comparative international development consistently focuses on a handful of indicators. The standard assessment outcomes employed by the World Bank, the United Nations Development Program (UNDP), the World Health Organization (WHO) and other global institutions are those which measure variations of Gross Domestic Product (GDP), literacy rates, average life expectancy, and infant mortality rates or use a composite indicator such as the Human Development Index (HDI).

GDP and related measures, including Gross National Product (GNP), Gross National Income (GNI), GDP growth rates and GDP per capita, show the size of the economy and approximate the wealth of a nation—wealth that may translate into public and private investment in inputs to well-being. GDP and GNP are often used interchangeable, although there are important differences between the two. GDP refers to the total market value of goods and services that are produced within the geographic boundaries of the nation during a specific time period, where as GNP includes the market value of all goods and services produced by residents of a country, even if they are living abroad. GDP/capita directly measures economic achievements while controlling for population size and is considered a proxy measure for the average citizen's access to wealth or resources with which to procure goods (that may be used in the creation of health). GNI is comparable to GNP. Where economic growth is viewed as the primary determinant of health, programs designed to grow national production and consumption are the desired tools for improving this notion of 'health'. A strong GDP or strong growth in GDP thus reflects a healthy nation.

Literacy rates measure social progress in building human capital and serve as a proxy for the average citizen's ability to process information. This reflects individual achievement, institutional achievements, as well as the creation, maintenance, and utilization of social and physical infrastructure such as public schools. Thus, the GDP-based indicators and literacy relate to a traditional view of development that focuses on economic forces, inputs and the goods which flow from such wealth.

Where health is viewed more as expanded capabilities and well-being, life expectancy and Infant Mortality Rate (IMR) and changes therein may be of greater concern. Changes in life expectancy are attributed to factors such as: improved ability to procure food which positively affects nutritional standards, improved sanitation, improved housing quality, improved health care access and innovations in medical technologies and techniques. Life expectancy represents an outcome which occurs over a life course and so is distinct in that it captures the idea of health as a process. But this measurement also gauges the trickle down impact of economic growth and social change which inform the various avenues to health as described above. Thus, one sees that at a macro level the indicators of a collective view of health relate directly and indirectly back to economic success. Infant mortality alone seems to be an outcome which reflects an immediate health concern. Environmental conditions and sanitation contribute to this outcome, as does the availability of clean health facilities and trained personnel. The Disability-Adjusted Life Year (DALY) attempts to quantify the overall burden of disease by assessing the years of healthy life lost due to premature (preventable) death and account for the loss of quality of life due to disability. This measurement combines mortality and morbidity.

The Human Development Index(HDI) isa composite indicator in that it combines data on three aspects of life—ability to have a decent quality of life, longevity, and knowledge. GDP per capita serves as a proxy for standard of living, longevity is measured by life expectancy, and knowledge is measured by literacy and gross school enrollment (United Nations Development Programme 2009b). The HDI is expressed on a scale of '0' to '1' with numbers near 0 indicating low levels of human development and numbers that approach 1 indicating high levels. As of 2014, Norway had the highest level of human development, as indicated by the HDI, with a score of 0.944 (United Nations Development Programme 2015). Now that we know some useful measures for health and development, we can explore global change in the 20th century and beyond.

1.3 A Century's Worth of Global Change in Development and Health

The world has changed in terms of life, death, and wealth.

In some parts of the world, the average life expectancy increased by greater than 50% in little more than a century whereas national wealth has expanded upwards of 300%! For example, England's GDP per capita rose by 298% (at constant market

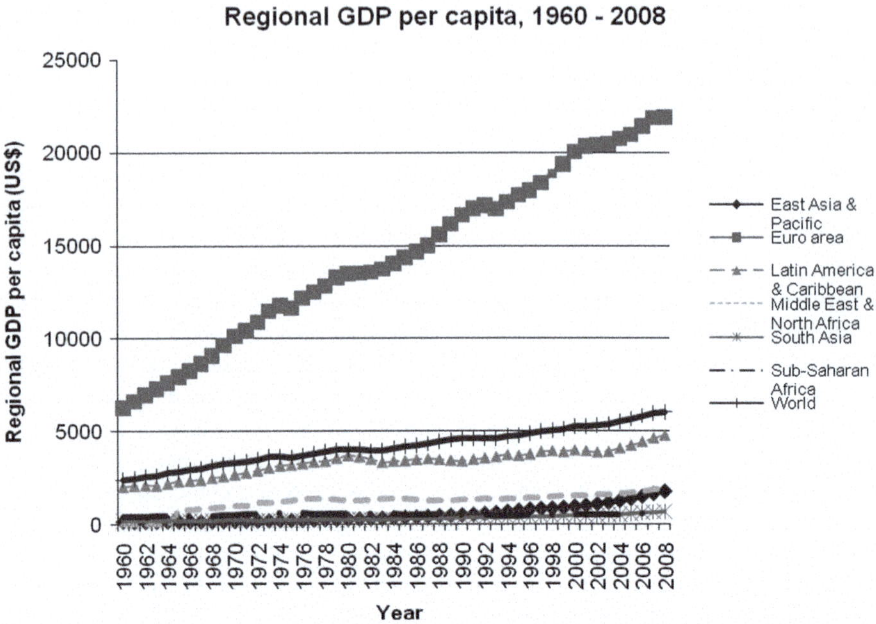

Fig. 1.1 Change in regional GDP/capita from 1960 to 2008. *Data Source* World Bank (2009)

prices) from 1900 to 1999 (Hicks and Allen 1999). The growth was not always steady. It fell approximately 24% between 1918 and 1921, so much so that the 1926 GDP per capita was lower than that of 1906 (Hicks and Allen 1999). Overall, the global average increased from approximately US$2400 to a little more than US $6000 in constant value (World Bank 2009). But not all regions shared equally in this gain. Figure 1.1 shows change in regional GDP since 1960. GDP per capita in the European region exceed the global average, and has grown at a faster rate than the global mean (World Bank 2009). South Asia and Sub-Saharan Africa had GDP per capital levels lower than US$500 in the 1960s, and maintained comparatively low levels. At this time, South Asia averaged only $US186 per capita compared to Sub-Saharan Africa's US$437 (World Bank 2009). By 2008, the regional average for South Asia had risen to US$682, overtaking the GDP/capita of Sub-Saharan Africa which stood at US$619 (World Bank 2009). The growth was not constant. Annual GDP growth fluctuated year to year. Between 1960 and 2008, there were several distinct periods in which the economy had negative GDP growth rates.

Life expectancy also changed. By and large, the regions with the largest economies also experienced the greatest change in health. The United States saw a rise in average life expectancy at birth from 49 years in 1900–1902 to 78 years in 2005 (Arias 2007). Between 1850 and 2007, the life expectancy of select European nations nearly doubled (Fig. 1.2). These gains in Europe proved consistent through World War I. Note that France, England and Wales suffered losses in life expectancy during and following the war. France suffered another decline during the Second World War,

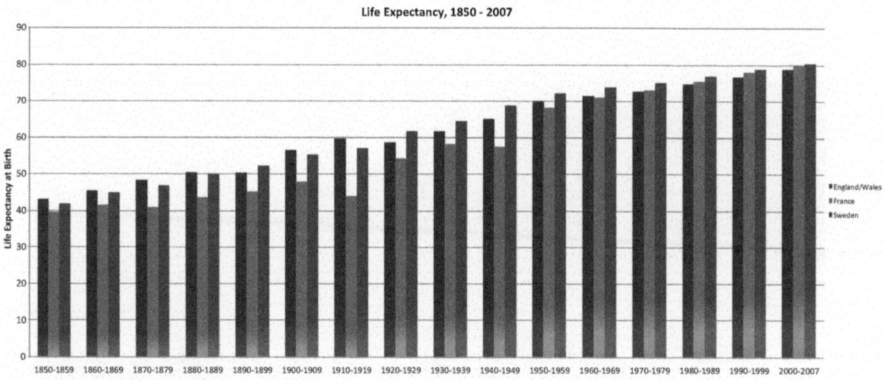

Fig. 1.2 Changes in life expectancy in select European countries, 1850–2007. Data for England/Wales includes entire United Kingdoms from 1920 forward. *Data Source* Human Mortality Database. University of California, Berkeley (USA), and Max Planck Institute for Demographic Research (Germany). Available at www.mortality.org or www.humanmortality.de (data downloaded on July 3, 2009)

proving that improvements in life expectancy can be won and lost. When life expectancy is broken down by sex (Table 1.1), further evidence of the fluidity is evident. The life expectancy for French males declined from 1910–1919, whereas females showed marginal gains. The weight of the loss of male life expectancy was strong enough to pull overall life expectancy down.[2] France recovered from these losses and today has one of the highest life expectancies in the world at 81 years (World Bank 2009). This illustrates the point that fluctuations in life expectancies, and other health indicators, may occur over short periods. Attention needs to be paid, and explanations sought, if variations are severe or enduring.

With average life expectancies in the 70s or higher, low infant mortality rates, and low levels of maternal deaths, Western nations are often used as a standard by which to gauge overall health achievement. Such goal-setting may be useful as the gains in the West were strong, but these occurred over the course of a century or more; a number of middle and low income nations made remarkable gains in terms of life expectancy over a shorter period of time. For example, China's crude death rate dropped from 25.1 per 1000 from 1950–1955 to 6.6 in 2000–2005 (World Bank 2009). The average life expectancy increased from 36 years in 1960 to 73 years in 2007 (World Bank 2009). Argentina, Chile, Sri Lanka, Costa Rica and Cuba are but a few of the other states that realized similar progress.

In other regions of the world, such as Africa, health gains were slower over the last century. The average life expectancy in Africa increased from 39 years in 1950–1955 to 53 years in 2005 (Fig. 1.3) and death rates decreased at a much

[2]Table 1.1 also shows a decrease in both female and male life expectancy in England and Wales from the period of 1920–1929 but this may be an artifice of combining two data sources. The data for 1920 forward includes all of the United Kingdom.

Table 1.1 Life Expectancy by sex, 1850–2007

	England/Wales		France		Sweden	
	Female	Male	Female	Male	Female	Male
1850–1859	44.85	43.06	40.43	38.83	43.91	39.83
1860–1869	47.39	45.39	42.27	40.86	46.61	42.93
1870–1879	50.91	48.4	42.33	39.56	48.38	44.96
1880–1889	54.09	50.41	44.81	42.29	51.24	48.32
1890–1899	55.56	50.36	46.72	43.61	53.53	50.91
1900–1909	60.15	56.63	49.83	46.16	56.52	54.05
1910–1919	63.44	59.77	51.53	37.94	58.32	55.59
1920–1929	60.52	56.63	56.41	52.15	62.8	60.57
1930–1939	63.57	59.47	60.89	55.35	65.7	63.39
1940–1949	67.55	62.39	62	53.38	70.15	67.51
1950–1959	72.51	67.16	71.16	64.97	73.85	70.73
1960–1969	74.33	68.24	74.59	67.4	75.95	71.64
1970–1979	75.58	69.36	76.89	69.03	77.97	72.22
1980–1989	77.43	71.58	79.45	71.25	79.74	73.76
1990–1999	79.18	73.92	81.81	73.78	81.23	75.98
2000–2007	80.8	76.3	83.35	76.16	82.48	78.12

Data for England/Wales includes entire United Kingdom from 1920 forward

Data source Human Mortality Database. University of California, Berkeley (USA), and Max Planck Institute for Demographic Research (Germany). Available at www.mortality.org or www.humanmortality.de (data downloaded on July 3, 2009)

slower rate than in other regions of the world. Sub-Saharan Africa (SSA) currently has the highest infant mortality rates, the highest crude death rates, and the highest levels of maternal deaths. Life expectancy in Sub-Saharan Africa increased by only 10 years during the same time period in which China gained 37 years (World Bank 2009). Some Sub-Saharan African states experienced a decrease in life expectancy, a phenomenon attributed to high HIV/AIDS prevalence, and to conflict. Figure 1.4 shows the variation of life expectancy in three such nations. Uganda and Sierra Leone experience a decline during the 1990s, but then resumed small but upward gains in life expectancy. Malawi experienced a decline until 2005.

Figure 1.3 shows that the rate of improvement in population health varied around the world, but both Europe and North America were early outliers with higher life expectancies and lower death rates than other regions by the 1950s. These regions proved to be early innovators in terms of experiencing changes in both human health and development.

The general trends in longevity provide but a small part of the picture of population health. How long people live, what makes them sick, when and how they die can change over time, and these changes can occur with social and economic change. If we consider global population dynamics since the 1800s, several major trends become apparent. First, the average income increased. Second, the average

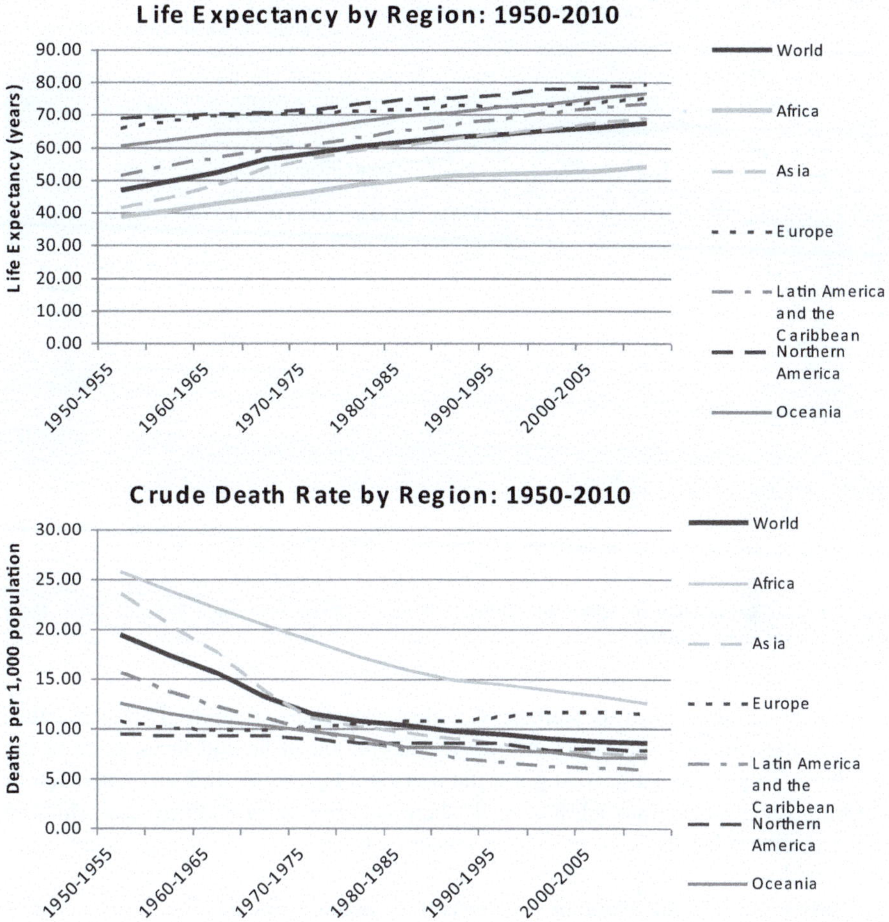

Fig. 1.3 Regional life expectancy and crude death rates, 1950–2010. *Data source* United Nations (2009)

mortality rate decreased. Third, the average life expectancy rose. Looking at it another way, the average age of death changed. Fourth, the number of infants who survive into childhood also rose. Two models explain how these trends interact, and how they shape and are shaped by societal forces. These are the **demographic transition model** and the **epidemiological transition model**.

The demographic transition model attempts to explain how the average age of death and average life expectancy impact each other, impact population growth, and interact with the socioeconomic structure of society. According to this model, there are four stages through which societies can transition. The first stage is one in which there are high death rates and high birth rates. Life expectancy is low and death rates for infants and children are high. As a result, the **total fertility rate (TFR)**, or

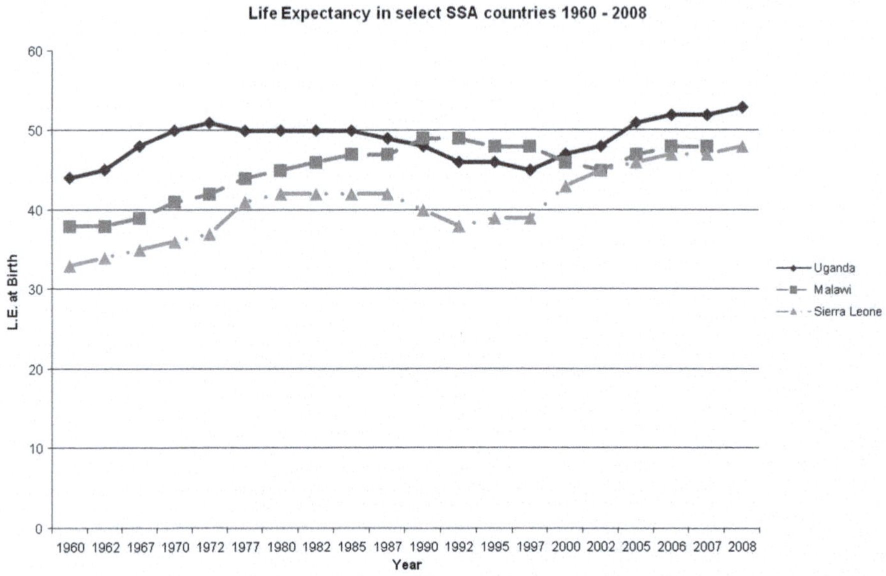

Fig. 1.4 Life expectancy in select Sub-Saharan African nations between 1960 and 2008. *Data source* World Bank (2009)

number of children born to women of child bearing age, is high. This is because families theoretically seek to maximize the likelihood of having the service of the children—to provide labor to support the household activities and survival, such as working on a farm—into adulthood. If there is a higher probability that children will die, then a family is more likely to have more children. This stage is generally associated with agrarian societies.

During the second stage of the transition, death rates decline. This stage is generally associated with urbanization. In theory, with urbanization come higher concentrations of population and greater technological efficiency. Such efficiency allows for an increase in production of goods to fulfill basic needs, such as increased food production. This change creates a surplus of food and an attendant decline in the need for agriculturalists. This in turn allows for greater specialization in skills further inspiring innovation that impacts income, living standards, medical care, diffusion of knowledge and changing social norms. The creation of surplus food means that there is a safety net against disaster. All of these factors contribute to a decrease in the overall number of deaths and increasing life expectancy. Because people are dying less frequently, but high birth rates continue, this stage is associated with population growth.

The decreasing death rate has a domino effect on birth rates. With greater likelihood of survival, families no longer need to have as many children to ensure that an appropriate number survive into adulthood. As a result, the third stage of the demographic transition is marked by low death rates, declining birth rates and increased life expectancy. Societal changes, including changes in access to education, jobs, contraception and female empowerment contribute to stage three. Population growth begins to level out and may decline. This stage is typically associated with fully urbanized, 'modern' societies, although there are exceptions to this rule. China, for example, reached a stage of low birth- and death-rates, and low natural growth during a period of rapid, but not full, urbanization. It reached a TFR of 2.01 in 1990–1995 and is now considered to be in Stage IV of the transition (United Nations 2009). China's one-child law contributed to this change by regulating behavioral change which may otherwise have taken several generations to impact. Restrictions on migration to urban centers also impacted urbanization and, potentially, the demographic transition.

The fourth stage entails low birth rates, low death rates and replacement level fertility rates. A country is considered to be at stage four if its total fertility rate is less than 2.1, which is considered replacement level in that enough males and females are born to perpetuate but not increase the population. Countries such as the United States (2.04 TFR), Chile (2.0 TFR) and Sri Lanka (2.33 TFR) are examples of countries in stage four (United Nations 2009). The demographic transition model allows for a theoretical state of population stability with zero growth, but in reality presents a somewhat less pristine picture. In some countries, fertility rates are below replacement level and so the population is declining. Italy (TFR 1.26 and population growth 0.53) and Japan (TFR 1.30, population growth 0.12) are two such examples (United Nations 2009). This situation has led for some to argue that the demographic transition model requires a fifth stage, that of shrinking population. Others discuss the need to revise the model to account for migration.

The epidemiological transition model is concerned with what causes people to die and how this influences life expectancy and population structures. The first stage of the epidemiological transition denotes a society in which infectious disease causes the majority of deaths. Life expectancy is low and there are many young people. Zimbabwe is an example of a country in the first stage of the epidemiological transition. Eighty-five percent of the deaths in Zimbabwe are caused by communicable disease, and average life expectancy is 45 (World Health Organization 2010c). The second stage denotes a transition from infectious to chronic disease. Because infectious disease persists, there is a dual burden of disease. Life expectancies are increasing and more people are living into the middle ages. The Philippines may be an example of a stage two country as 44% of its deaths are due to communicable disease, and life expectancy is 71 (World Health Organization 2010a). In the final stage of the transition, chronic disease and diseases of aging are the main causes of death. Life expectancy is high and many people are middle aged or elderly. Table 1.2 shows the main causes of death in the United States in 1910 and in 2005. You can see that infectious disease dominated the top causes of death in 1910. By 2005, pneumonia and influenza remain problematic but otherwise chronic disease is of greater concern than communicable disease. These data show that that the U.S. is currently in the third stage of the epidemiological transition. England and Wales present another example of change. In 1880, infectious disease caused 33% of the deaths in England and Wales, but

Table 1.2 Primary causes of death in the U.S. in 1910 and 2005

Rank	1910	2005
1	Tuberculosis	Heart disease
2	Heart disease	Malignant neoplasm
3	Diarrhea and enteritis	Cerebrovascular disease
4	Pneumonia	Chronic lower respiratory disease
5	Nephritis and bright's disease	Unintentional injuries
6	Accidental death	Diabetes mellitus
7	Cancer	Alzheimer's disease
8	Cerebral hemorrhage, apoplexy	Influenza and pneumonia
9	Congenital debility, icterus, sclerema	Nephritis, nephrotic syndrome and nephrosis
10	Typhoid	Septicemia

Data sources 2005 data National Center for Health Statistics (2007). *Health, United States, 2007 with chartbook on trends for health in the Americas*. Hyattsville (Maryland): National Center for Health Statistics. page 186
1910 data from Dept of Commerce and Labor, Bureau of the Census. 1912. *Mortality Statistics: 1910*. Washington DC: Government Printing Office

only 17% of the deaths in 1997 (Hicks and Allen 1999). Newly emerging infections such as HIV/AIDS and re-emerging threats such as tuberculosis and malaria have impacted the causes of death around the world. They demonstrate that communicable disease will likely always present a health concern. When determining what stage of the epidemiological transition any given society is in, one must consider not the complete absence of infectious disease but rather its relative contribution to mortality.

1.4 What Accounts for the Difference in Regional Change?

Since the 19th century, many parts of the world have transitioned from infectious disease to chronic disease as the major health concern, while other areas remain entrenched in the early stages of the epidemiological transition, with communicable disease accounting for the bulk of mortality and morbidity. Still other areas face the challenge of taming infectious disease while also addressing the growing demand of health care for non-communicable disease. By and large, however, people have never lived so long nor have so many lived so well. Various theories explain why and how longevity and quality of life have improved. Some theories look at socio-economic determinants of health and explain the health transformation in terms of improvements in living standards, whereas others look to technological innovation, and revolutionary thought. Another cluster of theories explains health gains in terms of improved access to care, and scientific and medical innovations. These competing theories create a lively debate and provide policy-makers with alternative tools and routes to consider in an effort to impact human development. A discussion of the various factors contributing to improved well-being over the last century follows.

1.4.1 Standard of Living

The standard of living theory argues that an increase in access to material goods improves quality of life and health outcomes. Economic, social and technological change over the last century in many parts of the world has increased income and access to material goods. Rising national income was central to improved living conditions in that increases in national income provided resources for national investment in social services such as public health and education and other goods (Kunitz 2007). Rising national income was tied to increased industrial activity which translated into increased employment (Kunitz 2007; McKeown 1976). Individuals had job opportunities and the ability to earn money thereby raising their household incomes. This furthered opportunities to invest in the family and in future generations through means such as education.

Improved nutrition, another aspect of improved standard of living, has long been recommended for good health. The ancient Greeks, for instance, recommended milk and exercise as the means to live a healthy life (Thomas 1999). Increased agricultural production in Britain during the 17th and 18th centuries created a surplus of food and labor, which were both necessary for the industrial revolution. McKeown (1976) argued that improved access to nutrition was possible because of the agricultural and industrial revolutions, and that improved nutritional standards, resulting from economic growth, fueled England's health and demographic transition from the late 1700s. Another agricultural revolution, the Green Revolution, occurred in the latter part of the 20th century. The Green Revolution introduced high yield crops and new farming techniques to developing countries. These innovations were successful in creating food surplus in many nations and demonstrated that now, as before, nutrition is a component of population health and development. These examples demonstrate that neither income, nor nutrition, nor any single factor fully account for changes in population health. Rather, there is a cyclical relationship between health and the inputs to improved living standards.

1.4.2 Public Investment, Health Infrastructure, and Public Health Campaigns

Another explanation for the improvement in population health holds that the creation of public health infrastructure and public health campaigns played an important role in controlling infectious disease and decreasing environmental risk. With growing populations and growing population density came an increased need to monitor population health and intervene when necessary. Public health crystallized during the industrial transformation. Its focus was on the health of communities rather than individuals, with particular import given to disease prevention, control of epidemics, and control of some endemic diseases. An **epidemic** can be an outbreak of a novel disease or can occur when the number of cases of a known disease exceeds the typical number experienced in that area or region. **Endemic** diseases are ones that persist in an ecosystem or population. Early public health action entailed assigning responsibility for monitoring health and enforcing public policy, procuring finances and personnel, allocating resources, establishing health priorities and developing strategies to address the main health concerns (Brunton 2004a, b; Kunitz 2007). The division of responsibility for public health varied across nations in the 19th and early 20th century. In Sweden and Germany, local governments assumed the bulk of responsibility for public health whereas in England and Wales the central government had more authority (Brunton 2004a; Kunitz 2007). Public health included controlling infectious diseases and providing for a safe and sanitary environment, although what constituted safe and sanitary changed over time and across cultures (Brunton 2004a). Industrialization added concern for pollution, working conditions and urban living conditions and cleanliness (Kunitz 2007).

Public investment in health and wellbeing increased as a result of economic growth and as a result of urbanization that was occurring in Western Europe during the Industrial Revolution. The promise of employment that new industry afforded brought waves of migrants from rural to urban centers. With increased population density came increased avenues for the spread of disease but also increased opportunities to stem disease through public investment in water, hygiene, sanitation, housing construction, and workplace standards (Brunton 2004b). Public health responsibilities evolved to address these issues as well as provide monitoring and surveillance. This investment not only benefited industry by providing healthy workers, but was justified in terms of public health and the economies of scale high population densities afforded (Brunton 2004b). Whereas it may not have been economically feasible to provide waste disposal for far-flung rural communities, it could be justified in urban centers and indeed, could even generate a profit (Brunton 2004b). Too, urbanization and economic growth brought specialization and resources for research and development in a myriad of fields.

Public health campaigns targeted specific diseases for prevention or control. The reasons for targeting specific diseases included social, economic, and military concerns (Worboys 2004). We have already discussed the sanitation and prevention campaigns for yellow fever associated with American expansionism and the construction of the Panama Canal. The control and eradication of smallpox is another, more recent example of a public health campaign success. This disease was pervasive around the world and killed as many as 30% of those infected (World Health Organization 2010b). Individual state efforts at control met with unequal levels of success. For example, at the turn of the 19th century, smallpox caused as much as 20% of the total deaths in England. A smallpox vaccine was introduced to England in 1798 but its availability and use were limited. Federal law made the vaccine mandatory in 1852, and rigorous enforcement of this law followed (Aiello et al. 2008a). Although smallpox prevalence decreased in England over time, it remained a global threat. In the early 1960s, smallpox still posed a threat to 60% of the global population (World Health Organization 2010b). The existence of this disease in other countries throughout the world meant that it could be re-introduced at any time. A coordinated global campaign to eradicate this disease was therefore undertaken in 1967 under the aegis of the WHO. The campaign was a success and smallpox was eradicated in 1980 (World Health Organization 2010b).

Other public health innovations included targeting specific populations, rather than diseases, for intervention. For example, many sanitary reforms in industrial England targeted the middle class because the poor were thought to be beyond sanitary and moral redemption. These campaigns achieved only a modicum of success because they failed to impact factors that contributed to disease spread, such as tight living quarters in slums and limited access to sanitary water sources. Disease control efforts therefore expanded to target the poor (Brunton 2004b). Today, health campaigns often target sub-populations, based on excess disease burden and vulnerability. Such targeting is considered an efficient and cost-effective public health strategy.

Another important innovation of the early 20th century was that of targeting diseases for which there is known treatment or known ways of prevention. This seems like common sense, but proved important in conserving finite resources for impact rather than prestige. An early example of this is seen in the hookworm campaigns of the 1920s. Although neither life-threatening nor considered to be of primary public health import, hookworm was debilitating. There existed a known cure and a known means of prevention, thereby making hookworm a viable target for elimination (Birn 2003). The hookworm campaign was not sexy, but it was impactful.

1.4.3 Medical Innovations

Medical innovation also proved important in changing the global health situation. Unlike public health, which targets populations and prevention, medicine is directed towards the individual and towards treating or curing a disease and minimizing the negative effects of ill health in the individual. Here, we refer to biomedical, allopathic medicine, or Western clinical medical practice. The so-called medical gaze is concerned with the individual and with the constituent parts of the individual—the organs, biological systems, cells, and microscopic organisms (Foucault 1994; 1997). This gaze relates to germ theory and clinical practice. Germ theory posited that a single, isolatable organism was responsible for a specific illness. Adherents of germ theory operationalized it by looking at and within the sick individual for the agent of illness. This divorced the individual from his/her physical and social environment as the gaze shifted internally from the whole being to body parts. Public health workers targeted interventions based on environmental conditions or vulnerable sub-populations; adherents of the biomedical model isolated and targeted at a somatic scale.

Clinical practice and germ theory revolutionized how we conceived of and treated disease, but also dehumanized the causes and experience of being ill, and obscured the impacts illness has on social networks outside of the patient. This gaze moved medicine from a stance of blaming supernatural forces, miasmas, and even immoral activity as creating illness to blaming micro-organisms. For example, during the Industrial Revolution the high number of cases of cholera, tuberculosis and other communicable diseases in urban slums was blamed on immoral lifestyles of men and women living together rather than on the social factors which forced overcrowding and deprived people of access to clean water and adequate housing (Brunton 2004b). Understanding that water-and air-borne bacteria caused these diseases allowed the medical community to develop new avenues of prevention and treatment which attack the agent and transmission cycles rather than attacking afflicted individuals. Medical practice lent itself to improvement in treatment technique as well as diagnoses which contributed to declining mortality. For example, in the late 1800s, even before the cause of tuberculosis was fully understood, clinicians found that by isolating patients with active TB, they could limit the spread of the disease (Thomas 1999).

Medical innovation added new weapons to combat disease and improve the quality of life. Wide-spread use of penicillin beginning in the 1940s precipitated a sharp decline in death rates, especially from diseases such as syphilis, pneumonia and staph infections (Aiello et al. 2008a). Vaccines against diseases such as pertussis (whooping cough), tetanus and diphtheria have proven effective in decreasing childhood mortality and lifetime disability.

1.4.4 Technological Innovation

Technological innovation was a driving force in public and private sanitation and in medical practice. Such innovation drew together new technologies and techniques to target priorities in population health. Public and private sanitation merged engineering advancements, new technologies and concerns with population health. Innovations ranged from simple to complex. When John Snow, one of the forefathers of epidemiology, identified sewage-polluted water as a source of the London cholera epidemic of 1854, local authorities posed a simple solution: remove the handle of the suspect wells. Of course, sustainable interventions were more systemic. In Snow's case, he found that several public water pumps drew water downriver from the Thames, a river polluted with open sewage from the expanding industrial center of London. Long-term improvements in sanitation meant altering how sewage was disposed of, and where and how water was obtained. In London, this entailed construction of a massive underground sewerage system to transport waste away from the population center (George 2006). It also included creating sanitation regulations, delineating institutional responsibility, and creating enforcement bodies. In 1866, England made local authorities responsible for sanitary regulation and enforcement (Aiello et al. 2008b). It may not be coincidental that in 1866, the year after sewer authorities were created and city draining began, a cholera epidemic ended. Of course, England was not alone in its sanitation improvements and codification of matters pertaining to air, water, garbage, waste and public health.

Other examples of technological innovation include water drainage and chlorination. Environmental engineering such as wetlands drainage removed mosquito-breeding areas and contributed to the decline of diseases such as yellow fever and malaria. The last yellow fever epidemic in the U.S. occurred in 1905. Broad-based water chlorination began in the U.S. in the early 1900s. It contributed to a drop in death rates from 600 per 100,000 at the turn of the century, to 400 per 100,000 by 1920 (Aiello et al. 2008a).

1.4.5 Behavior Change

Changing behaviors were also important to the health transition. During the 1800s, dysentery, typhoid and cholera were common causes of death. All were spread through unsanitary environmental conditions and fecal contamination of food and water. Typhus, spread by lice, was a prolific killer that gained strength through overcrowding and lack of household cleanliness. In military hospitals people were as likely to die from infection as from battle wounds. Prisons and workhouses became lodgings of collective suffering and disease. Improved personal cleanliness including use of soap, access to and use of laundry, improved sewage disposal, and the airing of surgical facilities and households all contributed to improved living and longevity (Aiello et al. 2008b). Florence Nightingale, a nurse famous for her care of wounded soldiers during the Crimean War, was one of the pioneers advocating improved sanitation and hygiene for better health on and off the battlefield. Hand washing and sterilization practices in surgery and in hospitals reduced nosocomial infections and improved the likelihood of survival (Aiello et al. 2008b). Improved personal hygiene practices were equally important in controlling infections (Aiello et al. 2008b). Personal hygiene included the aforementioned changes in hand washing, bathing, and laundry as well as changes in toilet habits and in child birth practices. Change had to occur at the individual level, but also at the societal level. For example, Aiello et al. (2008b) estimates that laundry costs prior to a public campaign to expand access to laundry facilities amounted to 1/6–1/3 of the weekly salary of an average worker, creating a clear disincentive for behavior change. Improving hygiene and sanitation practices entailed public reforms to make access to soap, clean water, and improved latrines affordable and available.

1.4.6 Access to Care

Improved access to care also contributed to improved health (Aiello et al. 2008a, b; Barry 2005; Foucault 1994; Thomas 1999). Increased access to care was made possible by revolutionary social thinking, by which provision of care to the poor became equally prioritized as provision of care to those who could pay, and by changes in how health care was financed. In the U.S. and much of Europe from the 1800s through the early 1900s, generally only those who could pay for health care received it. This meant that the middle and upper classes had access, but the poor did not. And yet, a number of transmissible diseases of concern for the broad public were concentrated among the poor. Advocates for public health argued that interventions needed to be directed to the poor as they, too, deserved improved health. Some doctors advocated for government provision of hospitalization and care for the poor who were afflicted with diseases such as tuberculosis; religious and charitable organizations also stepped up to provide care (Aiello et al. 2008b; Barry 2005; Brunton 2004b; Thomas 1999). By the 20th century, states began experimenting with social insurance and community insurance—schemes to distribute the cost burden for health care across a broader risk group (Brunton 2004b; Kunitz 2007; Thomas 1999). Access to care became defined not only by how the care would be paid for, but by where facilities were located and who could access them geographically and culturally.

1.4.7 Political Will

These numerous contributors to improved health would have come to naught had there been no avenue to communicate innovation, no willingness on the part of individuals to modify their own behavior, and no political will to invest in human well-being. Such will is difficult to quantify, but may prove to be one, if not the most, important factor contributing to improved health. As Dréze and Sen (1991) argue, political systems and political choice impact well-being. Their famous study on famine showed that it was not lack of food which caused widespread suffering and death, but distortions within the political economic institutions which created shortages. The creation of social welfare systems in Europe following WWI attests to the impact political will can have on creating access to health inputs including income and access to health care. Health achievements in the late 20th century by economically poor states such as Cuba, Costa Rica and Sri Lanka further attest to the import of political will. Think what would have happened in 1854 London had the authorities never intervened in the cholera epidemic. Would England have enjoyed its epidemiological and demographic transitions so early?

1.5 A Model for Exploring Health and Development

This discussion hints at the complexity of both health and development as well as the importance of cross-sectoral connection. One could argue that the economic growth of the Industrial Revolution could not have occurred without improvement to population health. If high mortality rates were left unchecked, labor shortages would have prevented industry from blossoming. It is equally compelling to say that without the wealth generated from industry, investment in health, education, technologies and public services would not have been possible, so health outcomes would have stagnated.

This connectedness ties together processes of health and development as well as different institutions that function across diverse geopolitical scales. Consider the role of different government bodies. During the English cholera epidemic, a physician working in the local community, conducting interviews with individuals in households across different neighborhoods isolated an important source of the epidemic. Local authorities acted to eliminate the primary source, and to change the local environment. But the problem of water contamination was not limited to a single neighborhood, nor was it even confined to the urban area. Open sewage ran into the Thames, which carried the contaminants down river. Community and citywide actions had to be coordinated to address the threat. But the installation of a new sewerage system, and the regulatory framework necessary to ensure its successful functioning, took more than just the local government. Funding for and coordination of responsible parties required regional and national efforts. At the national level, legislation to guarantee sanitary standards and proscribe responsibilities was passed.

Innovations in health care can come from local, national, and international levels. Such innovation and investment served health and development domestically and internationally. The expansion of empire carried national interests across boundaries and intermingled old and new problems in health and development as well as presented an arena for creative solutions. Innovations created for the domestic sphere could be carried overseas. Likewise, colonial medicine sought to address new problems and applied the solutions abroad and domestically. Colonial medicine may have been directed towards preservation of military and economic strength, but it resulted in public and clinical health resources and knowledge being transferred around the world from both colonizer and colonized.

Each scale, geographic and institutional, entails a different perspective on health and development, with distinct goals and distinct foci. The highest level, the meso-perspective, is global wherein opportunities and threats that come about through the interaction of ecosystems lay. At the global level, one sees institutions that discern global trends and coordinate responses to accentuate the positive and mitigate the negative. One sees opportunities for international cross-subsidies and technology transfer that is typically directed to nation-states.

National level concerns are those of population health and national resources. Here, the needs of the many outweigh the needs of the few. Development stratagems, health system design, resource allocation and wide-reaching policy are the tools of the nation-state. The gauge of success lies in macro-level measures, population trends, and sectoral performance. At a macro level health has less to do with the physical, mental, and social well-being of any one individual and more to do with the security of the state economic and political enterprise. Health is conceived of as an aggregation of numbers and averages which purports to express myriad aspects of individual well-being. Such 'health' is often used as a tool to demonstrate development of the nation-state—a non-corporeal entity. While a state can thrive, or can diminish, it cannot feel pain. From this perspective, it is the collective which must be protected.

If one considers the macro-perspective, the concern is with the organization of institutions within the catchment area of the nation-state, the region, or the world. Macroeconomic theory guides much of the discussion about both health and development at an aggregated level. Interest lies in the comparison of performance over time and across regions. The focus on nation-state maintains a focus on the good of a system or institution measured across indicators in which wealth accumulation and financial distribution maintain dominant positions when the macro view is outward focused. As the macro view shifts more inward, to conditions within the nation-state, comparisons are made between territories and between diverse groupings within a state. Attention is paid to distribution of resources and of disease. Inequalities become more closely linked to manifestations of social systems, institutions, and culture and the experience of inequality in suffering begins to take on a narrative. These are the concerns of Chaps. 2 and 3. Chapter 2 analyzes the conceptualization and utility of health to the broader international community and international organizations. Definitions, approaches to creating good health and development and changes in the specific foci and instruments to address the same as utilized by the WHO and World Bank are presented. In Chap. 3, the tools of the aforementioned agencies will be placed in the context of population health and the (economic) health of the state. We will explore these interactions and conceptualizations using case studies from Chile and Sri Lanka.

The local and community levels add socio-cultural context and a more nuanced appraisal of opportunities and challenges. At the local level, one tends to find fewer financial resources than at the national level, but greater knowledge about the multiple dimensions of sickness and health be it physical, social, or economic, and greater understanding about capabilities and needs. At the community level, assessment tools carry us beyond quantified measures and seek to incorporate unique community, cultural and individual experiences which inform the web of causation. These arenas seek to understand how changes are manifest in households and communities, and try to relate these micro changes to macro goals and structures.

At an even smaller scale one has the households and the individuals. Here is where suffering is personal; grandiose national rhetoric is meaningless save for how it translates into goods and services that the individual can use in her or his daily struggle to survive. Here is where one sees choices informed not by antiseptic, distant science or dehumanized national priorities, but by the hierarchy of priorities one juggles to live each day, week, month, or year. This level, too, is the realm of biomedicine that addresses the most basic input to population health—the individual. Individuals who make up the community translate what the grander scale view sees as numbers into a lived experience. The concern becomes focused on the material, physical, mental and emotional resources that are necessary to heal, to survive or to thrive. In Chap. 4, we look at community health and explore how NGOs and civil society address the needs of community, and gaps in provisions, with the intent of improving how health is manifest in community either through direct investment in health programs or through economic and human development programs (investing in social capital). Chapter 5 will explore the specific challenges of communities in war or in social collapse.

Connection across these different scales and institutions is not always based on geographically proximate relationships. Transnational cooperation entails a multiplicity of views, priorities and practices focused on specific issues. The rise of public-private partnerships represents an evolving aspect of international, national and local development. Chapter 6 will look at emergent public-private partnerships, conceived of at an international level but operationalized at the local level, in an effort to better understand the potential future of health and development. The conclusion will summarize what has been learned from different approaches and different scales, and point to convergence of health and development in the 21st century.

1.6 Conclusion

In summary, as we approach the enterprises of obtaining health and achieving development, we need to be aware that there are multiple approaches to obtaining these goals. Diverse institutions create definitions and tools to understand a shade, a nuance, a sector of what, taken together, may inform a truly holistic view of health and its interaction with development. No single perspective on health or development is correct. Under examination, competing views prove to share commonalities regarding the inter-relation of aspects of the development process and aspects of improving population health. But the competing views also create apparently dichotomous policy choices that built tension and trade-offs between health and development rather than building cohesion.

Three tasks lie ahead. If we assume that an understanding of what creates a healthful state of being is essential to creating instruments to bring about this desired state, we must first understand how we recognize 'health' across the macro- and micro-scales. The first task, therefore, is to understand how different actors define health and development. The second task is to look at how these definitions inform policy and actions designed to alter health and/or development. Our final task is to look at the varied landscape of health and development, and linkages across the different actors and bailiwicks, to better understand where common interest lies and where diverse skills can converge in order to better address the needs and peculiarities of the one as well as the needs and peculiarities of the many. These are our tasks in the chapters which follow.

Discussion Questions

1. How does state security differ from human security?
2. How did the conditions of industrialization increase public concern for health?
3. How did colonization and the growth of empire motivate investment in population health?
4. Describe how economic interests and public health interests intersect, and provide an example.
5. Access the World Development Indicators via http://databank.worldbank.org/ddp/home.do (note that the World Bank provides free access to select indicators. Many academic institutions and public libraries have membership which provides access to all indicators).

   - Select a low income and a middle income country.
   - Explore the indicators found under the "Economic and Policy Debt" category and the "Health" categories.
   - Select several economic and health indicators and explore how they change over a period of twenty years.

6. Access the Human Development Statistics available at (http://hdr.undp.org/en/statistics/. You should select the link "getting and using data". From the next page, select "Build you own tables".

   - Select a low human development and a middle human development country.
   - Select several of the indicators that would be used to measure health and several that would be used to measure economic development.
   - Do this for several years to see how these measures have changed over time. Discuss the change you see.

7. Do the WDI statistics match those from the Human Development data?
8. Select two of the countries you explored above. Use the Global Health Observatory data to explore five health indicators. To do this, go to http://www.who.int/gho/en/ and select the "Database" link. This will take you to a page with instructions on navigating the database.
9. Write a summary about the change in development and health for each of the countries you accessed in question 8, using the indicators you obtained in questions 5, 6 and 8.
10. Tell what stage of the demographic and epidemiological transition the countries you discuss in number 9 are in, and why you believe this to be the case.
11. Describe the main elements of the standard of living theory and the main elements of the argument that medical innovations led to improved health, and describe what these two theoretical approaches have in common.

References

Aiello, A., Larson, E., & Sedlak, R. (2008a). Hidden heroes of the health revolution: Sanitation and personal hygiene. *American Journal of Infection Control, 36,* S128–51.

Aiello, A., Larson, E., & Sedlak, R. (2008b). The health revolution: Medical and socioeconomic advances. *American Journal of Infection Control, 36,* S116–27.

Arias, E. (2007). *United States life tables* 2004. National Vital Statistics Report (p. 56). Hyattsville, MD: National Center for Health Statistics.

Avery, R. E., & Haskins, W. (Eds.). (1913). *America's triumph in panama: Panorama and story of the construction and operation of the world's giant waterway from ocean to ocean*. Chicago, IL: Regan Printing House.

Barry, J. (2005). *The great influenza*. New York: Penguin.

Birn, A. (2003). Revolution, the scatological way: The Rockefeller foundation's hookworm campaign in 1920 s Mexico. In D. Armus (Ed.), *Disease in the history of modern latin america: From malaria to AIDS* (p. 176). Durham and London, UK: Duke University Press.

Brunton, D. (2004a). *Medicine transformed: Health, disease and society in Europe 1800-1930*. Manchester, UK: Manchester University Press.

Brunton, D. (2004b). Dealing with disease in populations: Public health, 1830–1880. In D. Brunton (Ed.), *Medicine transformed: Health, disease and society in Europe 1800–1930* (pp. 180–210). Manchester, UK: Manchester University Press.

Camaroff, J. (1993). The diseased heart of Africa: Medicine, colonialism and the black body. In S. Lindenbaum & M. Lock (Eds.), *Knowledge, power & practice* (pp. 305–329). Berkeley, CA: University of California Press.

Chaillé, S., & Sternberg, G. (1879). *Preliminary report of the Havana Yellow-Fever Commission*. Annual Report of the National Board of Health (p. 26). Cited in Delaporte (1991).

Delaporte, F. Arther Goldhammer (trans.). (1991). *The history of yellow fever: An essay on the birth of tropical medicine*. Cambridge: MIT Press.

Dréze, J. & Sen, A. (1991). *Hunger and Public Action*. Oxford University Press: UK.

Foucault, M. Sheridan Smith, A.M. (trans) (1994) *Birth of a clinic: An archeology of medical perception*. New York: Vintage Books.

George, R. (2006). *The wasteland*. Slate Online Magazine. http://www.slate.com/id/2139945/entry/2139950/nav/tap1/. Accessed July 24, 2009.

Gilles, H.M. & Warrell, D.A. (Eds.). (1993). *Bruce-Chwatt's Essential Malariology* (3rd Ed.). London, UK: Arnold.

Hicks, J. & Allen, G. (1999). *A Century of Change: Trends in UK Statistics since 1900*. Research Paper 99/111, Social and General Statistics Section, House of Commons, December 29, 1999.

Jacyna, L. S. (2004). The localization of disease. In D. Brunton (Ed.), *Medicine transformed: health, disease and society in Europe 1800-1930* (pp. 1–30). Manchester, UK: Manchester University Press.

Kleinman, A., & Kleinman, J. (1997). Moral transformations of health and suffering in chinese society. In A. Brandt & P. Rozin (Eds.), *Morality and health*. London, UK: Routledge Inc.

Kunitz, S. (2007). *The health of populations: general theories and particular realities*. Oxford, UK: Oxford University.

McKeown, T. (1976). *The modern rise of population*. London, UK: Edwin Arnold.

The Rockefeller Foundation. (2010). http://www.rockefellerfoundation.org/who-we-are/our-history/1913–1919. Accessed June 13, 2010.

Thomas, D. (1999). *Captain of death: The story of tuberculosis*. Rochester: University of Rochester.

United Nations Development Programme. (2009a). *Human development report 2009*. Houndsmill, UK: Palgrave MacMillan.

United Nations Development Programme. (2009b). Technical Note. http://hdr.undp.org/en/statistics/indices/hdi/question,68,en.html. Accessed on November 23, 2009.

United Nations Development Programme. (2015). Human Development Report 2015. New York: UNDP.

United Nations. (2009). World population prospects 2008 revisions population database. United Nations. http://esa.un.org/unpp/p2k0data.asp. Accessed December 7, 2009.

Warren, A. (1951). Landmarks in the conquest of yellow fever. In G.K. Strode (Ed.), *Yellow Fever* (pp. 1–38). New York: McGraw-Hill Publishers.

Worboys, Michael. (2004). Colonial and imperial medicine. In D. Brunton (Ed.), *Medicine transformed: Health, disease and society in Europe 1800-1930* (pp. 211–238). Manchester, UK: Manchester University Press.

World Bank. (2009). World Development Indicators. http://0-ddp-ext.worldbank.org.bianca.penlib.du.edu/ext/DDPQQ/member.do?method=getMembers&userid=1&queryId=6. Accessed April 23, 2010.

World Health Organization. (2010a) Philippines*: Health Profile*. http://www.who.int/gho/countries/phl.pdf. Accessed 31 May, 2010.

World Health Organization. (2010b). *Smallpox*. http://who.int/mediacentre/factsheets/smallpox/en

World Health Organization. (2010c). *Zimbabwe: Health profile*. http://www.who.int/gho/countries/zwe.pdf. Accessed May 31, 2010.

Chapter 2
International Organizations and Their Approaches to Fostering Development

Abstract Multilateral agencies define and operationalized health and development in a variety of ways. The World Health Organization (WHO) and the World Bank are two dominant actors in health and development. Each espouses a different ideal of health as it relates to the process of development. The WHO defines health as a human right, and focuses on health outcomes as inputs to and the result of development. The World Bank's approach to development focuses largely on macro-economic growth as input to human capabilities. The World Bank became a leading actor in international health policy in the 1990s when it operationalized health as an outcome of financial and health care systems. This chapter looks at programming efforts by the WHO and the World Bank to foster development via investment in health or through macro-economic adjustment. Results are mixed. Efforts to improve primary care were successful in improving health outcomes of children under five, but made little impact on maternal mortality. Structural adjustment programs achieved moderate success with medium- to long-term economic growth but increased health inequities. These mixed achievements resulted in an effort by the United Nations to foster a multi-sectoral approach to development espoused in the Millennium Development Goals and Sustainable Development Goals.

Health and development are central concerns for national and international governance because the preservation and improvement of health and the improvement of economies and capabilities that define development contribute to stability and prosperity of nation-states as well as to the regional and global communities of which they are a part. Investment in health and development is predicated upon the assumption that the constituents of the nation-state, that is its territory, people, culture and way of life, are to be maintained and preserved as they contribute to the bodies politic and economic. Competing priorities and strategies that address economic growth, state security, human security and population health suggest that the relative import of health or development, and the impact each has on the other, remains contentious and forms what can best be described as the 'chicken or the egg' debate: Is development a necessary precursor to improvements in human

S.A. Johnson, *Challenges in Health and Development*,
DOI 10.1007/978-3-319-53204-2_2

health, or is human health necessary to achieve development? The position an institution or nation-state takes in this debate will dictate its policy approach. The implications are clear. If one believes that development is a precursor to health, then one accepts that resources should be put into growing the economy, alleviating poverty, and building institutions and structures that further political stability from which human development will follow. If, on the other hand, one adheres to the latter ideal, then investment in improving the human condition would be at the forefront. Once a critical threshold in population health is achieved, then economic and other forms of development will follow.

2.1 Health and Development as Concepts in the International System

How one defines and understands health or development will have significant bearing on programmatic operations. The conceptualization of health varies across institutions, actors and time, but is broadly interpreted in one of three ways. One such understanding of health is that it has intrinsic or independent value. Health is an inalienable right of human beings. A second understanding of health defines its value based on it being a contributing factor to other goals, such as economic development or state security. Within this framework, population health directly impacts economic growth by producing healthy workers who perform effectively and efficiently without creating a financial drain on the health care system. A healthy population further contributes to economic well-being by creating opportunities for children to be educated. If children are likely to live into adulthood, parents are more likely to invest in education. The education in turn translates into increased future earning potential for the children, their households, and broader society because better educated populations can command higher salary and can attract greater investment. A healthy population contributes to state security because it is able to attend to its basic needs. If a population can work (assuming there are employment opportunities), then citizens can provide for basic needs such as housing, food, and other material goods and/or reductions in absolute poverty. Where famine, malnutrition, or gross inequalities in other health aspects of a population do not exist there may be less probability of social cleavage, discontent, political and social instability. Thus, internal threats to state security decrease. When states function rather than fail, there is regional and global stability and peace. A healthy population produces young men and women who are physically able to serve in the military, thereby contributing to military preparedness and strength.

A third notion of health views health as an outcome of physical, social and institutional factors. It is thus a malleable state that must be built by adopting multiple avenues of influence and including multiple sectors within the scope of health-oriented policy. Each of the three interpretations of health implies a different notion of what policy actions contribute to good or poor health, and will therefore influence policy formulation.

These conceptions of health are neither stagnant nor are they mutually exclusive in that international actors may subscribe to one or several of these notions of health when defining agendas and prioritizing actions. The dominant understanding of health within an institution may shift over time as we will see in this chapter. Given the variability of goals within both the health and development communities, such change in definition and utility is not surprising. Neither the project of improving population health nor engaging in development is stagnant. As agendas are set and policies implemented, knowledge continues to grow through information gathering, program and policy assessment. Such assessment entails learning from what has and has not been successful. Both failures and achievements are utilized to craft new approaches to the continuing goal of betterment of society, options and capabilities. The conceptualizations of health utilized in the global community since the mid-20th century reflect the history, tensions and dominant concerns of the international community.

Development, like health, is interpreted in a variety of ways. At its most basic understanding, development means economic growth and poverty alleviation. Actors who used this definition focus policy on finances and economic growth. Health, thereby, may flow out of economic growth, the rationale being that increased national income translates into increased fiscal resources to invest in health inputs such as sanitation, improved food, health systems and so forth. However, a more holistic understanding of development sees *human* development as "the process of enlarging people's choices, by expanding human functionings and capabilities." (UNDP 2000:17). The publication of the first Human Development Report by the United Nations Development Program (UNDP) in 1990 was an international call to more broadly acknowledge the ideal of human development and human capacities. This more holistic interpretation suggests economic growth is only one foci and that other sectors such as education, health, and environment are equally important. Sustainability of these sectors, and indeed the ability to offer equal options to current and future generations, continues to be an important factor in sustainable human development.

At the macro- and meso-level of nation-states and global governance there are competing views as to whether economic growth or human well being is of higher priority. The competing models offer two very distinct approaches to attainment of either health or development; one argues economic growth comes first, the other suggests that health does. The relative prioritization informs policy focus and action.

While it is broadly accepted that development, in its many manifestations, and investment in health are necessary for stability and prosperity of nation-states and the broader global community, there remains a division in policy and action across global actors. This division forms the basis of this chapter in which we will examine how health and development have been broadly defined by international actors since the 20th century, and how such definitions were used to formulate distinct policy approaches espoused by international organizations (IOs). We will examine the formation of global governance following World War II by first looking at the political forces that informed the United Nations Charter. We will then examine how political forces and norms influenced and reformed the focus, scope, and actions of the World Health Organization (WHO) and International Bank for Reconstruction and Development (the IBRD, a.k.a. the World Bank). We will examine the impact of maternal-child health programs, a tool in delivering primary health care, and structural adjustment programs as a policy for obtaining macro-economic equilibrium. Finally, we will explore the movement towards a multi-sectoral approach espoused in the Millennium Development Goals (MDGs) and subsequent Sustainable Development Goals (SDGs).

2.1.1 International Health Before WWII

Infectious disease had long been a concern for international and domestic security, a concern which spurred the creation and coordination of specific codes to limit the spread of disease and mitigate its human and economic impacts. *Yersinia pestis*, plague, presented one of the early challenges to international health. Plague is believed to have originated in Asia. It ravaged Asia, the Middle East, and Europe between the 1300s and 1844 and remains endemic to parts of Asia, Africa, Europe and the Americas even today. The worst recorded epidemic, the Black Death, peaked in Europe between 1347 and 1351 and killed between one quarter to one third of the population in Europe and the Middle East (Watts 1997). The disease spread along trade routes over land and sea. In addition to being one of the earliest recorded pandemics, plague was also one of the earliest documented agents of biological warfare. In 1346, the Tartars laid siege to the city of Caffa. The Tartar community had suffered from the plague. They engaged in battle against the Genoese, who were secured in the walled city of Caffa. The Tartars reportedly catapulted plague-ridden bodies over the city walls hoping to disable their enemy with disease (Wheelis 2002). As the Genoese returned home to Italy, they carried the plague with them. The disease quickly established a foothold and spread throughout Europe.

Public authorities took action to limit the spread of the plague. These actions included the use of isolation and quarantine to control the spread of infectious disease. **Quarantine**, derived from the Italian *quaranta giorni*, or forty days, is the separation of individuals who have been exposed to a disease but have not yet developed symptoms from contact with other unexposed individuals. **Isolation** refers to physically separating people who develop a specific disease from contact with others. The city-states of Italy established Public Health Councils to address the health threat posed by plague (Gomez-Dantes 2001; Watts 1997). The City of Venice instituted a formal quarantine system to control the plague epidemic. Under the quarantine law, incoming ships had to remain at anchor for forty days before they would be allowed to dock. Health regulations in Italy included sanitation (disposal of bodies), limiting movement of infected and exposed individuals, financing of medical care, and economic support for those impacted by market closure (Watts 1997). Proscriptions against population movement were adopted throughout plague-ridden areas. Other actions included closing marketplaces and cordoning off entire cities, limiting trade, domestic and international mobility.

Over time, quarantine regulations became the most powerful tool the international community had to limit the spread of infectious disease. Quarantine and isolation were used against such diseases as cholera and yellow fever in the 1800s. The growth of interstate commerce and travel during the Industrial Revolution along with the coalescence of modern nation-states, contributed to a growing call for international coordination of health responses. The European cholera epidemic (1830–1847) led to the first International Sanitary Conference in 1851. Representatives from 11 European nations developed transnational quarantine policy (Stern and Markel 2004). Interamerican cooperation solidified under the aegis of the Pan American Sanitary Bureau (Stern and Markel 2004). In Europe, the *Office International d'Hygiéne Publique* (OIHP) in Paris became the chief coordinator of public health activities, such as monitoring and assessing disease occurrence and possible risk factors, providing technical advice to address health risks and improve health outcomes, and coordinating different actors to address specific health threats. Additionally, the OIHP had the authority to convene meetings, draw up international conventions, and administer quarantines (Gomez-Dantes 2001; Stern and Markel 2004). The League of Nations Health Organization (LNHO) formed in 1922, providing health supports which were parallel to the OIHP. In the years following the first world war, OIHP came to dominate quarantine policy while the LNHO began looking at disease prevention and health promotion. The LNHO also began efforts to address social determinants of health, and the specific vulnerabilities of motherhood, childhood and poverty (Gillespie 2002; Gomez-Dantes 2001; Stern and Markel 2004).

Interest in social medicine grew in the early part of the 1900s (Rodríguez-Ocaña 2002; Weindling 2004). **Social medicine** holds that social forces such as income, ethnicity, and institutional arrangements create social inequity from which health inequity follows. This medical perspective represents a broad reinterpretation of public health etiology in which disease comes about via a three-way relationship between agent, host, and environment. It was a subject of debate in the late 1800s and then re-emerged in health rhetoric following World War I, challenging the exclusivity of focus as practiced by adherents of bacteriology and germ theory. A division in the health community emerged between those who focus on the individual causes of ill health and those who focus on social causes. This division influenced rhetoric and policy throughout the 20th century into the 21st century.

During the 1920s and 1930s, the LNHO, under the leadership of Ludwik Rajchman, expanded the organization's scope of concern beyond that of disease control, medical nomenclature and drug standardization to include emphasis on economic needs, employment, nutrition and social insurance as important constituents of good health (Gillespie 2002; Kunitz 2007). Social insurance was more than state-sponsored insurance, which had been gaining adherents at the turn of the century. **State insurance** provided for government-funded medical care of the poor and sick through municipal clinics, free hospitals and convalescent homes. Countries such as Germany, France and Russia were early innovators in such practice. Despite such efforts, however, care was fragmentary. State efforts were frequently small compared to private care provided by charitable or religious organizations or private fee-for-service care that precluded the poor. **Social insurance**, or social welfare, expanded the notion of state insurance to include other social aspects. It is a social safety net which includes income support, nutritional support, provision of housing and access to medical care for highly vulnerable populations such as the elderly (who no longer earn income), women, children and the poor whose physical or social circumstances prevent equal ability to access essential goods. Deficiencies in these goods make people more susceptible to death and disease; those highly vulnerable groups have fewer resources with which to mitigate harmful outcomes. In some cases, they are less able to respond to risks because of physical reasons. For example, women of childbearing age may be particularly vulnerable to physical conditions associated with childbearing, such as nutritional deficiencies, which can compromise their immune systems and make them susceptible to other diseases. These populations may be more vulnerable because of social or institutional structures as well. Consider the legal status of women in some areas following World War II where women were not allowed to enter the work force either because of formal rules or informal social norms. Those women who had engaged in work as part of the war effort were expected to return home at war's end. Their means of economic support was tied to spousal income or family wealth. In some regions, women were not allowed to own property. With no independent means of support, women were dependent upon the largess of men or upon social policies which would provide access to material support.

Progressives argued that societal obligations include the provision of social safety nets for these populations and for broader society. The growth of social medicine, state insurance and social insurance was a countervailing force to the biomedical perspective that concentrated on a specific disease and a pharmacopic or biophysical cure. In social medicine, health became entwined with labor, employment, and the political economy—in other words with the broader development landscape. Although full agreement as to the inclusion of social insurance within the health policy domain and purview of LNHO was never fully accepted, the debate about the appropriate catchment area for health had begun. The LNHO, the International Labor Organization (ILO) and a number of nation-states entered the fray. Support for social insurance was especially strong in a number of European states. This expanded conceptualization of health and the role of government in providing access to health care and more expansive social welfare continues to be debated in international and domestic spheres even today.

The LNHC was joined by the ILO and the International Red Cross in this expansive understanding of health which would play an important role in establishing the mission of the WHO in the latter part of the century. Neither the OIHP nor the LNHC were able to operate during World War II, and fell apart thereafter. In the power vacuum which followed the close of war, public health campaigns focused on humanitarian aid efforts (even before such a term had been coined) and were delivered piecemeal. It is in the power void that the story of current intergovernmental organizations (IGOs) engaged in health and development began.

2.1.2 *The United Nations and the Modern Story of Health and Development*

The modern story of health and development at the international level begins at the close of World War II with the formation of the United Nations (UN) and its agencies. The UN has proven to be the pre-eminent institution for cohesive global governance despite the challenges it faces. The UN was founded as the successor to the League of Nations in 1945. At the time of its founding, the global community was recovering from two bloody conflicts and a global depression. The international community had to address rebuilding regional and global economic and social structures. In addition, the global community had to address its own complicity in creating the conditions which led to war. It would do this by creating a system with universal membership for nation-states to work together to ensure global security. Collective action would be used to mitigate social and economic conditions which could lead to regional or global conflict. Internationally accepted norms were created which included the primacy of sovereignty in domestic affairs, the responsibility of collective action, and the duty of nation-states to strive to protect peace.

At the end of the Second World War, the global community engaged in institution building with the intent of creating global prosperity and limiting the potential for another global conflict. The foci of these endeavors included peace-building, conflict mitigation, economic growth, state and international security, and human prosperity. The global community faced the short-term challenge of rebuilding vast regions that were physically and economically devastated. Such reconstruction entailed addressing the immediate needs of people and states as well as the longer term needs for political, economic and social stability. Defeated nations could not be subject to punitive or solely extractive economic and social policy, nor could they be left to attempt redevelopment on their own without risking a recreation of the desperate conditions which led to the Second World War. Development and reconstruction required short term responses, emergency aid, as well as long term planning for global security which would be predicated upon state and human security. The UN was formed to provide a global forum of diplomacy and create governance tools in the interest of maintaining world peace and security.

The United Nations Charter was adopted on June 26, 1945 with the goal "to save succeeding generations form the scourge of war." (United Nations 1945) To do this, the UN Charter provided rules to respect human rights, rules to respect the rights of sovereign, peace-loving nations, and an international forum for grievances and conflict mitigation. With the formation of the UN, the ideal of collective responsibility in protecting internationally defined norms was put forward. It was followed three years later with the Universal Declaration of Human Rights which defined social, civil, economic and political rights of individuals and charged nations-states to collectively protect these rights. Among these rights is the right to health and the attainment of the same. The Universal Declaration of Human Rights (UDHR), adopted on December 10, 1948, reads:

> Everyone has the right to a standard of living adequate for the health and well-being of himself and of his family, including food, clothing, housing and medical care and necessary social services, and the right to security in the event of unemployment, sickness, disability, widowhood, old age or other lack of livelihood in circumstances beyond his control.
>
> Motherhood and childhood are entitled to special care and assistance. All children, whether born in or out of wedlock, shall enjoy the same social protection. (Universal Declaration of Human Rights Article 25)

The specific representation within the UNDHR focuses on a holistic understanding of that which is necessary for overall physical and social well-being, including clothing, housing, food, employment and control over monetary and material resources necessary for an adequate standard of living. It speaks to the promise not only of health, but of a minimal status of human well-being or development. Health is not limited to the ability to access medical care or be free from sickness. Mothers and children are singled out as requiring special recognition and protections because of physical, social, economic and political factors which make them more vulnerable to illness, disease, and social insecurity. The UNDHR definition suggests that health cannot be separated from being human, nor is it understood to exist in a single, natural state. Rather, by defining health within a broader scope of living standards, it is implicit that health can be produced and altered by external forces. It is also implicitly linked to some level of economic development in that housing and employment inform the basic rights and inputs for health.

The UN would also disseminate information and resources to assist members in building social and economic conditions which would ensure prosperity and deter future conflict. The charter pledges to "promote higher standards of living, full employment, and conditions of economic and social progress and development." (United Nations 1945) In other words, part of the UN mission is to engage in the project of development.

The UN Charter entailed the creation of specialized sub-committees and units which focus on specific concerns. The principal organs of the UN include the General Assembly, Security Council, Economic and Social Council, Trusteeship Council, International Court of Justice, and the Secretariat. The UN Economic and Social Council (ECOSOC) is the main body responsible for coordinating economic and social work. In addition, numerous departments and programs exist to address specific aspects of the greater UN charter. Text box 2.1 contains a brief description of a number of UN agencies. Among those programs working on issues of health and development are the United Nations Development Program (UNDP), the United Nations Educational, Scientific and Cultural Organization (UNESCO), United Nations Human Settlement Program (UN-Habitat), the World Food Program

(WFP), United Nations Population Fund (UNFPA), and the United Nations Environmental Program (UNEP). Together, these bodies monitor global trends germane to social and economic conditions, identify needs and strategies to address the same, and provide technical assistance and resources to implement change. The agencies also coordinate diverse actors and resources. The UN further has the power to create specialized agencies.

Text Box 2.1

PRINCIPAL ORGANS of the United Nations

Trusteeship Council supervises the administration of Trust Territories; suspended operation on November 1, 1994. (www.un.org/en/mainbodies/trusteeship)

Security Council, consisting of 15 Member States, is responsible for the maintenance of international peace and security. (www.un.org/sc)

General Assembly has representatives from all 193 Member States and is the primary deliberative and policymaking organ of the UN. (www.un.org/ga)

Economic and Social Council coordinates the international economic, social, cultural, educational, health and related work of the 14 UN specialized agencies, functional commissions and five regional commissions. (www.un.org/en/ecosoc)

International Court of Justice is the judicial organ of the UN, whose role is to settle legal disputes and give opinions in response to legal questions. (www.icj-cij.org)

Secretariat consists of the Secretary-General and other staff and carries out the day-to-day work of the UN, including the administration of policies and programs. (www.un.org/en/mainbodies/secretariat)

PROGRAMS AND FUNDS

UNCTAD (United Nations Conference on Trade and Development) helps developing countries integrate into the world economy by acting as a forum for intergovernmental negotiations, conducting research, policy analysis, and data collection, and providing technical assistance. (www.unctad.org)

ITC (International Trade Centre), a joint agency of the World Trade Organization and the United Nations, helps developing countries achieve sustainable development through small business exports. (www.intracen.org)

UNODC (United Nations Office on Drugs and Crimes) assists Member States in their efforts to counteract illicit drugs, crime, and terrorism through field-based technical cooperation projects, research and analysis, and support in the ratification of international treaties and the development of domestic legislation. (www.unodc.org)

UNEP (United Nations Environment Program) provides leadership in caring for the environment by assessing environmental conditions and trends, developing international agreements, strengthening institutions, integrating economic development and environmental protection, and facilitating the transfer of knowledge and technology. (www.unep.org)

UNICEF (United Nations Children's Fund) seeks to protect the rights of children and promote children's full potential by addressing such issues as poverty, violence, disease, and discrimination. (www.unicef.org)

UNDP (United Nations Development Program), works with countries to build and share solutions to development challenges, including democratic governance, poverty reduction, crisis prevention and recovery, environment and energy, and HIV/AIDS. (www.undp.org)

UNIFEM (United Nations Development Fund for Women) seeks to advance women's rights and gender equality and works primarily in the areas of women's economic security and rights, violence against women, HIV/AIDS, and gender justice in democratic governance. (www.unifem.org)

UNV (United Nations Volunteers) contributes to peace and development globally by promoting volunteerism and advocating on behalf of volunteers. (www.unv.org)

UNCDF (United Nations Capital Development Fund) provides investment capital, capacity building, and technical advisory services to Least Developed Countries (LDCs) to promote microfinance and local development. (www.uncdf.org)

UNFPA (United Nations Population Fund) promotes health and development by helping countries use population data to develop policies and programs. (www.unfpa.org)

UNHCR (Office of the United Nations High Commissioner for Refugees) coordinates international activities to protect the rights and well-being of refugees and resolve refugee problems. (www.unhcr.org)

WFP (United Nations World Food Program) provides food aid to fight hunger in emergencies and to reduce chronic hunger and undernutrition. (www.wfp.org)

UNRWA (United Nations Relief and Works Agency for Palestine Refugees in the Near East) carries out direct relief and works programs as well as advocacy for Palestine refugees. (www.unrwa.org)

UN-HABITAT (United Nations Human Settlements Program) promotes the development of socially and environmentally sustainable towns and cities with the goal of providing adequate shelter for all. (www.un-habitat.org)

SPECIALIZED AGENCIES

ILO (International Labour Organization) promotes labor rights, social justice and protection, and opportunities for decent employment for men and women worldwide. (www.ilo.org)

FAO (Food and Agriculture Organization of the United Nations) seeks to achieve food security by improving nutrition, agricultural productivity, and the lives of rural populations, and by contributing to the growth of the world economy. (www.fao.org)

UNESCO (United Nations Educational, Scientific and Cultural Organization) promotes international cooperation and dialogue in the fields of education, science, culture and communication. (www.unesco.org)

WHO (World Health Organization) is the health authority within the UN system and is responsible for providing leadership on global health matters, establishing health norms and standards, promoting evidence-based health policies, providing technical support, and monitoring health trends. (www.who.int)

World Bank Group's mission is to fight poverty by providing resources, sharing knowledge, building capacity, and creating partnerships in the public and private sectors. (www.worldbank.org)

IBRD (International Bank for Reconstruction and Development), a lending arm of the World Bank, aims to reduce poverty by providing loans, guarantees, risk management tools, and analytical and advisory services to middle and low income countries. (www.worldbank.org/ibrd)

IDA (International Development Association), a lending arm of the World Bank, aims to reduce poverty by providing interest-free credits and grants for programs that increase economic growth, reduce inequalities, and improve living conditions. (www.worldbank.org/ida)

IFC (International Finance Corporation) promotes the development of the private sector in developing countries through investments and advisory services. (www.ifc.org)

MIGA's (Multilateral Investment Guarantee Agency) *promotes foreign direct investment (FDI) into developing countries by providing guarantees to the private sector.* (www.miga.org)

ICSID (International Centre for Settlement of Investment Disputes) provides a space for the arbitration of international investment disputes. (www.worldbank.org/icsid)

IMF (International Monetary Fund) fosters global monetary cooperation, exchange rate stability, and international trade growth, and helps member countries to achieve balance of payments and poverty reduction. (www.imf.org)

Fifty-one nations constituted the original UN membership. By 1974, the number was 138. Today, there are 193 members recognized as sovereign states by the UN. Of particular import is the increasing number of developing countries with UN membership. The number increased as former colonies and territories gained independence or organized into independent states. Developing countries did not have individual political or economic power, but en masse controlled a newly empowered voting block which questioned the prevailing economic and political ideologies of development. After three decades of development, 70% of the world's population resided in developing countries, but these countries controlled only 30% of global income (United Nations 1974).

During the post war period, the global community engaged in reflection surrounding the collapse of global empires and independence of former colonies. As independence movements took hold, questions arose not only about nation-building, but also about how to improve the quality of life across disparate topographical, political and social milieus, and about how best to achieve global security. The self reflection begged the question as to why certain areas of the world prospered and achieved certain standards of living, whereas other parts of the world did not. Development economics and development studies grew out of these post-war and post-colonial concerns. Development studies were initially dominated by western intellectual traditions and a conceit that the standards and norms achieved in the western world were highly desirable and should be replicated throughout the world. This intellectual bent has influenced and continues to exert pressure on international norms and the development agenda in the IOs. Neo-Marxism, post-modernism, and feminism have posed modest challenges to this tradition, but by and large development programs remain firmly entrenched in Western economic and political thought.

2.2 The World Health Organization

The World Health Organization (WHO) is the unique IGO charged with global monitoring and evaluation of health trends. The WHO is a specialized agency within the United Nations system which directs health policy/priorities and coordinates health-related action. The need for a global health authority was rooted in the tradition of international coordination of public health campaigns to combat the spread of infectious disease. This was a role previously filled by the LNHO and OIHP which collapsed during WWII. The UN Relief and Rehabilitation Administration provided emergency health care and food following the end of the war, but had a short-term charter for such provision. The need for a new coordinating agency in the ruins of war was clear, but the new agency's structure, powers and purview needed to be negotiated. In 1946, U.S. Surgeon General Thomas Parran and Sir Wilson Jameson of the British Ministry of Health initiated the planning process for the new health agency under the aegis of ECOSOC (Gillespie 2002). Representatives of regional, national, and international health organizations were invited to participate, but the process itself was dominated by the United States and European powers as these nations had both experience in issues of international public health and had established health offices around the world. Because ratification by 26 states was necessary to establish a specialized agency within the UN system, the Interim Commission for the World Health Organization was careful to define the scope of the agency in a manner which would attract both socially liberal and more conservative signatories. Ratification by the U.S. was critical to ensure financial support of the WHO and make the agency viable immediately and into the future (Gillespie 2002). The United States thus became one of the most influential powers in shaping policy, programs and actions. The WHO Constitution was adopted by 61 states on July 22, 1946 and entered into force on April 7, 1948.

The writing of the WHO constitution was littered with controversy as to the scope of both the agency's power and the scope of understanding as to what makes for good health. The controversy had its roots in a growing division among medical and policy leaders which pre-dated WWII, but was exacerbated by the post-war balance of power and growing division between capitalist and communist nation-states.

Given the international interest in defining and redefining the state's role in health creation, it should be no surprise that social insurance proved to be a contentious issue during the formulation of the WHO charter. The WHO's predecessors defined health in terms of specific diseases and had therefore limited its operations to disease monitoring and control, and dissemination of best practices (Gillespie 2002). Rajchman and his adherents' reconceptualization of health to include the political economy challenged national sovereignty and market liberalism. Critics saw social insurance as an unwelcome tool of state intervention in markets in areas where free-market capitalism was embraced (Gillespie 2002). The opponents of social insurance argued that it related to politics, the market, and labor more directly than to health. The question became whether or not the new international health agency should be given a charter which may permit clear authority in sectors not traditionally considered part of public health. The strongest opposition to including social insurance within the scope of the WHO came from the United States and Britain (Brunton 2004; Gillespie 2002; Kunitz 2007; Weindling 2004; Worboys 2004). Given the political brinksmanship necessary to obtain the U.S. vote, the focus on social medicine and social insurance was attenuated (Gillespie 2002). But the U.S. was not the only vote needed to ensure longevity of the WHO. Language that defined health as a confluence of the physical, social and mental spoke to a number of the European powers' concern for social medicine. Concessionary provisions in the articles of the constitution left room for reinterpreting the agency's focus and definition of 'health' in the ensuing decades.[1]

The definition of health contained within the WHO charter represents both a challenge to medical imperialism rooted in a Western biomedical basis and as mandate for the WHO to work on a social agenda which included social constituents of health.

> Health is a state of complete physical, mental and social well-being and not merely the absence of disease or infirmity. (WHO 2008c).

This definition validates both Western and traditional interpretations of health, and provides for mandates to focus not merely on the single body, but also on broader socioeconomic conditions which act upon health and create inequalities across diverse groups. The WHO Constitution provided for a broad purview in the topics which the agency could investigate as related to health and its determinants, but a modest role in terms of actual powers to implement policy.

---

[1]Gillespie points to a concession that allows the WHO to study social security in conjunction with other agencies as another action that was necessary to secure votes from European countries.

The mission is to provide leadership in shaping health policy and setting the global health research agenda and to provide technical expertise on global health through monitoring and assessment of health trends, dissemination of information, establishment of norms and standards, and technical support for member states. While the WHO has the power to adopt conventions, agreements and international health regulations, it lacks enforcement power. The WHO can make recommendations and advocate specific policy approaches and research agendas and can call for international conventions and proffer binding treaties, but power to act upon recommendations remains the sovereign right of nation-states. Rather, the WHO provides technical guidance on public health issues, and coordination of actors and institutions. The WHO also coordinates donor-funding for special programs. The organization and operation of professional medicine is also outside of the WHO's scope. Although the WHO defines diseases and response protocols, it does not regulate medical practice or offer professional accreditation. Its purview is very much that of public health rather than biomedicine. The WHO's power is further hobbled by financial constraints, which allow for only modest investment in research and implementation. The agency's annual budget of US$ 4400 million in 2016–2017 is funded by membership fees and voluntary donations, and is but a fraction of the World Bank's annual lending which totaled 64 billion dollars in 2016 (WHO 2015c; World Bank 2016).

2.2.1 WHO Early Years: Health as a Biomedical Condition

The WHO was a traditional (WHO 2009d) public health authority in its early years. Its mission was much like the LNHC before it: to monitor and analyze international health threats, to standardize professional nomenclature, and to provide technical guidance for disease management. The ideal of the intrinsic value of health was always at the forefront of the WHO mission; programmatically, however, the WHO focused on health as a narrowly defined outcome of human and infective agents. Even before the final charter was signed, the Interim Commission of WHO identified communicable diseases as the primary threat to global health (Gomez-Dantes 2001). Malaria was first among these concerns, followed by tuberculosis and 'venereal disease' (Gomez-Dantes 2001). During the 1950s and 1960s the WHO embraced the health revolutions provided by technological advancement and focused on the eradication of specific diseases to the exclusion of economic or social constituents of health. Vaccination, antibiotics, and insecticides became the tools for global campaigns to combat infectious disease. The focus provided mixed success. An anti-yaws campaign proved highly successful. Campaigns to decrease the health burden of measles and control wild polio had initial success. Later years, however, would see failures of measles vaccination and the emergence of wild polio albeit at a significantly lower rate than that experienced prior to the WHO campaign.

2.2.2 *Malaria and Smallpox Campaigns*

In 1955, the WHO undertook the eradication of malaria, one of the great plagues of humankind. **Malaria** was an enemy of colonial expansion, an enemy of states made free following the war, an enemy of those living in tropical and temperate climates. It is a parasitic disease spread to humans via mosquito bites. Although the disease had been the target of regional eradication efforts for considerable time, technological innovations of the mid-century combined with international organization suggested that this old enemy could be destroyed once and for all (Gilles and Warrell 1993; Najera-Morrondo 1991). The campaign entailed widespread use of chemicals, in particular, dichlorodiphenyltrichloroethane (DDT), to kill vectors. Prophylactics would eliminate the human reservoir. The vision of health with the anti-malaria campaign presented health as an outcome included agent, host and a broader ecology. During the post war years, malaria was eradicated in the United States, parts of Europe, and the Middle East, and declined in parts of Latin America and some parts of Asia (Gilles and Warrell 1993; Newman 1965). No such success was experience in Africa and other parts of Asia. By the 1970s, temporary gains began to erode and the disease resurged in Latin America and Asia. Today, an estimated 250 million people are infected each year, and almost one million people, mostly children, die (WHO 2009c). Social and economic costs are manifold.

In the 1960s, the WHO continued to target specific diseases, and undertook the most successful disease eradication program to date: the elimination of smallpox. At the time WHO launched its smallpox eradication campaign, 60% of the world's population was at risk of this disease (WHO 2009d). The disease killed nearly one quarter of those whom it infected. Survivors often bore pox mark scars or were blinded as a testament to their dangerous encounter. The WHO's launched its campaign in 1967. The last naturally-occurring case was found in Somalia in 1977 (WHO 2009d). In 1980, the World Health Assembly certified that smallpox was no more.

2.2.3 *WHO: Health as a Human Right*

By the early 1970s, the number of member states in the UN had more than doubled from its initial membership as a result of decolonization and formation of newly independent nations in the global South. This ushered in the era of the New International Economic Order (NIEO) which was a concerted effort by UN members representing the global South to create a more just distribution of global economic power and resources between the global North and the global South. It was also a period in which the inequities—in economic status and population health—between the 'haves' and the 'have nots' of the world became a focus for international political rhetoric. These concerns also came at a time when public dialogue reengaged with ideas of social determinant of health. A revolution in thought about how to improve health inequalities between the developed and developing world was called for, one which included social determinants and well as an understanding of historical context and power structures. Such concerns were reflected in the 1970s with a refocusing of health as a right and as a component of economic and social development. On September 12, 1978, attendees at the International Conference on Primary Health Care signed the Declaration of Alma Ata. This reaffirmed the commitment of the global health community to the ideal of health being a human right, and declared, "… that the attainment of the highest possible level of health is a most important world-wide social goal whose realization requires the action of many other social and economic sectors in addition to the health sector." (WHO 1978) Social justice and the health divide between nations spoke to concerns of the NIEO. The declaration said that state governments had the duty to provide basic health care and coordinate health services, and acknowledged that local actors are essential in creating healthy communities (WHO 1978).

The Declaration marked the beginning of the era of primary care. The WHO directed programs and policies towards achievement of the goal of universal access to primary care in an atmosphere where there was a growing realization of the importance of intersectoral coordination for health outcomes. In describing eight essential areas of primary health care, the Declaration addressed social and biomedical aspects of health. The eight elements of primary care were health, education, nutrition, access to water and sanitation, maternal and child health care, immunization, prevention and control of locally endemic disease, treatment of common diseases and injury, and provision of essential drugs (WHO 1978). Despite the Declaration's affirmation of the economic sector's contribution to community well-being, no explicit economic goals or inputs were described. Efforts to place health at the fore of economic and social policy remained hobbled by the comparative lack of power and resources of the WHO and many state ministries of health. A global scaling up of primary care would not be achieved easily. Perhaps the greatest consistent success came in expanding vaccination coverage vis-à-vis the Expanded Program on Immunization (EPI) launched in 1974 which will be discussed later in this chapter (Jamison et al. 2006). The era from 1978 to the late 1980s saw WHO focus on health as an outcome associated with broad socio-cultural milieu, in that success would be gauged by changes in the overall health profile of populations and communities, rather than changes in any the health burden of any one disease.

2.2.3.1 Primary Health Care

Primary health care includes an array of strategies to prevent disease, to target endemic diseases of particular public health import, provide basic needs such as clean water and sanitation, and provide access to health care for common conditions that require low levels of technology and technical expertise. Maternal and child health is a prime focus of primary care based on the impact improved child survival and maternal health have on social, epidemiological and demographic change. Primary care services are often among the most cost effective interventions in that the inputs are low cost and result in direct cost saving through prevention or mitigation of more severe health sequelae, and result in indirect savings in terms of opportunities costs. When we consider global change in primary care since the 1970s, global immunization coverage and improved access to safe water and sanitation are clear achievements. But the full promise of primary care is yet to be realized and gains that have been made are threatened. Economic contraction and declining GDPs mean that financing for primary care is in jeopardy; national revenue is more tightly constrained and competition for resources is greater, and foreign aid is neither sufficient nor sustainable (WHO 2008a, b). A shortage of qualified health care workers impacts the developed and developing world (WHO 2008d).

Since the Alma-Ata conference, the WHO is and has been a major proponent of primary health care including maternal and child health (MCH). Preeminent among MCH are childhood vaccines and programs targeting maternal health. These two programs are emblematic of the successes and failures of primary health. Progress increasing global immunization coverage is one of the great success stories of public health, but it is not without a down side as evidenced by backsliding in immunization rates and continued loss of life to vaccine-preventable disease. Maternal health is one of the more sensitive indicators of human development in that it reflects access to skilled health services, pre- and postnatal care, nutrition, education, female empowerment, social and economic development. Maternal health is considered important for its intrinsic value and for the multiplier effect it has on child and household health and attendant societal impacts. Despite being on the global agenda for nearly four decades, gains in maternal health are inconsistent and well below what is feasible and equitable.

Maternal health refers to the health of a woman during her pregnancy, at childbirth and in the post-partum period, a period generally considered to be 42 days (WHO 2005a). Complications which result in maternal death or disability can occur before giving birth, during delivery, or when recovering from child birth. Of the causes of maternal death, hemorrhaging is the most common and accounts for 25% of the deaths, followed by infection (15%), complications related to unsafe abortion (13%), pre-eclampsia and eclampsia (12%), and obstructed labor (8%) (WHO 2010). When maternal health complications do not kill, they can damage a woman physically, emotionally and socially. Birth complications can damage a woman's reproductive organs. If the damage is severe enough, the woman may not be able to have children, and may therefore lose social status and economic protection. Obstetric fistulas are another complication which, if not surgically mended, cause loss of bladder or bowel control among other sequelae. This can also lead to social and economic isolation, lose of personal dignity, and mental illness (Wall 1998).

Direct obstetric complications are only one part of the maternal health equation. Complications which occur during pregnancy rather than during childbirth are difficult to measure but are believed to account for one out of every four maternal deaths (WHO 2007). A study in Zambia found that 40% of the referrals made to a teaching hospital were related to pregnancy complications, not childbirth (WHO

2007). Such complications may be a result of a condition developing because of the pregnancy. For example, a woman may develop high blood pressure related to the pregnancy. Disease and pre-existing conditions also cause complications during the course of pregnancy. Malaria, anemia and maternal malnutrition can be exacerbated by pregnancy and result in maternal mortality, still birth, and infant mortality. An estimated 10,000 women die each year during pregnancy as a result of malaria (WHO 2007). HIV is another complicating factor in maternal and infant mortality.

Between 1990 and 2005, global maternal mortality decreased at less than 1% per year (WHO 2007). These data reflect the dismay of the international community which found little to cheer about in terms of progress in maternal health. Some regions demonstrated improvement in maternal health. South-east Asia, for example, improved access to antenatal care, that is care received during pregnancy, by 34% (WHO 2005c). But during the same period, African nations improved access by only 4% (WHO 2005c). Only a third of births in Niger are attended by skilled health personnel (Save the Children 2008). Between 1990 and 2005, maternal mortality ratios declined by 5.4% (WHO 2007). The largest decline was in East Asia (47.1%), the smallest in Sub-Saharan Africa (1.8%) (WHO 2005a, b, c). Around the world more than half a million women will die because of poor maternal health care and ten million will suffer pregnancy-related injuries (WHO 2007). Ninety-nine percent of these deaths will occur to women living in developing countries (WHO 2007). One million children will be left motherless (WHO 2010). **Maternal Mortality Ratios (MMR)**, the number of maternal deaths per 100,000 live births (or 1000 depending upon conversion), are as high as 2100 per 100,000 live births in Sierra Leone, 1800 in Afghanistan and Niger, and greater than 1000 in several African nations (WHO 2007). Progress has been slow and uneven. Figure 2.1 shows the unequal progress in reducing maternal mortality by region. The global community agreed it could do better. It committed to improving maternal care with the Millennium Development Goal (MDG) 5 to reduce 1990 MMRs by 3/4 by 2015.

Maternal health can be enhanced by improving access to adequate health care and by improving the position women have in society. Neither task is easy. Adequate health care entails having access to clean and sanitary facilities, proper equipment, and trained personnel. Maintaining financial commitment to facilities and care, and adequate levels of trained staff has proven difficult. The WHO, World Bank and other IGOs have long advocated health districts and local clinics to provide essential services such as maternal care. Health systems failed due to stagnant funding, inadequate flow of aid and loss of health care workers to the private sector or over international borders (WHO 2005c). Capacity and quality of services are not equal across nations or even within nations as can be inferred based on the outcomes described in Fig. 2.1. Access to care relates to obstetric care and antenatal care.

When one considers that maternal mortality is a function not only of the risk associated with the specific pregnancy, but also with the number of pregnancies a woman experiences during her reproductive years, it becomes clear that family planning and access to safe abortion are also important elements of maternal care (WHO 2007). Family planning includes access to knowledge about reproduction as

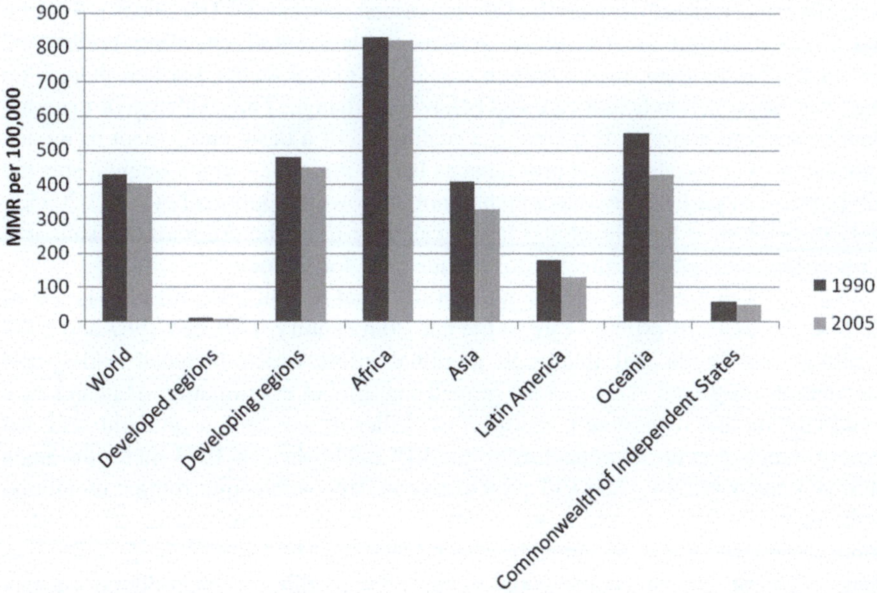

Fig. 2.1 Changes in maternal mortality between 1990 and 2005. *Data source* Maternal mortality in 2005: estimates developed by WHO, UNICEF, UNFPA and The World Bank (2007). Derived from data on page 17

well as access to birth control methods. Although access to contraception has risen from 10% of the population in the 1960s to 59% of the population, there remains a large gap between need and availability. An estimated 87 million unwanted pregnancies occur each year; there are 46 million abortions of which some 40% are unsafe (WHO 2005c). Addressing family planning includes education and access, but it also includes looking at the position women have in any given society. Family planning and abortion services continue to be controversial around the world. Such programs suffer funding cutbacks and political backlash based on cultural acceptability and social mores—at times driven by donor rather than local community morals (Thornton 2008).

Institutional capacity, and failures of the same, are one part of the equation in maternal health, a part which lends itself to technocratic and economic solutions. The social aspect is more difficult to address. Maternal health care needs to involve societal knowledge of pregnancy and birth, societal norms about health seeking behavior, and critically, the empowerment of women. Where women do not have the same legal rights as men, or are not valued socially as much as men, they may be excluded from care (WHO 2005c). Social norms may dictate what is appropriate care for a woman, and may dictate whether or not she may show pain let alone be allowed to seek care. Where women do not have equal decision-making powers or are excluded from economic and social circles and hierarchies because of gender, their health may be jeopardized. They may also be subjected to violence and abuse.

Such disempowerment is magnified if the women are poor (WHO 2005c). Societal and cultural change is difficult to realize as they entail changing norms and behaviors at individual, community, national and global scales. Further, there is no one 'true' approach to health care and behavioral change. The challenge of maternal health care is to address such care as a scaling up of a basic entitlement or human right rather than to caste such programs as health initiatives which target a specific sub-population particularly one which is not empowered politically (WHO 2005c). Only through such high level and large scale buy-in of the program can sufficient support be garnered and directed to provide care for women.

In contrast to the limited gains made in maternal health, immunization is one of the true successes of primary care in the late 20th century. Between 1967 and 1977 smallpox was eradicated thanks to a global effort which included widespread vaccination programs. This victory proved that global coordination of health care could take on and overcome a centuries-old killer. It was both a symbolic and real victory which provided momentum to the EPI established in 1974 under the aegis of WHO and UNICEF. The EPI principles entailed establishing routine childhood immunization for six of the most relevant vaccine-preventable diseases: measles, polio, diphtheria, pertussis, tuberculosis and tetanus. The logic of the program was manifold. First, immunization would increase the likelihood of childhood survival and was thus an investment in the future. Second, decreases in infant mortality are associated with declining total fertility and movement along the demographic transition. This in turn relates to lower dependency ratios and improved standard of living and improved human development within the broader population (WHO 2001, 2009a). Third, vaccinations are an efficient public health intervention in that there is a targeted group, minimal contact with the health system is necessary, and no major lifestyle changes are required (WHO 2009a). Fourth, vaccination programs benefit the individual who receives the vaccine as well as the broader community through herd immunity. Thus, immunizations were a public good. Fifth, immunization is cost effective. In the mid-1990s, the cost for the six basic EPI vaccines was US$1 per child (WHO 2005a).

The initial obstacles to the EPI campaign were logistical, fiscal and related to technical capacity. The primary obstacle was that the necessary vaccines were manufactured in the developed world but would be used in the developing world (Lee et al. 1997). Technological transfer for vaccination campaigns entailed the costs of the vaccines as well as the logistical support to transport and administer vaccines while maintaining cold chain and ensuring trained personnel managed the programs (Lee et al. 1997). To meet these challenges, the WHO, UNICEF and their partner agencies created innovative processes and partnerships. Initial financial obstacles were overcome through bilateral and multilateral aid and donations. The actors developed public-private partnerships to provide low cost equipment to transport and store vaccines while maintaining the cold chain (Lee et al. 1997). Procedures for vaccine administration and personnel training were established. Monitoring and surveillance followed. The administrative mechanisms were in place to evaluate program successes and failures, and modify approaches as programs became established and data gathered. For example, during national immunization days all children under age 5 receive polio vaccines regardless of previous vaccination status (Keegan and Bilous 2004). This innovation created a larger population catchment and circumvented the difficulties associated with vaccination eligibility tied to paper records. In-country vaccination networks provided an established health system which can be utilized to deliver other health care (Lee et al. 1997).

As technology and knowledge advanced, immunization campaigns changed. The resurgence of yellow fever in the 1980s resulted in WHO adding yellow fever to the list of recommended vaccines (Keegan and Bilous 2004; Lee et al. 1997). The development of a hepatitis B vaccine also resulted in a change to the EPI vaccines. There are new foci for international campaigns such as the Global Polio Eradication Initiative, formed in 1988, and the Global Immunization Vision and Strategy put forward in 2005 by WHO and UNICEF (WHO 2009a). The Vaccine Independence Initiative helps countries assume financial responsibility for vaccination programs (Lee et al. 1997).

The immunization program has made some remarkable achievements. When EPI was established, only 5% of the world's children were vaccinated against these diseases. Today, 79% are (Lee et al. 1997). Since the launch of the Global Polio Eradication Initiative, polio cases dropped by 99%—five million people were spared paralysis associated with the disease (WHO 2005a). Ninety-five percent of WHO member states now provide Hepatitis B vaccines, although with mixed coverage rates (WHO 2015a, b). Global mortality from measles decreased by 74% between 2000 and 2007 (WHO 2009a).

But not all news is good news. The vaccination programs are showing strain and, in some cases, losing ground as financing dries up and personnel are no longer trained. Vaccination coverage dropped by 5% or more in 41 countries since 1990 (Lee et al. 1997). DTP3 coverage which began to fall in the 1990s has stabilized (Keegan and Bilous 2004). Coverage in the African region averages only 56% (Keegan and Bilous 2004). In 2002, 1.4 million children died from vaccine-preventable diseases (Keegan and Bilous 2004). The reasons for the stagnation and failure include social change, war and humanitarian crises, poverty and unsustainable external support for immunization (Keegan and Bilous 2004; Lee et al. 1997; WHO 2009a).

Even with one of the most successful health campaigns, we cannot escape economics. The success of the vaccination programs was partially dependent upon foreign aid and multilateral funding, funds which are unsustainable. Further, as nations experienced economic contraction or fought wars, prioritization changed and funding for primary health care eroded. The economics of vaccination campaigns have also changed. Vaccination costs for the initial six targeted diseases were low and there was an economy of scale. Newer vaccines are more expensive. The cost of a hepatitis B vaccine, including administering the vaccine, are between US$ 20—US$ 40 per child, an expense beyond the ability of some nations to pay (WHO 2005a). Global alliances have formed to try to overcome some of the obstacles to obtaining and maintaining high levels of vaccination coverage. For example, the Global Alliance for Vaccines and Immunization (GAVI) provides funds to poor counties with low vaccination coverage. It also brought together public and private actors to address development and sustainability of vaccines for both the developing and developed world.

But the strain on primary care remains. It is interesting to see the different achievements in terms of MCH. Vaccination programs targeting children are widespread with visible impact on morbidity and mortality. Maternal health is less clearly defined and associated with no single intervention. Vaccination entails a one (to three) time encounter with the medical system; maternal health entails a bare minimum of one but frequently more contacts. There is also a difference in terms of the political value placed upon children as opposed to women which differs from nation to nation. Obstacles of maternal health include a dearth of basic medical materials and training. None the less, poor countries such as Mozambique are investing in low cost medical training for nursing assistants and mid-wives. The logistical and technical obstacles are certainly no greater than those initially faced by EPI. Perhaps the ultimate barrier is political will to value women as much as children, and rearrange power structures and norms to ensure women equal chances of living health filled lives.

2.2.4 Social Determinants of Health and the WHO in the 21st Century

The WHO maintains the position that health is a human right but throughout its history, the agency has had little power to enforce this view and has achieved only a modicum of success in harnessing collective action to promote health based on any intrinsic value. The WHO has been more successful in operationalizing health as an outcome related to the control of specific diseases and ascribing value to states and a planet free from certain diseases both in terms of alleviating suffering, thus ensuring health as a right, and protecting various social and economic interests. The end of the 20th century saw a renewed interest in the linkage between socioeconomic, political and physical environment and health outcomes captured in studies of social epidemiology and the language of social determinants of health, as well as health as an input into the same. The work of medical anthropologists such as Nancy Scheper-Hughes, Arthur Kleinman and Paul Farmer became greatly influential in reconsidering the micro- and macro-level factors which alter health outcomes of entire groups of people and contribute to what Kim (2000a) refers to as the deserted places: areas in which health declines even while health indicators for the broader community improves. **Epidemiology**, the field of medicine which specifically examines the occurrence and distribution of disease within a population, began looking beyond the more traditional environmental determinants to the broader social order and its influence in creating risk exposures in susceptible populations. The sub-field of social epidemiology, which examines "... how social conditions give rise to patterns of health and disease in individuals ...", became firmly established (Berkman and Kawachi 2000:10). Health was once again understood to be the product of numerous factors but increasingly these factors were seen to occur outside the geographic and institutional boundaries of any one nation state. Of growing concern was the role macro-economic policy had in creating vulnerabilities and limiting the ability of nation-states, local communities and individuals to respond to health risks.

This interest is infusing new directions linking health and development.

2.3 The World Bank

Macroeconomic stability and financial relationships are another important aspect of global peace, security and development. The Bretton-Woods institutions were created in 1944 to better manage the global economy through rebuilding the shattered economies of both the defeated and the victorious in the war, and by creating international resources and policies to further economic growth from which, in theory, prosperity and peace would follow. The Bretton-Woods institutions are the International Bank for Reconstruction and Development (IBRD or the World Bank) and the International Monetary Fund (IMF) which are distinct yet complementary organizations. The World Bank's mission was to rebuild the shattered infrastructure of Europe and Asia and provide technical and financial assistance to create the conditions of economic and political stability, growth in trade, and improvement in living standards. The IMF's role was to manage and promote international monetary cooperation and trade. Its initial focus was to provide short-term loans to nation-states for investment in capital expenses and structures deemed necessary for economic growth, and also provide countries with assistance in overcoming balance of trade problems. Such issues were initially viewed as being short-term necessities of economic growth. The role of the IMF evolved partially due to the Debt Crisis of the 1980s, the financial crises of the 1990s, and the global recession. Its role is no longer limited to monetary policy and short-term balance of payments issues. Rather, the IMF is engaged in macro-economic management of monetary and fiscal policy, longer term debt negotiation and restructuring, and global financial stability. It serves developed as well as developing countries as witnessed by the US$ 2.1 billion loan to Iceland initiated in 2008 (Anderson 2008).

Of the two Bretton-Woods institutions, the World Bank was created specifically to address global development. As the full title indicates, its initial *raison d'etre* was post-war reconstruction. Only after a modicum of stability was achieved in rebuilding could the World Bank focus on the project of development. Today, the World Bank is the largest public development institution in the world with annual lending totaling US$24 billion. It consists of five institutions, including the original IBRD, the International Development Association (IDA), the International Finance Corporation (IFC), the Multilateral Investment Guarantee Agency (MIGA), and the International Centre for the Settlement of Investment Disputes (ICSID). The IFC was added to the World Bank Group in 1956 to assist with and coordinate private sector investment. The IDA was created in 1960 to provide interest-free loans and technical assistance to only the poorest nations. In 1966, the ICSID was created as a forum to settle disputes arising between investors and national governments. MIGA is the most recent addition to the World Bank Group. It formed in 1988 to better encourage foreign direct investment (FDI) through the provision of risk insurance to protect investors against political risks in developing nations (Bretton Woods Project 2006).

The broad mission of rebuilding and redevelopment allows a great deal of leeway in terms of programmatic operation. The World Bank policies and priorities continue to change to address the evolving geopolitical and economic landscape. At its inception, the programmatic focus was to rebuild the physical and economic structure of Europe and Asia. Allied bombing left a devastated landscape which necessitated construction of infrastructure for transport, communications, commerce, and governance. The bank emphasized the creation of infrastructure throughout the 1950s. It reasoned that in order for nation-states to function in the global network, they needed not only roads and buildings but capital equipment and materials for industrial production. Modernization theory, which held that societies move from rural/agricultural base to urban/industrial base, was dominant. Through investment in industrialization, it was believed that the ultimate goal of increasing national income would be achieved as states would have the tools to produce for and compete in an international economy. It followed that once the tools and structures were in place, the human resources necessary for production would need to be addressed. Thus, the bank turned its attention to investment in education, agriculture and the basic needs of the populace in the 1960s.

But the project of development is not easy nor is any outcome assured. Despite increased levels of urbanization and industrialization, many poor countries remained poor and inequities in wealth distribution increased. By the early 1970s, the World Bank became increasingly focused on programs to reduce the number of people living in poverty and providing for the necessities of a minimal standard of living, or **basic needs**, which included caloric intake, housing, and income generation.

2.3.1 The World Bank: Evolution of Development

During the last 40 years, the primacy of economic growth and market liberalization underpinned the World Bank's agenda, policies and actions. The neoliberal model infused the work of the World Bank and continues to guide the agency's program. However, despite the philosophical underpinning, the World Bank did not operate with a single unaltered vision. It modified how it operationalized its policies in response to critiques and evidence of program achievements and failures. As a result, the World Bank development platform transformed from one with a narrow focus on macro-economic growth and fiscal responsibility to the detriment of the social sector, to a program of growth with provision of social safety nets and targeting of interventions to the most vulnerable segments of society. In other words, the institution proved flexible and adapted to earlier program failures. Three programmatic eras related to health and development policy are evident. The first era is marked by the Structural Adjustment Programs (SAPs) and their attendant impact on macroeconomic stability, government spending and currency valuation. This is followed by the World Bank as a health systems authority. Finally, there is an era of using Poverty Reduction Strategies (PRS) for development.

2.3.1.1 Structural Adjustment Program

With the onset of the Debt Crisis in the 1980s, World Bank directives re-iterated the primacy of economic growth and economic management as a central tenant of development. The SAPs were the primary tool in the bank's toolkit for dealing with shrinking or debt-ridden economies. The success of the SAPs is widely debated. While they benefited some countries' macro-economic performance over the course of five to ten years, they also heightened inequality within and between nations, limited the sovereign decision-making ability of some nations, and caused a decrease in social conditions and human development outcomes in a number of states (Kakwani et al. 1990). The bank's response was to retool the macro-economic focus of the SAPs, by allowing governments more flexibility in fiscal management, and allow for maintenance of social safety nets. Today, growth of national income, poverty alleviation and reduction of income inequality remain strong foci but with rhetoric, and various degrees of supporting action, around developing pro-poor policies and building human capacity.

In 1982, Mexico's Finance Minister declared that Mexico could no longer make payments on its national debt. The reason was that the debt service on commercial loans exceeded the country's earning power. The low interest loans entered into in the 1970s, when commercial banks were flush with petrol dollars, had transmogrified into massive debt with increasing interest rates. This occurred against a backdrop of rising oil prices. Mexico was not alone in its pending default. A number of developing nations could not service their debt. This constituted the Debt Crisis. The threat was a grand scale of default which could have ruined large commercial lenders based in the developed world, and destabilized the global economy. The solution to what was feared to be a global economic collapse was intervention by the World Bank and IMF. The institutions offered to renegotiate debt schedules and loan money to governments to cover balance of trade deficits so long as the debtor nation agreed to abide by a set of fiscal and monetary policies. These were the SAPs.

With the Debt Crisis, an opportunity arose for international finance institutions to implement neoliberal principles on a broad scale. The underlying tenant was simple. "Economic growth was viewed as the best form of social policy, and social spending itself was considered an obstacle to growth." (Ewig and Kay 2008:250) The guiding principles of the SAPs were also known as the **Washington**

Consensus, so named because the Washington-based international financial institutions recommended this package in response to the Debt Crisis. The SAPs used monetary and fiscal measures, and employed market liberalization with the intent of achieving fiscal balance, decreasing inflation, and spurring outward-oriented economic development. Although these policies did not directly address human development, the actions necessitated by the SAPs caused a dramatic restructuring of government social services, contraction of social safety nets, and reduced the agency of poor populations. **Conditionalities** for receipt of loan adjustment and financial assistance were the order of the day, with an eye towards fiscal balance and monetary stability and market liberalization. Such stability would come through a focus on economic growth rather than investment in human capabilities.

As part of the structural adjustment, debtor nations were required to reduce public spending. This action would serve three purposes. First, it would reduce the imbalance in government revenues versus expenditures—an imbalance which was viewed as especially problematic in states such as Chile with entrenched welfare programs (Ewig and Kay 2008). Second, such reductions would lower government consumption and thereby bring down inflation (Gershman and Irwin 2000). With a reduction of government spending particularly in the social sector, subsidies for imported goods such as food would be decreased or removed. This would cause a reduction in demand for the imported goods and potentially impact the **balance of payments**—that is the amount of money spent on imports compared to that earned on exports. This third aspect of fiscal restraint addressed the balance of payment deficit—one of the main triggers of the debt crisis.

Economists attribute part of the trade imbalance to over-valued exchange rates. Rather than maintaining an artificial value in the international market with fixed exchange rates, the currencies of developing countries were floated in the international market. Devaluation resulted. Residents of nations undergoing restructuring lost buying power in the local and international markets (Gershman and Irwin 2000; Kim et al. 2000a; World Bank 2004). This, coupled with a reduction in public subsidies for goods such as food, fuel and medical imports, meant that the poorer members of society could no longer afford the essential inputs to health and well-being.

Market liberalization was yet another tenant of the SAPs. Trade barriers were removed and public facilities were privatized. Industrial protections and occupational safety regulations were weakened or removed (Armada et al. 2001). Public services were privatized, including social services. This, coupled with the reduced public spending, resulted in increasing unemployment as public sector employees were laid off (Kim et al. 2000b; Oppong 2001).

The outcomes of the SAPs are heavily debated. The achievements of the SAPs may best be measured by looking at long-term economic trends. Over the course of ten to twenty years, some countries which implemented these programs achieved economic growth and modest improvement in GDP/capita (see Table 2.1). Living standards increased in conjunction with rising national income (Kunitz 2007).

Table 2.1 Change in macro-economic features, measured by GPD growth, change in GDP/capita and balance of payment (BoP), in of select countries that undertook structural adjustment programs

		1980	1990	2000	2005
Argentina	GDP growth (annual %)	4.2	−2.4	−0.8	9.2
	GDP per capita (constant 2000 US$)	7535	5607	7694	8097
	Current account balance (BoP, current US$)	−4,774,000,000	4,552,000,000	−8,980,617,893	5,274,866,972
Bangladesh	GDP growth (annual %)	0.8	5.9	5.9	6.0
	GDP per capita (constant 2000 US$)	226	255	335	401
	Current account balance (BoP, current US$)	−702,138,191	−397,909,577	−305,831,651	−176,224,669
Egypt, Arab Rep.	GDP growth (annual %)	10.0	5.7	5.4	4.5
	GDP per capita (constant 2000 US$)	867	1135	1423	1539
	Current account balance (BoP, current US$)	−436,428,572	2,327,000,000	−971,000,000	2,102,800,000
Ghana	GDP growth (annual %)	0.5	3.3	3.7	5.9
	GDP per capita (constant 2000 US$)	239	218	255	290
	Current account balance (BoP, current US$)	30,200,000	−223,200,000	−386,500,000	−1,104,610,000

		1980	1990	2000	2005
Peru	GDP growth (annual %)	3.1	−5.1	3.0	6.8
	GDP per capita (constant 2000 US$)	2256	1657	2049	2351
	Current account balance (BoP, current US$)	−101,100,000	−1,419,000,000	−1,545,828,520	1,147,610,229
Tanzania	GDP growth (annual %)		7.0	5.1	7.4
	GDP per capita (constant 2000 US$)		275	274	330
	Current account balance (BoP, current US$)	−521,165,462	−558,926,906	−498,600,924	−864,330,117

Data source World Bank (2009b)

However, the question as to whether or not such growth was worth the price paid, especially by the poor, remains subject to debate. The SAPs have been widely criticized for causing social strife and failing to achieve their stated goals. The SAPs did not reduce the debt burden of the nations the programs were intended to help. In fact, by 1997, in numerous cases debt had grown (Gershman and Irwin 2000). The programs removed the public safety nets for the poor and created 'health shocks' in which health indicators actually got worse, albeit for a brief period of time (Armada et al. 2001; Kim et al. 2000b; Oppong 2001; World Bank 2004). The programs undermined investment in growth and in some cases, by undermining human development and removing the human benefits of a welfare state, set countries back in terms of development (Farmer and Bertrand 2000; Gershman and Irwin 2000). The programs also resulted in unequal growth, rising inequality and exacerbated poverty (Armada et al. 2001; Farmer and Bertrand 2000; Oppong 2001; World Bank 2004). Further, it is argued that the programs violated the international principle of sovereignty in that the national governments had little leeway in negotiating the SAP conditions. Critics argue that such conditions were set to further hegemonic interests of the United States and other large economic powers which control IMF and World Bank policy through an unequal voting structure (Armada et al. 2001).

The World Bank responded to the criticism as evidenced by the shift to targeted interventions for the poor which occurred in the 1990s. The bank continues to work with issues of macro-economic stability but its strategies evolved to incorporate lessons learned from the failures of the SAPs, and to provide supports for vulnerable populations. The more recent Poverty Reduction Strategy (PRS) places a premium on protecting social supports for the vulnerable, targeting programs to benefit the poor, and includes a participatory process in which national and community stake-holders are represented in policy debate and roll-out. PRS have been praised for allowing nation-states greater flexibility in agenda setting, allowing greater ownership of development policy, in safeguarding public safety nets, in protecting health outcomes (generally maternal and child health), and in providing for greater participation across political and geographic scales. At the same time, evidence suggests that participation in PRS process is varied and dependent upon existence of a strong civil society; although input may be sought from different sectors of society, decision-making is not jointly undertaken; the parameters of PRS are not flexible enough to manage external shocks such as the global economic contraction of the current debt crisis; continue to be heavily biased by donor preferences; and do not allow enough for context specific factors to alter policy prescriptions (Booth et al. 2006; Braathen 2006; Gottschalk 2005). The long term impact of this strategy remains to be seen. Whether the poverty reduction strategies represent a true shift in World Bank action as opposed to mere rhetoric remains subject to debate.

Although the structural adjustment policies of the 1980s focused on overall economic performance, many of the conditionalities attached to loans and debt relief touched upon social services including health. Cost-cutting programs, privatizing of social services, and cost recovery ideas were introduced in the 1980s, and continued through the 1990s. It was during this latter period when the World Bank presented a cohesive health platform and rose to the fore of global health actors. This occurred when the bank revisited its previous work which, rather than furthering the mission of poverty alleviation was found to foster inequality and breed poverty (World Bank 2004). The new era of the World Bank thus saw economic efficiency continue as a concern, but such concern was married to an ideal of addressing inequity.

2.3.1.2 World Bank as a Health Authority—World Development Report 1993

The World Development Report in 1993 saw the World Bank embrace the notion of health as an outcome of economic growth thereby recognizing health as a credible focus for development policy. It also placed import on health as a constituent of economic growth. In this, the World Bank perspective differs from the

WHO-espoused notion that health is a human right which therefore, based solely on its inherent and natural value, should be at the apex of policy concerns.

Economic growth has traditionally been of central concern to the World Bank, and it was the dominant focus of this particular World Development Report. The opening paragraph of the 1993 Report marks gains in life expectancy, decreases in childhood mortality and the elimination of smallpox as successes in trickle down effects from national economic prosperity and embraces the standard of living thesis. "Not only do these improvements translate into direct and significant gains in well-being, but they also reduce the economic burden imposed by unhealthy workers and sick or absent schoolchildren." The report proffers policy options that encourage economic growth: "Economic policies conducive to sustained growth are thus among the most important measures governments can take to improve their citizens' health." (World Bank 1993:7)

Health improvement will trickle down from growth in the national economy because such growth translates into increased money for public goods, such as education and health care, and increased incomes which impact health through higher standards of living. Health is an outcome of value because it translates into money, but to obtain it, one must have money to invest. This position revitalized the debate as to how economic development and health impact each other. This interpretation also positioned the World Bank as a global health authority.

Part of this new authority was undoubtedly tied to the World Bank's finances. Unlike the WHO, the World Bank had resources to act upon its convictions. The World Bank commits over US$ 50 billion every year to projects (World Bank 2016). For example, its lending for health and social services amounted to US$ 2.7 billion in 2007—a little more than the amount the WHO hoped to raise in donations to meet its total operating budget (World Bank 2009a). Loans, grants and debt-restructuring would be available to those nation-states which adopted the practices put forward in the development report. The WHO could offer technical guidance but the World Bank could pay to make things happen. The practices recommended in the 1993 report included investing in human capital, encouraging government provision of primary health care and public health interventions such as vaccination, decentralization of health services, improvements in efficacy through (re)structuring of fees to incentivize appropriate care uptake and ensure cost recovery mechanisms, and promotion of competition for health care vis-à-vis opening insurance markets where appropriate. The most important elements of the health reforms espoused by the World Bank were provision of primary care, decentralization and privatization. The focus of these latter two programs was health system reform rather than improvements in population health, and hastened in an era of health commodification (Armada et al. 2001; Gomez-Dantes 2001).

Parts of the report repackaged principle elements of the SAPs, including privatization, but there were some important departures. Decentralization was viewed as a more efficient way to deliver necessary health care and was put forward as a central tenant of health care restructuring. The sustainability of health care could be achieved by using cost effective methods and cost recovery mechanisms such as user fees, an idea that was in keeping with free market principles. Importantly, the report departed from the neoliberal ideology which guided the SAPs in that it discouraged conditionalities for receipt of funds, argued for investment in human capital, argued in favor of equitable distribution of health care goods by programs targeting the poorest 20% of the population, and acknowledged the different capabilities of poor versus very poor nations.

As the World Bank focused on health, it entered into a series of contradictory policies intended to make public provision of health care more cost effective and make service delivery more efficient through privatization and competition. One on hand, World Bank programs encouraged public provision of primary health care and essential health services which would especially benefit the poor. The bank's directives encouraged public financing and provision of primary education especially for girls. At the same time, however, the World Bank emphasized the mixed public and private financing for health care vis-à-vis insurance, and the introduction of private provision of health care, competition, and cost recovery mechanisms including user fees which created financial burdens upon the poor.

A major criticism of the Bank's entrée into health care was that the policies put forward commodified health and, as such, was counter to the ideal of health being both a basic human right and provision of the same being an obligation of government. Further, the argument that the Bank's policies were swayed largely by donor nations, to the disadvantage of the recipient nations, continued.

Efforts to decentralize health care services and to better target the poor proved to vary widely in terms of impact. In many nations, public health services favored tertiary care such as hospitals which tended to be located in urban areas thus excluded rural, typically poorer areas services.[2] The ideal of decentralization was to empower regional and local governing bodies to decide upon which services and health interventions were most necessary and suitable within the local context. Decentralization would shift power away from the administrative center, typically in the urban capital, and disrupt problems which cronyism and patronage wrecked in terms of hiring, concentration of personnel, and flow of financial resources. These actions would allow health care to be better targeted towards the poor. At the same time, social service would be pared down to exclude subsidizing the non-poor and wealthy classes.

These policies failed to account for differential abilities and costs associated with decentralized provision of health serviced. The differences in technical capabilities at regional and local administrative levels were not provided for. As a result, decentralization efforts failed because highly skilled medical practitioners maintained an urban bias; municipal amenities and salaries were simply not enough to attract skilled practitioners (Oppong 2001; World Bank 2004). Further, the administrative capacity of municipal authorities was seldom up to par and

[2]This argument is strongly made in the 1993 World Development Report. However, evidence suggests that in highly urbanized regions such as Latin America poor were equally concentrated in urban areas. Great attention was paid to access barriers presented to the urban poor in the late 1990s and into the 21st century.

training/capacity building were not addressed. In some cases, poor management persisted and, even with additional revenues from decentralization, the local authorities still could not pay for the services needed by the local populace (World Bank 2004). In other cases, decentralization actually increased cost of service delivery (World Bank 2004). In El Salvador, for instance, despite overall increases in public funding of health care, the funds which were allocated to the rural sectors decreased in part because the government, following a model of increased competition, contracted with NGOs to provide health care (Smith-Nonini 2000). In African, Latin American and Asian nations, decreases in public spending and resultant low levels of salaries for health care professionals created a 'brain drain' with medical staff either concentrating in urban areas or relocating to other countries which offered higher wages (Oppong 2001; World Bank 2004). In addition, some nations continued to suffer from trade imbalances which caused the import of essential drugs to slow or stop (Oppong 2001). The decentralized health authorities were often left without necessary drugs or medical supplies.

Cost sharing and recovery mechanisms were implemented as a method to contain escalating costs of health care provision and to provide revenues to invest in public health and deteriorating health infrastructure. These mechanisms included the introduction of user fees on a sliding scale and self-funding for insurance. Evidence shows that the cost sharing mechanism essentially excluded the poor from accessing health care (Farmer and Bertrand 2000; Oppong 2001; Shaw and Ainsworth 1995; World Bank 2004). Increased user fees were shown to decrease health care utilization by the poor, to delay health seeking behavior such that treatment costs escalated and health impacts worsened because the disease progressed to a more severe state; people turned to traditional healers, informal consultants, non-Western medicine and/or self treated because of lower costs (Farmer and Bertrand 2000; Oppong 2001; Shaw and Ainsworth 1995; World Bank 2004). Privately-funded insurance programs prove unviable for the extremely poor, those with irregular salaries, and are of limited success in rural areas. Even in markets where payment did not present an obstacle, lack of information and coordination between public and private insurance can confuse the consumers, lead to underutilization of insurance, and result in cost and performance inefficiencies in the insurance market. Further, both decentralization and introduction of competition in financing and provision of health services necessitate having a strong, local civil society which can be social advocates. Where civil society is weak, many of the benefits continue to be captured by the elite (Ewig and Kay 2008; Gershman and Irwin 2000; Raczynski 2001). Insurance programs have met with moderate success in middle income areas; evidence from low income and highly indebted poor countries (HIPC) shows insurance programs tend to be weak because of insufficient numbers who can afford to pay into the system, inadequate risk pooling due, in part, to fragmentation across plans, and poor incentives for competitive insurance markets (Medici et al. 1997; Oppong 2001; Shaw and Ainsworth 1995; World Bank 2004).

Privatization occurred in both the financing of health care delivery, through public and private insurance programs, and in the delivery of services. The balance between public and private responsibilities is highly contentious in the developed and the developing world. The health reforms to the UK's National Health Service which occurred under Margaret Thatcher and Tony Blair speak to the constant struggle to find affordable, equitable mixtures of public-private finance and provision. During the writing of the first edition of this book, the United States was in the process of creating a major health care initiative to provide equitable access to health care through public and private means. The result was the Patient Protection and Affordable Care Act (PPACA). During the revision, for the second edition of this book, the U.S. was debating whether or not to dismantle the PPACA. Economists consider health care incentives to be among the most perverse in terms of using price points to signal certain behaviors. Given the struggles of high income countries to balance equity in care with consumer choice, satisfaction and free market principles, it is little wonder that low- and middle-income countries struggle with privatization.

The failures of privatization in low- and middle-income countries were numerous. The combination of shrinking budget allocations for social services and the entry of private actors into health care resulted in a contraction of service provision (Armada et al. 2001; Oppong 2001). While ideally private competition would create more effective, competitively priced service delivery, such a theory was based upon a notion that all markets are equally attractive. This simply did not prove to be the case. For example, in some rural areas sparse population and the low income levels meant that economies of scale for health care delivery could never be realized, and that people would not be able to pay for medical care (World Bank 2004). These two factors alone would be enough to dissuade private health care providers from operating in the area. It would be difficult to get a single private enterprise to provide services, let alone allow for competition.[3] With the lack of private entrants in the high cost, high risk areas, provision falls to the public sector. However, with constrained fiscal and human resources, and in some cases the loss of more profitable markets to the private sector, the public sector proved not capable of providing adequate levels or types of health services (Oppong 2001; Smith-Nonini 2000; World Bank 2004). The response to the noted failures of the first phase of health care reform was to address logistical problems with program implementation, and further evaluate context-specific barriers.

The emphasis on delivery of primary services put forward by the World Bank clearly resonated with the WHO's primary care platform. Likewise, the policy proposals for decentralization re-enforced the import placed on local authorities in understanding improving population health in a way no bureaucrat living in an urban center far away for the area in question could understand. Less resonant were the cost-recovery mechanism, privatization and health system reform. The WHO espoused the program of health system reform during the 1990s. Some see this as a failure of the WHO to maintain an interest in broad social determinants of health

[3]This phenomenon is not limited to the developing world. For example, lack of quality and service options are problems experience in the rural United States.

(Armada et al. 2001; Gomez-Dantes 2001). However, the action speaks to a degree of *real politick* which cannot be ignored. Developing nations and the WHO faced very real financial and operational constraints. To the extent that health care provision favored urban and tertiary sectors over rural and primary sectors, progress towards the goal of universal provision of primary care could be gained through reallocating resources to local level administrations.

Throughout the 1980s and 1990s, the failure of macro-economic policies and dominant development theory that health impacts will trickle down through economic growth fueled continued debate and research on the relative importance of health and development with an intent of creating better policy. Critics of the SAPs argued that the focus on macro-economic policy constrained a nation's ability to address real concerns and vulnerabilities of its population, exacerbated societal inequalities, and hurt the poor. Further, critics argued that the financial IGOs adopted a cookie cutter approach to macro adjustment policy which failed to account for different cultural and geographic milieus, and institutional capacity which contribute to a nation's prospects for economic growth. Although the extent of SAPs impact on health and human development was not fully understood at the time of its writing, the 1993 World Development Report did address this latter concern by making a case for addressing each nation's unique capacities.

2.3.1.3 Towards Change

The continued dissection of the failures of SAPs and development programs, growing alarm about the negative impacts of globalization, and increased acceptance of a broader definition of development to include increasing capabilities created an opening for multiple disciplines to contribute to the dialogue about improving development and human well-being. Researchers turned to anthropology and the role of culture to explain successes and failures in the arenas of development and political science. Social scientists outside of the economic discipline, worked to dispose of the racist (but sadly prolific) idea that when economic policies failed it was because some cultures were innately inferior. Rather, critics questioned the economic policies and institutional structures of IGOs and the global market in setting goals based on a single, western model of development, ignoring cases which went against dominant theory, and setting certain countries up for failure based on unrealistic goals and inappropriate conditions. These debates changed both health and development policy.

The impacts of the World Bank development program and health reforms are varied across region of implementation and across timeframe. In the long term, there is evidence of improvement in aggregate indicators of both health and development (Kim et al. 2000a, 2000; World Bank 2004). Health sector reforms have demonstrated some cost savings and efficiency gains in middle income countries (Medici et al. 1997). The impacts are more varied in low income nations or HIPCs. To the extent that program failures caused a re-evaluation of World Bank operations which now include explicit provisions to protect the vulnerable, and provisions for a participatory process, one can argue this, too, is a long-term success. The long term sustainability of the programs remains in question. However, the short term costs of the reforms are great. The contraction of social services under the SAPs created a health shock which had the greatest negative impact on the poorest members of society, those least able to mitigate risks of economic and health service contraction. As a result, short term health indicators for some groups worsened. For example, infant mortality rates in Peru decreased during the early 1990s period of economic restructuring. The occurrence of sickness increased more than 20% while medical purchases dropped by 50% in some sectors of society (Kim et al. 2000b). The contraction of the health care structure equated to a collapse of the monitoring, surveillance, prevention and treatment—the keystones of public health. This collapse was associated with disease outbreaks, strengthening of the HIV epidemic, and increases in incidence and prevalence of endemic diseases (Kim et al. 2000b; Oppong 2001; World Bank 2004). The opportunity costs associated with the disease retrenchment are immeasurable. Further, the short-term impacts include increased inequity in both health and income (Armada et al. 2001; Medici et al. 1997; World Bank 2004). The human and fiscal costs associated with redressing this are incalculable. What remains unknown is whether the individual health and development situation of the countries which participated in the World Bank programs would be better or worse had there been no intervention at all.

2.4 The Beginning of Convergence—State and Human Security

At the end of the 20th century, a shift in geopolitical forces altered the priorities for the global community to address. The end of the Cold War momentarily dispersed fears of a nuclear apocalypse. There was a sense that all societies would benefit from the dismantling of the global stand-off between the U.S., the U.S.S.R., their satellite nations and proxy conflicts. The monies once spent maintaining the war machine could be redirected to social goods… the so-called **peace dividend**. The integrity of the nation-state in the ideological stand-off was no longer of sole import because of increasing integration across economic, political, social and cultural spheres with heightened globalization and fluidity of the principle of sovereignty in defining and addressing global issues. At the same time, there was a shift in development thought and a new paradigm of **sustainable human development**, a process that incorporates social, economic and environmental spheres, became central in development rhetoric. The social aspect incorporates the capabilities approach developed by Amartya Sen, an approach that defines development as expanding people's choices, as well looking at social structures and processes that impact human well-being. This speaks to human development. Sustainable human development strives to ensure that future generations have the same opportunities as the current generation—speaking to sustainability. This re-examination of development, peace-building and the role of multilateral institutions looked back to the original goals of the survivors the global warfare and rediscovered a *raison d'être* which focused on people rather than states. That reason was human security.

> The concept of security has for too long been interpreted narrowly: as security of territory from external aggression, or as protection of national interests in foreign policy or as global security from the threat of a nuclear holocaust. It has been related more to nation-states than to people. … Forgotten were the legitimate concerns of ordinary people who sought security in their daily lives. For many of them, security symbolized protection from the threat of disease, hunger, unemployment, crime, social conflict, political repression and environmental hazards. (UNDP 1994:22)

For decades, the international community remained narrowly focused on state security to the exclusion of a more anthropocentric approach. **State security** is concerned with external threats to the borders, institutions, and governance of nation-states. It emphasized maintaining military defense, state territories and protecting national interests. But at its inception, the UN Charter promised freedom from fear and freedom from want; state security would provide freedom from fear but human security would speak to freedom from want. **Human security** spoke to security of individuals in their home, in their work, in living their lives. It spoke to the UN Charter's promise to harness economic and social progress as a means to foster human well-being and dignity from which peace would follow. The collapse of the Soviet Union illustrated one of the short-comings of the state security paradigm in that it had come to focus almost exclusively on external threats to the nation-state. But the Soviet Union did not fall in battle against a foreign military. It collapsed because of economic and social disorder. This reminded the international community that a broader interpretation of state security, one that included internal threats to national integrity, was a real concern. The 1994 Human Development Report reminded the global community of the promise initially laid forth by the UN and positioned human security as a valid, complimentary paradigm to that of state security. Governments were responsible for protecting their people as well as territory from the threats of conflict, repression, disease, hunger, and want. The main threats to human security include economic opportunities of households as well as states, security of food, health, environment, personal security from external forces and domestic forms of oppression, protection of community, political participation and democratic institutions.

With the growing acceptance of the sustainable human development and human security models, health emerged as a critical input not only to economic success but to the very preservation of state and regional security upon with international governance was built. Throughout the 1990s, the import of health grew, transcending mere rhetoric of IGOs and nation-states and actually becoming a central component in the international agenda and policy-making forums.

This is not to say health never factored into international security concerns. In fact, the threat infectious disease—whether introduced deliberately or accidentally—posed to military, to the civilian population, and to socioeconomic structures were well understood for hundreds of years. With the epidemiological transition, chronic diseases entered the radar of policy-planners. Towards the close of the 20th century, the developed world was especially concerned about the implications of an aging population on health and financial security of the household and government institutions. The growing discussion of health in state and human security brought the global community back to the early ideal of health being necessary for global peace and stability as seen in the UN Charter and in the *Office International d'Hygiéne Publique* and the League of Nations before that.

International protocol for addressing disease threats to state security were codified by the WHO in 1951 under the International Sanitary Regulations. The International Health Regulations (IHR) replaced the International Sanitary Regulations in 1969. The IHR listed specific diseases which were to be monitored and reported vis-à-vis a global monitoring network, and set forth reporting and control protocol. Resurgent and newly emerging infections proved a challenge to the international community. Malaria re-emerged as both a regional and global threat. In fact, this single disease was found to limit economic growth in endemic countries by as much a 1.3% of GDP per year as compared to malaria-free nations (Gallup and Sachs 1998). The HIV/AIDS pandemic touched nearly every country in the world. Cholera and plague resurged; and the world acknowledged that 'tropical diseases' like malaria presented a persistent threat. In 2002–2003, the emergence and rapid spread of Severe Acute Respiratory Syndrome (SARS) showed that diseases spread quickly in the globalized landscape, and cost money and lives. The infection spread to 30 countries and caused 623 deaths worldwide (WHO 2003). Global economic costs are estimated to be as high as US$ 30 billion in Asia alone (Saywell et al. 2003). Among the nations which experienced greatest morbidity, mortality and/or economic losses were Singapore and Hong Kong, and Canada. The SARS epidemic proved to be just one of several health crises which threatened global security—human and economic. The pandemic of H1N1 influenza A virus (aka 'swine flu'), and the 2014 Ebola epidemic served as further prompts to global action to preserve security in the face of disease.

The IHR lacked teeth and coordination until the 21st century when international interest in state and human security converged, the symbiotic relationship between economic growth and health was understood and accepted in global power centers, the costs to global economics and security for ignoring health problems became clear, and international action began to back-up rhetoric. The world health community began the slow process of revising international instruments to better address disease threats in 1995. The result was a major revision of the IHR which was adopted in 2005. The number of internationally notifiable diseases expanded to include wild polio, novel strains of human influenza, and SARS. In addition, member states must notify WHO of any "Public Health Emergency of International Concern" (PHEIC) which includes biological, chemical, infectious, and radioactive threats. The health threat is to be reported regardless of the source of origin, a provision which allows for reporting zoonotic infections, or animal-based disease, which may pose a threat to the human population by leaping species. The IHR 2005 also created an extensive international network for disease surveillance and mechanisms for coordinated response to public health risks to minimize impact on international trade and traffic (WHO 2005b). The revised code attempts to foster a scaling-up of national public health capacity.

The strength of the IHR is that it created a disease intelligence network, surveillance and monitoring serving as the backbone of the global public health system. Although the regulations are legally binding to the signatories compliance with the IHR is voluntary as the WHO has no enforcement capacity. Positive and negative incentives are used to encourage compliance. The positive incentives include access to technical expertise, assistance in mobilizing funding to comply with the enhanced monitoring and reporting protocol, and logistical support for outbreak verification and response. The threat of international disdain should a state fail to comply with the IHR creates a negative incentive to moderate behavior. The SARS outbreak serves as one such example. China reported the outbreak of a novel disease in February, 2003 stating that it had detected 305 cases of this new disease (WHO 2003). Subsequent investigation proved that China has obscured the facts (WHO 2003). The outbreak had actually been detected in November and the number of cases was more than double the initial figure (WHO 2003). The international community chastised China for failing to report a public health threat which did indeed create a global crisis (WHO 2003). Critics said that had China reported the initial outbreak, actions could have been taken to limit the geographic spread, health impact and economic damage. However, the economic and political costs of disease stigma, and being labeled as a source or impacted country, are high and create perverse incentives which can cause states to hide disease outbreaks. National short-term interests may supersede a longer-term global perspective.

The revision to the IHR represented a change in health policy which occurred over nearly two decades. In the 1990s the WHO and UNDP tried to redefine health as an input into development whereas the World Bank emphasized economic growth's pre-eminence in triggering human development and expanding economic opportunities. The perspective shift associated with the human development and human security models created research and debate but encouraged little in terms of reorienting international health policy until the scares associated with the anthrax attacks in the United States in 2001 and the SARS epidemic showed that economic and military strength were no protection from global threats from disease. These cases also solidified the rise of human health as a concern for state security and showed that state and human security were inextricably linked.

Health had been gaining in-roads into the state security discussion since the collapse of the Soviet Union and the growing realization that HIV/AIDS was a ubiquitous and growing problem. A 1998 USAID report stated that HIV/AIDS was impacting military preparedness around the world, with an especially tenacious foothold in Africa, and therefore represented a clear and present threat to international security and peace (Peterson 2002). In January 2002, the UN Security Council convened to address the threat HIV/AIDS posed to regional and world security. This marked the first time in UN history that a disease was addressed as a security issue. Health intersected with state security in that an alteration in population health could create social effects which could destabilize or alter domestic political structures. As domestic institutions falter, regional instability could result.

HIV/AIDS was already proving it could erase decades of development progress by killing the most able-bodied age cohorts. The average life expectancy in

Southern Africa decreased from 60 in 1985 to 1990 to 53 in 2000–2005, a decrease many attribute to HIV/AIDS World Bank (2009b). In some countries, the loss was much greater. HIV/AIDS struck at the most economically productive age cohort. It was also the cohort of parents and primary care-givers to young children. Malawi alone has around 2 million AIDS orphans (Mutume 2001). Without parents, who will take care of the children? In some cases, child care falls to aging grandparents, creating societal strains which are exacerbated by the needs of the elderly. In other cases, the state provides care. In still other cases, the children are left to fend for themselves. Homeless and unguided, the hope of the future generations fall. The children leave school. With their exodus goes the hope not only for their own social and economic development, but for the country's future development prospects which are predicated upon having a healthy, productive, and educated population.

Health is linked to state security in a variety of ways. Health risks, chronic and communicable, endanger the lives of citizens at home and abroad. The military is not immune to these risks. As military men and women become sick or die, the military weakens and may not be adequately able to respond to other security challenges. Social and political stability may be at risk if a society is confronted with excess morbidity or mortality (Peterson 2002). A single event or disease could hamper development prospects for years, and reverberate across a broader population which may not have initially been exposed to the first disease. In 2001, the United Nations Food and Agriculture Organizations (FAO) found that a food security crisis was being exacerbated by HIV which was expected to kill an estimated 26% of the agricultural workforce in 10 African nations (FAO 2001). Those dependent upon the agricultural production would suffer too. If a single disease could take away 1.3% of economic growth potential in a year, the implication for economic distress from several health hazards across multiple years was staggering. The ultimate concern was that disruption in population health could not be isolated as it could cause a shift in the political, social, economic or military balance of power. International thought about health was changing. A critical mass of research and rhetoric had been reached. The international community could no longer address health as an isolated sector, nor as a domestic social issue. It was global, and it was important for peace, security and prosperity. In 2014, the UN Security Council and UN General Assembly again confronted a health threat to peace and security as Ebola raged through West African. The UN created its first ever health-focused mission as we will discuss in Chapter Five.

2.5 Convergence in the 21st Century

The 21st century began with two seminal events which firmly united health and economic development as being in a symbiotic relationship from which neither could be divorced from the other. These two events were the formation of the Commission on Macroeconomics and Health (CHM) and the Millennium Development Summit which resulted in the MDGs.

The CMH was founded in 2000, under the aegis of the WHO, as an attempt to bridge diverse views about the primacy of health or economic growth. The commission turned prior emphasis on health trickling down from economic development, or simply being good in and of itself, to health being a foundation to economic development. The CMH's 2001 report declared:

> Health is a priority goal in its own right, as well as a central input into economic development and poverty reduction. The importance of investing in health has been greatly underestimated, not only by analysts but also by developing-country governments and the international donor community. Increased investments in health as outlined in this Report would translate into hundreds of billions of dollars per year of increased income in the low-income countries. There are large social benefits to ensuring high levels of health coverage of the poor, including spillovers to wealthier members of the society. (WHO 2001:16)

The CMH became a leading researcher on links between socioeconomics and health, as well as an advocate for addressing macroeconomic policies and structures which have the power to impact population health through intended and unintended consequences. The CMH represented a confluence of health conceptualization in that it places health as both an outcome of various factors and processes as well as an input into the same. This conceptualization would be carried into the Millennium Development Goals (MDGs) and the Sustainable Development Goals (SDGs).

2.5.1 Millennium Development Goals

The same year, the United Nations hosted the Millennium Summit, which brought together world leaders to strategize ways in which to meet human development targets. This meeting focused on multiple pathways to achieving sustainable human development. It addressed the ideals of building human capacity and human capital as well as global sustainability. The group adopted the United Nations Millennium Development Declaration which established eight goals UN members would strive to achieve by 2015. Three of the eight goals explicitly address population health. A guiding ideal of the MDGs is that they would provide a focus for the global development agenda. Nation-states, IGOs and other actors would use the MDGs to inform programs and goals. Further the goals acknowledge the need for public and private spheres to operate together as they will both benefit by improvements in human development (Table 2.2).

As 2015 approached, the global community began evaluating the impact of the MDGs and making plans for post-2015. The Millennium Summit and MDGs were a hallmark in development and health in that they represented a convergence of the North and the South, explicitly addressed the cyclical relationship between health and economic development, and invited public—private partnerships. The conceptualization of health as an input and an outcome to other desirable goods was complete.

The evaluation of the MDGs revealed successes and failures, and provided lessons to be incorporated into the next iteration of global development goals—the SDGs. Several of the goals, such as Goals 7 and 8, lacked clarity (UN System Task

Table 2.2 Millennium development goals

Goal 1: Eradicate extreme poverty and hunger
Goal 2: Achieve universal primary education
Goal 3: Promote gender equality and empower women
Goal 4: Reduce child mortality
Goal 5: Improve maternal health
Goal 6: Combat HIV/AIDS, malaria and other diseases
Goal 7: Ensure environmental sustainability
Goal 8: Develop a global partnership for development

Data source United Nations (2010) http://www.un.org/millenniumgoals/. Accessed 9 October 2009.

Team 2012a; UN General Assembly 2013). The quantitative targets in the MDGs failed to account for baseline regional disparities and placed unfair expectations on those countries that were the worse off (UN System Task Team 2012b). For example, a country with a higher percentage of its population living in extreme poverty would have to have a much greater reduction in absolute number of people living in poverty to reach the 50% reduction goal than would a nation with a lower percentage of people living in poverty. The process by which the MDGs were created was criticized for a lack of participatory process and failure to utilize strong evidence in creating and monitoring progress (United Nations 2015; United Nations General Assembly 2013; Preparatory Committee 2011). The MDGs failed to account for or adopt to existent or emergent problems such as climate change, changing demographics, the impact of conflict and the conflict spiral on national and regional development, and the global increase of non-communicable diseases (UN General Assembly 2013; UN System Task Force 2012a; Preparatory Committee 2011; UN 2015)

The MDGs did foster broad dialogue not only about development but also about the differential abilities and responsibilities of global actors. These goals proved to be the beginning of a process to encourage integrating development programs across multiple sectors and actors. The MDGs also succeeded in directing resources to the developing world, and demonstrated that state and non-state actors could successfully coordinate their actions to have real impact on human development (UN 2015; UN System Task Team 2012a). There were also remarkable achievements in terms of specific goals.

The most lauded achievement of the MDGs was reducing by half the percentage of the global population living in extreme poverty, defined as $ 1.25 a day. Nearly half of the world's population lived in extreme poverty in 1990. This number dropped to 14% by 2015 (UN 2014; UN 2015 pg 4; UN System Task Team 2012a). While critics note that poverty reduction in China accounts for a significant portion of this change, the decrease remains import. The target of halving the proportion of the people without access to safe drinking water and basic sanitation was also met. By 2015 it is estimated that 91% of the global population had obtained access to safe drinking water (UN General Assembly 2013; UN 2015). Although the target of universal access to education was not met, primary school enrollment in developing regions increased from 83% in 2000 to 91% in 2015 with the highest gains in Sub-Saharan Africa (UN 2015).

There was notable progress in the health-related goals, but much work remains. Under-5 mortality rates fell from 90 per 1000 live births to 43 per 1000—a significant gain but still short of the target of 31 deaths per 1000 (UN 2015). There was progress in improving maternal mortality, but neither the target for maternal mortality nor for access to reproductive health was met. Despite the targets for Goal 6 combatting HIV/AIDS, malaria and other diseases not being met, there were important gains in the battle against infectious disease. In terms of hard numbers, HIV incidence decreased by 1.4 million, and deaths from malaria and TB also fell (UN 2015). More than 12 million people gained access to antiretroviral therapy (ART) (UN 2015).

2.5.2 Sustainable Development Goals

The year 2015 marked the deadline for achieving the MDGs but it did not mark the end of global efforts targeting development. The United Nations undertook a two year process to develop the next iteration of global development goals. This time, the UN strove to have a more inclusive process that would produce goals applicable to both the developed and the developing world, while addressing the gaps in the MDGs. This began with the United Nations Conference on Sustainable Development in June 2012, the Rio +20 conference, at which participants called for a process that would include input from multiple stake-holders. As a result, the UN established the United Nations Open Working Group (OWG) for creating the new development agenda.

The OWG consisted of 30 seats shared by 70 countries. These countries were grouped by geographic region and rotated meeting attendance among group members (Sustainable Development 2015). The OWG sought input from multiple stakeholders both within and outside of the UN system via surveys, discussions, and on-line discussions. These tools included the My World 2015 survey (www.myworld2015.org), a broad-reaching internet survey that allowed laypeople to vote on what they saw as the six most urgent development needs. The OWG delivered its final synthesis report to the General Assembly in December, 2014. This report became the basis of the SDGs, which were adopted by the General Assembly on September 25, 2015 (A/RES/70/1) (Table 2.3).

The SDGs consist of 17 goals with 169 separate targets that include human rights, equality and sustainability as core values (UN General Assembly 2015; UN System Task Team 2012a). The goals purport to focus on inclusive social and economic development, environmental sustainability, and peace and security (UN General Assembly 2015; UN System Task Team 2012a). The goals are both applauded and condemned for being aspirational rather than obtainable. The goals

Table 2.3 Sustainable development goals

Goal 1: End poverty in all its forms everywhere
Goal 2: End hunger, achieve food security and improved nutrition and promote sustainable agriculture
Goal 3: Ensure healthy lives and promote well-being for all at all ages
Goal 4: Ensure inclusive and quality education for all and promote lifelong learning
Goal 5: Achieve gender equality and empower all women and girls
Goal 6: Ensure access to water and sanitation for all
Goal 7: Ensure access to affordable, reliable, sustainable and modern energy for all
Goal 8: Promote inclusive and sustainable economic growth, employment and decent work for all
Goal 9: Build resilient infrastructure, promote sustainable industrialization and foster innovation
Goal 10: Reduce inequality within and among countries
Goal 11: Make cities inclusive, safe, resilient and sustainable
Goal 12: Ensure sustainable consumption and production patterns
Goal 13: Take urgent action to combat climate change and its impacts
Goal 14: Conserve and sustainably use the oceans, seas and marine resources
Goal 15: Sustainably manage forests, combat desertification, halt and reverse land degradation, halt biodiversity loss
Goal 16: Promote just, peaceful and inclusive societies
Goal 17: Revitalize the global partnership for sustainable development

Source United Nations. http://www.un.org/sustainabledevelopment/sustainable-development-goals/. Accessed 27 July 2016.

are both action-based and rights-based with a focus on equity, evidence-based practice, and enhanced monitoring and evaluation.

The new goals have an explicit focus on pathways to economic well-being including the traditional call for increased economic growth, increased productivity, and poverty reduction. However, the OWG synthesis report was critical of using GDP as a standard measure for gauging economic success (UN 2014). While there is a call for more just and inclusive trade, consumption and labor systems, the SGDs lack dialogue about reform. The new goals maintain the push for renewed partnerships across public and private entities, and between the global North and global South which were found in the MDGs. However, they also have a new emphasis on South—South partnerships and capabilities, and highlight the potential contributions from middle income countries, as well as the unique challenges they face.

Addressing climate change is both an explicit goal (Goal 13) and an aspect of six other goals.

The promotion of health and well-being is a singular goal (Goal 3) with 13 specific targets which attempt to address health in a more holistic manner than did the MDGs. This new manifestation addresses the notion that "Health is a precondition for and an outcome and indicator of all three dimensions of sustainable development…" (WHO 2015b:5). The targets include goals from the MDGS—improving maternal mortality and infant mortality, and addressing HIV/AIDS, malaria, and TB—but adds a new health agenda focusing on non-communicable diseases, sociobehavioral illness and industrial harm. Goal 3 addresses not only health outcomes but inputs to sustainable health care. It calls for Universal health coverage and access, strengthening research, development and accessibility of essential medicines, and improving the health work force.

2.6 Conclusion

We have seen how the WHO and the World Bank have separate but important roles in global governance and as drivers of health and development. We saw, too, that the institutions, their foci, and strategies change from internal and external pressures. The World Bank moved from a narrow definition of development to engaging in a more holistic approach to development with concern for social safety nets. Like the WHO, it also uses the MDGs to guide some of its operations. In the 21st century, the WHO was strengthened in its ideal of health as a human right by the MDGs and the work of the CMH by international financial institutions and the broad international political community.

Of the eight MDG goals, three explicitly focus on health. The MDGs call for creating global partnerships between public and private actors. The World Bank and the WHO are engaged in a number of such partnerships. Once such example, is the Global Fund to Fight AIDS, Tuberculosis and Malaria, a partnership we will learn more about in Chapter Six. The call for increased public-private partnerships recognizes the asymmetric economic powers and resources of the private versus public sector and underscores the message that public and private actors have common interests.

It is too early to tell what the SDGs will achieve in terms of action and outcomes. They represent a continuing evolution of the definition and operationalization of health and development. The SDGs emphasis the intertwining and dependency of multiple sectors to impact human development. In the new global vision, economic well-being is more than GPD growth, and health is clearly held to be both an input to and outcome of development. Health, livelihoods and adequate quality of life are held to be basic rights. The new goals are criticized for their breadth, lack of specificity, lack of measurability, and potential cost (Wiser 2015; Stewart 2015; Economist 2015). However, they do represent a movement towards a more holistic integration of well-being across economic, human and environmental spheres.

Discussion Questions

1. What are three ways in which health is conceptualized by international actors? Which view is closest to your own?
2. What aspects of social medicine differentiate it from biomedicine? How does the difference between the two impact the debate about health and development?
3. The charter of the WHO was heavily debated between countries that favored social insurance and those that did not. The role of the agency in regulating biomedicine was also a point of contention. Why do you think these aspects of health care were so contentious?
4. What are the health outcomes associated with maternal health? Describe technocratic and social routes that may be effective in decreasing maternal deaths.
5. Compare the obstacles associated with global vaccination to the obstacles associated with global improvements in maternal health. What important differences do you see? How might you address these?
6. What were the roles of the World Bank and the IMF when created in 1944? What are their roles today?
7. What are the structural adjustment programs? What polities did they entail?
8. What was the purpose of decentralizing health care? What were some of the (unforeseen) negative consequences?
9. Do you believe the WHO approach to development through health vis-à-vis primary care, or the World Bank approach to health through development via structural adjustment and health sector reform will yield better results in terms of development and human well-being? Why?
10. What global geopolitical factors contributed to the growing importance placed on human security at the end of the 20th century?
11. Compare the targets of the SDGs to those of the MDGs. Where do you see similarities in targets? Where are there differences? Select an SDG and discuss what you believe the greatest challenge is to its achievement.

References

Anderson, C. (2008, December 2). Iceland gets help to recover from historic crisis. *IMF Survey Magazine*. http://www.imf.org/external/pubs/ft/survey/so/2008/int111908a.htm. Accessed September 21, 2009.

Armada, F., Muntaner, C., & Navarro, V. (2001). Health and social security reforms in Latin America: The convergence of the World Health Organization, the World Bank, and transnational Corporations. *International Journal of Health Services, 31*(4), 729–768.

Berkman, L., & Kawachi, I. (Eds.). (2000). *Social epidemiology*. New York: Oxford University Press.

Booth, D., Grigsby, A., Toranzo, A. (2006) *Politics and Poverty Reduction Strategies: Lessons from Latin America HIPCs*. Working Paper 262. Overseas Development Institution. http://www.odi.org.uk/resources/download/1184.pdf. Accessed October 20, 2009.

Braathen, E. (2006) *A participatory pathbreaker? Experience with poverty reduction strategies from four South African Countries*. Working Paper 2006: 122. Norwegian Institute for Urban and Regional Research. http://en.nibr.no/uploads/publications/1df1db2bd58ca8ca81eb79e3c3fcf445.pdf. Accessed October 20, 2009.

Bretton Woods Project. (2006) http://www.brettonwoodsproject.org/item.shtml?x=537848. Accessed December 15, 2009.

Brunton, D. (2004). Dealing with disease in populations: public health, 1830-1880. In D. Brunton (Ed.), *Medicine transformed: Health, disease and society in Europe 1800–1930* (pp. 180–210). Manchester, UK: Manchester University Press.

Economist. (2015). *The 169 commandments*, March 28, 2015. http://www.economist.com/news/leaders/21647286-proposed-sustainable-development-goals-would-be-worse-useless-169-commandments. Accessed July 6, 2016.

Ewig, C., & Kay, S. J. (2008). New political legacies and the politics of health and pension re-reforms in Chile. In D. Beland & B. Gran (Eds.), *Public and private social policy: Health and pension policies in a new era* (pp. 249–268). Houndsmills, UK: Palgrave Macmillan.

Farmer, P., & Bertrand, D. (2000). Hypocrisies of development and the health of the Haitian poor. In J. Y. Kim et al. (Eds.), *Dying for growth: Global inequality and the health of the poor* (pp. 65–90). Monroe: Common Courage Press.

Food and Agricultural Organization of the United Nations (FAO). (2001). *The Impact of HIV/AIDS of Food Security*. CFS 2001/3. http://www.fao.org/docrep/meeting/003/Y0310E.htm#P87_4352. Accessed 6 February 2017.

Gallup, J., & Sachs, J. (1998). The economic burden of malaria. *American Journal of Tropical Medicine and Hygeine, 64*(1/2), 85–96.

Gershman, J., & Irwin, A. (2000). Getting a grip on the global economy. In J. Kim et al. (Eds.), *Dying for growth: Global inequality and the health of the poor* (pp. 11–43). Monroe: Common Courage Press.

Gilles, H., & Warrell, D. (eds.) (1993). *Bruce-chwatt's essential malariology* (3rd edn.). Boston: E. Arnold.

Gillespie, J. (2002). Social medicine, social security and international health, 1940-1960. In E. Rodriguez-Ocana (Ed.), *The politics of the healthy life: An international perspective* (pp. 219–239). Sheffield, UK: European Association for the History of Medicine and Health Publication.

Gomez-Dantes, O. (2001). "Health". In P. J. Simmons, C. de Jonge Oudraat (Eds.), *Managing global issues: Lessons learned*. Washington DC: Carnegie Endowment for International Peace.

Gottschalk, R. (2005). The macro content of PRSPs: Assessing the need for a more flexible macroeconomic policy framework. *Development Policy Review, 23*(4), 419–442.

Jamison, D., Breman, J., Measham, A., Alleyne, G., Claeson, M., Evans, D., et al. (Eds.). (2006). *Disease control priorities in developing countries* (2nd ed.). Washington, DC: World Bank.

Kakwani, N., Makonnen, E., & van der Gaag, J. (1990). *Structural adjustment and living conditions in developing countries*. Working Paper 467. Washington, DC: World Bank.

Keegan, R., & Bilous, J. (2004). Current issues in global immunizations. *Seminars in Pediatric Infectious Diseases, 15*(3), 130–136.

Kim, J. Y., Millen, J., Irwin, A., & Gershman, J. (Eds.). (2000a). *Dying for growth: Global inequality and the health of the poor*. Monroe: Common Courage Press.

Kim, J. Y., Shakow, A., Bayona, J., Rhatigan, J. Rubín, & de Celis, E. (2000b). Sickness amidst recovery: public debt and private suffering in Peru. In J. Kim et al. (Eds.), *Dying for growth: Global inequality and the health of the poor* (pp. 127–154). Monroe: Common Courage Press.

Kunitz, S. J. (2007). *The health of populations: General theories and particular realities*. Oxford: Oxford University.

Lee, J. W., Aylward, B., Hull, H. F., Batson, A., Birmingham, M. E., & Lloyd, J. (1997). Reaping the benefits: Getting vaccines to those who need them. In M. M. Levine, G. C. Woodrow, J. B. Kaper, & G. S. Cobon (Eds.), *New generation vaccines* (2nd ed., pp. 79–88). New York: Marcel Dekker.

Medici, A. C., London, J.L., Coelho, O., & Saxenian, H. (1997). Manager care and manager competition in Latin America and the Caribbean. In G. Schieber (Ed.), *Innovations in health care financing: proceedings from a World Bank conference*. Discussion Paper No. 365. Washington DC: World Bank.

Mutume, G. (2001). Malawi battles AIDS orphan nightmare. *Africa Recovery, 15*(3), 17. http://www.un.org/ecosocdev/geninfo/afrec/vol15no3/153chil5.htm. Accessed December 15, 2009.

Najera-Morrondo, J. A. (1991). Malaria control: History shows its possible. *World Health, 4*, 2.

Newman, P. R. (1965). *Malaria eradication and population growth with reference to Ceylon and British Guyana*. Ann Arbor: School of Public Health, University of Michigan.

Oppong, J. R. (2001). Structural adjustment and the health care system. In K. Konadu-Agyemang (Ed.), *IMF and World Bank sponsored structural adjustment programs in Africa: Ghana's experience, 1983–1999* (pp. 357–370). Aldershot, UK: Ashgate.

Peterson, S. (2002). Epidemic disease and national security. *Security Studies, 12*(2), 43–81.

Preparatory Committee for the United Nations Conference on Sustainable Development. (2011). *Synthesis report on best practices and lessons learned on the objective and themes of the United Nations conference on sustainable development*. A/CONF.216/PC/8. New York: United Nations.

Raczynski, G. (2001). Provision of social services in Chile: A search for a new model. In G. Mwabu, C. Ugaz, & G. White (Eds.), *Social provision in low-income countries: New patterns and emerging trends* (pp. 211–227). Oxford: Oxford University.

Rodríguez-Ocaña, E. (Ed.). (2002). *The politics of the healthy life: An international perspective*. Sheffield, UK: European Association for the History of Medicine and Health Publication.

Save the Children. (2008). *Mothers day report card*. http://www.savethechildren.org/newsroom/2008/best-worst-countries-mother.html. Accessed June 6, 2010.

Saywell, T., Fowler, G., & Crispin, S. (2003). The cost of SARS: $ 11 billion and rising. *Far East Economic Review*. March 24, 2003 on line at http://unpan1.un.org/intradoc/groups/public/documents/apcity/unpan009483.pdf. Accessed June 3, 2010.

Shaw, R. P., & Ainsworth, M. (Eds.). (1995). *Financing health service through user fees and insurance: Case studies from Sub-Saharan Africa*. Washington DC: World Bank.

Smith-Nonini, S. (2000). The smoke and mirrors of health reform in El Salvador: Community health NGOs and the not-so-liberal state. In J. Y. Kim et al. (Eds.), *Dying for growth: Global inequality and the health of the poor* (pp. 359–381). Monroe: Common Courage Press.

Stern, A. M., & Markel, H. (2004). International efforts to control infectious disease, 1851 to the present. *Journal of the American Medical Association, 292*(12), 1474–1479.

Stewart, F. (2015). The sustainable development goals: A comment. *Journal of Global Ethics, 11* (3), 288–293.

Sustainable Development (2015). *Intergovernmental process*. http://www.sustainabledevelopment2015.org/index.php/intergovernmental-processes. Accessed July 8, 2016.

Thornton, R. (2008). *Unimagined community: Sex, networks, and AIDs in Uganda and South Africa*. Berkeley: University of California.

United Nations. (1945). *United Nations charter*. http://www.un.org/en/documents/charter/. Accessed December 15, 2009.

United Nations. (1974). *United Nations declaration on the establishment of a new economic order*. http://www.un-documents.net/s6r3201.htm. Accessed September 6, 2009.

United Nations. (2010). http://www.un.org/millenniumgoals/. Accessed October 9, 2009.

United Nations. (2014). The road to dignity by 2030: Ending poverty, transforming all lives and protecting the planet. In *Synthesis report of the secretary-general on the post-2015 sustainable development agenda*. A/69/700. New York: United Nations.

United Nations. (2015). *The millennium development goals report 2015*. New York: United Nations.

UNDP. (1994). *Human development report 1994: New dimensions of human security*. New York: Oxford University Press.

UNDP. (2000). *Human development report 2000: Human rights and human development*. New York: Oxford University Press.

UN General Assembly. (2013). *A life of dignity for all: Accelerating progress towards the millennium development goals and advancing the United Nations development agenda beyond 2015*. Report of the Secretary-General. A/68/202. New York: United Nations.

UN General Assembly. (2015) Transforming our world: the 2030 agenda for sustainable development. Resolution adopted by the General Assembly 25 September 2015. A/RES/70/1. New York: United Nations.

UN System Task Force. (2012a). *Realizing the future we want for all: Report to the secretary-general*. NY: United Nations.

UN System Task Force. (2012b). *Review of the contributions of the MDG agenda to foster development: Lessons for the post-2015 UN development agenda*. New York: United Nations.

Wall, L. L. (1998). Dead mothers and injured wives, the social context of maternal morbidity and mortality among the Hausa of Northern Nigeria. *Studies in Family Planning, 29*(4), 341–359.

Watts, Sheldon. (1997). *Epidemics and history: Disease, power, and imperialism*. New Haven: Yale University.

Weindling, P. (2004). From germ theory to social medicine: public heath. In D. Brunton (Ed.), *Medicine transformed: Health, disease and society in Europe* (pp. 1880–1930). Manchester, UK: Manchester University.

Wheelis, M. (2002). Biological warfare at the 1346 siege of Caffa. *Emerging Infectious Diseases [serial online], 8*(9). http://www.cdc.gov/ncidod/EID/vol8no9/01-0536.htm. Accessed June 5, 2010.

Wiser, Scott. (2015). On the structure of global development goals. *Journal of Global Ethics, 11* (3), 280–287.

Worboys, M. (2004). Chapter 8 colonial and imperial medicine pgs. In D. Brunton (Ed.), *Medicine transformed: Health, disease and society in Europe 1800–1930* (pp. 211–229). Manchester, UK: Manchester University Press.

World Bank. (1993). *World development report 1993: Investing in health*. New York: Oxford University Press.

World Bank. (2004). *Health sector reform in Bolivia: A decentralization case study*. Washington, DC: World Bank.

World Bank. (2009). *The world bank annual report 2008: Year in Review*. http://go.worldbank.org/UQHC5XICN0. Accessed September 21, 2009.

World Bank. (2009b). *WDI on-line World Development Indicators*. http://databank.worldbank.org/data/reports.aspx?source=world-development-indicators. Accessed 23 Apr; 31 may 2010.

World Bank. (2016) *Annual Report 2016*. Washington DC: World Bank.

World Health Organization. (1978). *Declaration of alma-ata*. www.who.int/hpr/NPH/docs/declaration_almaata.pdf. Accessed September 4, 2009.

World Health Organization. (2001). *Macroeconomics and health: Investing in health for economic development*. A report of the Commission on Macroeconomics and Health Geneva: World Health Organization.

World Health Organization. (2003). *Severe acute respiratory syndrome (SARS): Status of the outbreak and lessons for the immediate future*. Geneva: World Health Organization.

World Health Organization. (2005a). *Immunization against diseases of public health importance. Fact sheet 288*. www.who.int/mediacentre/factsheets/fs288/en/index.html. Accessed June 6, 2010.

World Health Organization. (2005b). *International health regulations*. http://www.who.int/topics/international_health_regulations/en/. Accessed November 2, 2009.

World Health Organization. (2005c). *World Health Report 2005*. http://www.who.int/whr/2005/en/index.html. Accessed June 6, 2010.

WHO, UNICEF, UNFPA and The World Bank. (2007). *Maternal mortality in 2005: Estimates developed by WHO, UNICEF, UNFPA and The World Bank*. Geneva: World Health Organization.

World Health Organization. (2008a). Primary health care: Fiji's broken dream. *Bulletin World Health Organization, 86*(3). http://www.who.int/bulletin/volumes/86/3/08-020308/en/index.html. Accessed June 12, 2010.

World Health Organization. (2008b). Flawed by fair: Brazil's health system reaches out to the poor. *Bulletin World Health Organization, 86*(4). http://www.who.int/bulletin/volumes/86/4/en/. Accessed June 12, 2010.

World Health Organization. (2008c). *Constitution of the world health organization* (45th edn.). http://www.who.int/governance/eb/who_constitution_en.pdf. Accessed June 12, 2010.

World Health Organization. (2008d). *World health report 2008.* http://www.who.int/whr/2008/whr08_en.pdf. Accessed June 6, 2010.

World Health Organization. (2009a). *2009 state of the world's vaccines and immunizations* (3rd edn.). http://whqlibdoc.who.int/publications/2009/9789241563864_eng.pdf. Accessed June 6, 2010.

World Health Organization. (2009b) *Program budget 2008–2009.* http://apps.who.int/gb/ebwha/pdf_files/AMTSP-PPB/a-mtsp_4en.pdf. Accessed September 21, 2009.

World Health Organization. (2009c). *Malaria.* http://www.who.int/mediacentre/factsheets/fs094/en/index.html. Accessed December 15, 2009.

World Health Organization. (2009d). *Smallpox.* http://www.who.int/mediacentre/factsheets/smallpox/en/index.html. Accessed September 27, 2009.

World Health Organization. (2010). *Maternal mortality.* http://www.who.int/making_pregnancy_safer/topics/maternal_mortality/en/index.html. Accessed June 6, 2010.

World Health Organization. (2015a). *Global immunization data.* July 2015. http://www.who.int/immunization/monitoring_surveillance/Global_Immunization_Data.pdf?ua=12016. Accessed August 3, 2016.

World Health Organization. (2015b). Health in the post-2015 development agenda: Need for a social determinants of health approach. In *A joint statement from the UN platform on social determinants of health*. Geneva: WHO.

World Health Organizatin (2015c). *Programme Budget 2016–2017.* Geneva: WHO.

World Health Organization, United Nations Children's Fund, & World Bank. (2007). *Maternal mortality in 2005*. Geneva: World Health Organization.

Chapter 3
State-Led Growth and Development

Abstract The health of the state is a symbolic conceptualization of a collective entity that is made up of geographic territory, institutions, laws, and people. At the national level, health can intersect with concern for state and human security, macroeconomic performance and population health. Two dominant models of state investment developed in the late 20th century. One placed human development, with concern for health and education, at the forefront of policy concern; the second placed macroeconomic growth at the policy apex. Each approach entailed trade-offs which affect both short-and long-term outcomes and opportunities for the nation. Rapid, short-term economic growth can create monetary and material resources that can improve the availability of inputs to health but can also increase health inequalities. If the state does not intervene, these inequalities will cause long-term harm to the poorest, most vulnerable in society. Investment in human health and welfare can achieve equitable health coverage, access to care and gains in health outcomes. However, it can also lead to unsustainable and unsound budgetary practices that impact the macroeconomic performance of the state. Chile and Sri Lanka demonstrate the strengths and weaknesses of the aforementioned approaches to health and development.

National concern for health and development is manifest within the context of population health and the health of the state. **Population health** refers to an aggregation of individual level health measures that include life expectancy, maternal mortality ratios, and epidemiological profiles that show which diseases cause the greatest amount of death and disability. The health of the state relates to the conceptualization of a national 'body' consisting of geographic territory, institutions such as government agencies, rules and norms, and the citizenry. When the concern is with population health, policy focuses on the best ways to impact the health of many. Such a view by necessity may sacrifice the needs of the few or the one. When concern lies with the health of the state, national income and the integrity of geographic boundaries and political institutions are the key concerns. Creative tension therefore exists between concern for the people and concern for the state. Actions taken to guarantee the health of the nation-state may be deleterious to

S.A. Johnson, *Challenges in Health and Development*,
DOI 10.1007/978-3-319-53204-2_3

population health. Take, for instance, the act of going to war. Lives are sacrificed in battles waged to maintain the integrity of political institutions, national norms and territorial boundaries. By contrast, a nation-state may invest heavily in ways to better the health of the population by providing universal access to preventative care and unlimited curative treatments. Such action could result in short-term improvements in the people's health, but the state may exhaust its coffers and could go bankrupt. It may find itself unable to continue covering such costs, and unable to fulfill other state obligations or even protect its citizens. Of particular interest for health and development, therefore, are the trade-offs between macro-economic stability and the well-being of the populace via provision of health care.

In this chapter, we will explore these tensions through two case studies. Sri Lanka serves as an example of long-term investment in health with little economic growth. By the 1960s, Sri Lanka achieved health outcomes equal to those found in the developed world. It did this without heavy economic growth and, some argue, at the cost of economic growth. None-the-less, the investment helped the country maintain high levels of education and good health outcomes despite a 26-year old civil war that ended in 2009. Chile, on the other hand, is the darling child of multilateral development agencies such as the World Bank and IMF; it represents a success story in terms of achieving high levels of economic growth as well as restructuring and privatizing a troubled health care system that now provides nearly universal access to care with a modicum of financial sustainability. These achievements have come at the cost of widening inequity in quality and coverage of health care.

Before we begin looking at national policies in these two states, we must first understand the concept and context of the nation-state in the international system. Policy entails action and re-action to improve the well-being of the state. But the state is a non-corporeal entity. Disease analogies in reference to the status of the state abound—a state can hemorrhage money, turn red with the blood of its people, become sick and weaken, rot from within and so forth. Anthropomorphisms aside, a state cannot literally bleed nor can it feel pain or suffer the way individual members of society can. States are, however, the pre-eminent actors in international and domestic governance. So how then does one define state well-being and measure changes in state welfare?

To answer this, we must ask what is a state?

In its most basic manifestation, a state is simply a catchment area for political power. It is a centralized political entity that is defined by a geographic territory and by institutions, laws and norms that govern people. State institutions make and enforce domestic laws, raise revenues through taxation, and maintain a legal monopoly on the use of force for defense and enforcement. The state's actions are guided by law, norms and standards, and by individuals who speak on behalf of the greater entity. State institutions and leaders manage national discourse and agendas; the style of management and degree of openness in communication is a product of the type of government and political system within a state. The state also creates order-imposing structures to disseminate and enforce the rule of law. State institutions are products of rules and norms, and are also products of power structures and interest groups which form between people who make up the state's citizenry. Power structures impact rules which, in turn, impact the power structures. The extent of state powers is defined within a geographic space denoting national boundaries which fluctuate as the influence and power of a political entity flows and ebbs in conjunction with the political power of surrounding states. In other words, the state's influence and territory are products of the state itself, and of the other international actors. Shifts in internal political structures, military power, or economic performance can cause a domino effect in regional and global balance of powers (Eller 1999; Martinussen 1995).

A state's power represents and influences a broad populace which is what Benedict Anderson terms an imaginary community. "It is *imagined* because the members of even the smallest nation will never know most of their fellow members, meet them, or even hear of them, yet in the minds of each lives the image of their communion" (Anderson 2001, p. 6). In his writing on the roots of nationalism, Anderson describes the ties of a people that extend beyond their geographically proximate community or their membership in a group based on a shared ethnicity, history or geographic territory. He captures disparate scales of interests, from individual to regional to national, which come together in the formulation of state identity and policy. This is a useful model to apply as we explore the tensions between state, sub-groups, and individuals within the context of health and development.

With this in mind, we can answer the question posed earlier in this chapter, how does one measure a state's well-being? One could measure it based on qualitative assessments such as stability of political institutions, social stability, comparative political strength in a global system, strength of the military, or happiness of its citizens. If one believes that money is power, then the condition of a nation-state's economy may be a marker of well-being. One could look at absolute GDP or growth in GDP. One might also focus on the measures of population health described in Chapter One, and changes in the same over time, to understand the condition of a state. Frequently, analysts look to a combination of qualitative and quantitative data to understand the health of nation-states.

A state may function for the preservation of itself, a non-human entity, but its obligations include providing for and protecting individuals within its bailiwick. We saw in Chapter Two that international law grants a state authority over its own people, but places respect for human rights, maintenance of peace, and preservation of human health in a higher order category. If a state fails to respond to the needs of its citizens in these essential areas, the international community may. The state may be imaginary, but it is built upon the flesh and blood of real people whose well-being must be maintained for the state to function and remain autonomous. The level of well-being for which a state is responsible, and whose health must be maintained, are not universally defined nor consistently enforced. There is, therefore, variation and negotiation when prioritizing national agendas. The state's obligations in providing care to its citizenry, so long as there is not an indiscriminate amount of violence and death which may trigger a humanitarian intervention, are also not well defined. The norm of the individual's right to life, and of the government's obligation to protect such a right, does not offer guidance as to how best to preserve this right, nor does this right address issues such as quality. Even where the notion of health as a human right is accepted, there is no universal agreement as to how a government should best provide for or protect this right. Are the state's resources better directed to earning national income that can be used to purchase inputs to well-being, or are they better directed in providing health care directly? Where health care is provided, what should it look like?

3.1 Trade-Offs Between Internal and External Factors, Social and Economic Outcomes

In maintaining both state and population health, national policy must respond to internal and external factors. Table 3.1 lists internal and external factors which impact state and population health. Each variable may act independently or interactively. Food security, for instance, is an area in which domestic and international factors impact population health and state well-being. A state which has a plethora of natural resources and environmental endowments may be able to use those resources to provide for its populace, for example, by growing rice. The rice can be used for domestic consumption, or it can be exported and the international revenue earned saved as **foreign reserve** or used to import other types of food and goods. The amount of money earned from the sale depends upon international demand and international supply. If there is a high demand for rice, and very few countries produce it, then the money earned will be comparatively high. If however either demand is low, or there are many competitive suppliers, the amount of money earned will be low. In either case, the producing state has little influence over the ultimate price paid. If the rice-growing state has plentiful water resources, good soil, and favorable climatic conditions, it may be able to raise a variety of food for its people and so may not need to earn money on the international market to import foods. If, however, its natural endowments and institutional history are such that all it can grow is rice, then the populace may suffer from malnutrition barring any other intervention. Other foods would need to be imported to improve available food sources. What is imported will depend upon the international price earned for rice exports, international prices being earned for the imported good, and political and cultural preferences. This is an oversimplification, but demonstrates the interplay between domestic and international forces.

Although subject to domestic and international forces, the state has considerable leeway to define its actual role and responsibilities vis-à-vis its citizenry. Political systems, economic and social philosophies all come into play. Democratic political systems allow for a more expansive role of citizens to express their preferences, through voter choice, and to alter political power and policy, than do non-democratic systems. Welfare states assume a more active role in public provision for the health and well-being of their populaces than do non-welfare states by dedicating nation wealth to provide direct inputs to health, such as universal access

Table 3.1 A brief summary of international and domestic factors that can influence the policy options and overall well-being of a nation-state and its citizens

Internal (domestic)	External (international)
Natural resources	Market demand Prices
Labor force composition Education level Wage structure	Capital flow FDI
Political system Is it responsive to internal or external pressures? Political will to address needs of populace Inclusiveness Distribution of resources	Transnational governance Ability to control cross-border issues Capital flow Illicit markets Population movement Environmental impacts
Local market conditions Prices Demand Domestic availability	International market conditions Prices Demand Currency valuation
Strength of institutions Ability to attract investment Ability to regulate/enforce Ability to negotiate equally	Globalization FDI Multilateral institutions
Military	Regional/international military
Epidemiological profile	Infectious disease and openness of movement
Demographics	Migration
Social forces Interest groups	Regional stability
Financial resources Economic strength Availability of capital Debt	Global demand Multilateral institutions Conditionality Debt forgiveness

to care, and indirect inputs like salary support. Nation-states which rely upon private enterprise or market forces to provide for social goods assume less direct responsibility in the provision of inputs to the health and well-being of its people.

Ultimately there are trade-offs between the economic and social policy balance a nation pursues; the specific tradeoffs and available options are often the result of intersectoral and historical processes. For example, the Dominican Republic in the early 1980s found itself limited in terms of both economic and social policy options because of a historical trajectory. The Dominican Republic, like many Latin American nations, utilized Import Substitution and Industrialization (ISI) and monocrop agricultural production of sugar cane as its main development strategies through much of the 20th century (Moya Pons 1999). Rising sugar prices in the post WWII years contributed to growing foreign reserves and increased interest by the oligarchs in controlling sugar producing land. By 1960, the dictator Raphael Trujillo owned two-thirds of the productive sugarcane area in the country (Clemens and de Groot 1988). Trujillo was assassinated in 1961. After a disputed election, social unrest and invasion by the United States military, Joaquín Balaquer, a protégée of Trujillo, became president in 1966. He continued the dual approach of land concentration and ISI policies through the 1970s. All was well and good so long as sugar prices remained relatively high. But the prices eventually dropped with increased international competition, and resulted in decreased foreign earnings (Vedovato 1986). This decline came at a time when the price of oil, an important import, rose. By 1975, the economy was shrinking by more than 2% per year,[1] foreign debt was mounting and foreign reserves were nearly depleted (Moya Pons 1995, 1999; Espinal 1995). When Antonio Guzmán became president, he inherited an economic mess with few options available with which to make repairs. His response was to print money without backing, and increase public sector employment (Espinal 1995; Moya Pons 1995). The result was increased public debt and inflation.

The country subsequently experimented in fits and starts with structural adjustment programs which helped to stabilize inflation rates but wreaked havoc upon social supports (Espinal 1995; Moya Pons 1995). Reforms included austerity measures, free-floating the peso, reduction/elimination of public subsidies, and addition of a regressive sales tax. Current account balances improved, fiscal deficits declined, and inflation rates stabilized. But the free-float of the peso resulted in a dramatic reduction in its international purchasing power as it decreased from a one-to-one exchange rate against the US dollar to an eight to one exchange rate (Espinal 1995).

The Dominican Republic had built an economic and agricultural legacy based upon export of a single cash crop—sugarcane. Food for domestic consumption was imported. With decreasing foreign reserves, frozen credit (the result of defaulting on debt payments), and decreased currency value, the middle and lower classes were not able to purchase adequate levels of food. This, coupled with the elimination of public subsidies in the interest of fiscal balance, meant nutritional standards were about to take a nosedive. The result was civil unrest and food riots (Espinal 1995). Again, policy makers faced competing domestic (stave off civil unrest and provide food) and international (pay down loan balance, build up reserves) priorities. Their options were limited by this historical trajectory. By 1989, the Dominican Republic suspended debt payments. As a result, states that supplied oil and medical goods suspended shipments (Moya Pons 1995). The poor were again hurt as essential goods became unavailable.

Although the Dominican Republic eventually regained some fiscal and social stability, this case highlights the trade-offs between economic and social policy. It also shows how a state's historical trajectory can impact its options. Here, successive politicians inherited economic and social schemes set by previous administrations that did not necessarily represent the interests of the people. Economic policy that had once proven to be successful collapsed under a shift in international market forces, both with sugar prices decreasing and petroleum prices increasing.

[1]Calculation based on World Bank (2009a, b) data for 1970 and 1975.

Efforts to address economic stability created social suffering and instability. When policy makers attempted to respond to the social conditions, economic stability and development suffered.

Foreign Direct Investment (FDI), often touted as a panacea for development, is yet another example of competing international and national forces. FDI is a large portion of global financial investment. In 2008, the United Nations Conference on Trade and Development (UNCTAD) reported that US$ 1.5 trillion of FDI was invested globally (UNCTAD 2008). When a state lacks adequate natural endowments and/or institutional capacity to build international wealth on its own, it can seek foreign investment to stimulate economic growth. FDI is a developmental tool which is held to add revenues to national accounts, provide employment and even provide for human development through work-place training. States attract FDI by offering competitive advantages to investors, such as low employee wages, a skilled work force, tax incentives or less stringent regulatory frameworks that will decrease supply side input costs. The attractiveness of a state also depends upon institutional and political stability, strength of rule of law, and the perception that corruption is minimal or manageable. As such, FDI operates as both carrot and stick—investment can benefit national development but, in order to attract the investment, a stable, secure social and political environment is necessary. If a government doesn't clean up its act, there will be no FDI, or investors may pull out. Such pre-requisites may explain why more than half of global FDI in 2007–2008 was directed to only 10 countries.[2]

The quest for foreign investment may weaken state sovereignty and the ability of domestic governments to regulate business practices, including workplace safety, and activities tied to the investment may create externalities, such as pollution, that become the problem of the state government. Trade liberalization entails removal of protective tariffs that may cause domestically-based companies to become uncompetitive if they fail to alter their business practices. In some cases, the changes in business practices come by weakening organized labor and collective bargaining power, or weakening workplace health and safety regulations. Membership in trade organizations like the World Trade Organization requires policy-makers to accept operating rules that may hamper the national or local government's ability to regulate not only industry but other sectors such as environment (Esty and Geradin 1997). Although no government can be forced to enter a trade organization, the perceived financial benefits of such membership are great. Critics of trade liberalization further argue that globalization is dominated by economic interests of the high income nations that create an unequal playing field in which developing countries have few options but to join in the neoliberal marketplace in order to pay back foreign debt accrued via corrupt officials or as remaining vestiges of colonialism.

An example of the pros and cons associated with FDI and participating in the international market is seen in the heated debate regarding provisions of the North

[2]Calculated based on data in UNCTAD (2009).

American Free Trade Agreement (NAFTA) between Canada, Mexico, and the United States. With its enactment in 1994, NAFTA created the largest regional trading block in the world. The intent of the agreement was to provide preferential trade status to the three member nations via decreased regulatory barriers. Under NAFTA rules, regulations that would place an undue financial burden on industry were disallowed. If a nation violates this principle, industries based in any of the signatory nations can challenge the government of the offending nation under a litigating body created by the treaty (NAFTA Secretariat 2010). Critics argue that treaty provisions decrease the ability of local and national governments to regulate industries, and that industries reap the benefits of the dearth of regulation, such as higher profits, higher returns to stockholders, and lower prices to consumers, but those most affected by the negative impacts of industrialization receive nothing (Ruiz-Beltran and Kamau 2001; Frenk et al. 1994; Brown 2005). Indeed, they end up incurring additional costs through environmental degradation and decreases in health associated with pollution, and unsafe work environments (Ruiz-Beltran and Kamau 2001; Frenk et al. 1994; Brown 2005).

Economic and social inputs and impacts cannot easily be separated, nor can national and international forces be segregated. Policies which are directed towards the social sector affect finances and vice versa. Particularly when considering the long-term development horizon, there is a need to consider how investment strategies and policy will radiate across different sectors. A policy toolkit may not be able to foresee all complications, especially regarding international pressures. Good planning necessitates careful consideration of foreseeable consequences and mechanisms to evaluate policy success and shortcomings. In a landscape of limited resources, policy cannot provide all things to all parties—tradeoffs and prioritization are required. Two dominant approaches to national development entail investment in economic development typically through a liberal economic regime, or investment in human development as defined through public provision of education and social welfare which serve as the models we will explore in the case studies in this chapter. There are also mixtures of these two models, for example, Singapore which has a liberal economic system and state-funded health care.

3.2 Health Inputs

Before we begin our case studies, it will be helpful to better understand basic concepts in health care finance and delivery, and how policy shapes health care. The approach which a state adopts towards development, whether it embraces economic development or human development, influences the availability and quality of health inputs. It also determines which actors, public or private, are responsible for the provision of these inputs. Population health outcomes are determined by the physical environment (including weather and climate), sociopolitical context, economic resources, epidemiological profile, investment in social capital, and quality/coverage of health systems (Berkman and Kawachi 2000;

Kunitz 2007; Kawachi et al. 1999). Given the different avenues to impact health, a question arises as to where a government invests its resources? Are efforts best directed towards social welfare or towards economic growth? In considering options, a state needs to be concerned with potential outcomes, costs, and determining how to balance constraints in programmatic operation against outcomes which may not be realized until well into the future.

The balance between economic growth, fiscal sustainability, welfare programs and health care is a central debate among policy-makers, especially in countries with aging populations. Specifically, states must determine a. who is responsible for financing and delivering health care; b. how much of the population should have access to health care; c. what services and supports are considered vital to health d. who regulates care.

Of particular concern is the role of the state in health care provision. Arguments in favor of government provision include: there are economies of scale and administrative efficiencies which can be gained with a single payer (or large, diverse pool) system; increases in risk pooling that allow for more efficient and equitable care are created; and concerns with equity in coverage and quality of provision can best be addressed through government regulation. Arguments against government provision include cost inefficiencies, restrictions to market gains from competition (cost and quality), and unsustainable costs which drain government resources and create opportunity costs because the government cannot use the money spent on health care for alternative reasons.

A health system consists of the finances and services for health care. The services can be preventative and curative. Public and private sources can fund health care. The public sector can pay for health care by using government revenues collected from general taxes, the **Beveridge** model, or by drawing upon taxes which are earmarked specifically for health or social security, the **Bismarck** model. These revenues may be paid directly to service providers or may be pooled into an insurance fund. The Beveridge model is named after William Beveridge, one of the architects of the UK's National Health Service. The Bismarck model is so-named for Otto van Bismarck, who implemented a welfare state in 19th century Germany. Loans, grants and Official Development Assistance (ODA) are also sources available for government financed health care, but suffer from uncertainty in terms of availability and length of provision. Such funding may be considered a viable option for one-time systemic projects, such as reform or capital investment, but is often the only option for health system financing in low income countries but is not a sustainable funding source. Private sector financing includes direct, out-of-pocket payments made by individuals to a service provider, payments made by individuals to an insurance plan, or payments made by employers to insurance plans or service providers.

Health care services can be delivered by public or private agencies. Government services typically include public health responsibilities such as the provision of sanitation and control of epidemics of infectious diseases. The government may also be involved in preventative and curative care through a network of **primary care** clinics and health stations, **secondary** tier facilities which offer more complex curative services such as maternal care, and **tertiary** care facilities which provide specialized care. Secondary care facilities are generally found at the regional level. Tertiary care facilities are fewer and are biased towards urban locations. The government may pay for these facilities through central budgets and may directly employ staff as public employees with salaries, although variation in funding and staff exist. The government may also pay for care from private facilities either through direct payments plans or through public or subsidized insurance. Private provision includes non-profit and for-profit agencies which provide care to private individuals, private employers, insurance plans, or through government contracts. Payment mechanisms include fee-for-service and capitation.

Insurance plans provide a way for individuals and communities to pool their financial resources to create a bulwark against potential future illness. With future health uncertain, individuals are willing to contribute a small amount of money on a regular basis to guarantee their ability to cover unforeseen, potentially catastrophic, costs of illness or injury. Insurance schemes are successful when there is a mixture of individuals who will have both low and high health care needs. This is referred to as a **risk pool**. Health care studies show that the majority of members will require only a small percentage of the resource to cover necessary health care costs while a small minority of members will become extremely ill and require expensive treatment, thereby using up the majority of funds. The ability of an insurance plan to adequately cover its members' health care needs depends upon having a diverse risk pool. In general, the larger and more varied the population, the better the risk pool. If an insurance pool has only individuals who are unhealthy, the costs of health care may exceed the money available from the insurance payments, or premiums.

Economists associate several market failures with health insurance markets which justify government regulation. These include moral hazards, adverse selection, and imperfect information (Schieber and Maeda 1997). A **moral hazard** occurs when people over-consume health care provision or engage in risky behavior based on an assumption that health consequences will be limited because of insurance. In theory, an individual will use health services above and beyond his/her actual need if care is available at no cost. Or, an individual will engage in riskier behaviors, such as skydiving, if s/he has health insurance which will cover the cost of injury whereas an individual without insurance might not engage in such activities (Gladwell 2005). You can see that the moral hazard argument makes certain assumptions about individual behavior which may not be true. One could well imagine that the threat of pain and suffering associated with a skydiving injury is sufficient to prevent many people from engaging in this activity. Even when health care is available, people rarely enjoy going to the doctor. However, from an economic perspective the threat of moral hazard is sufficient to justify cost-sharing as a policy intervention. The portion of an insurance premium a consumer pays, co-payments for services, and set deductibles are all cost-sharing mechanisms that theoretically reduce the moral hazard (Gladwell 2005; Schieber and Maeda 1997). Cost-sharing is also used to fund health care delivery, and to make health care delivery financially feasible as we shall see in the case of Chile.

Whereas moral hazard is a demand-side failure, **adverse selection** and cream-skimming are supply-side failures. Adverse selection occurs when individuals with high health care needs purchase health insurance and those in good health, with little need for health care, do not. As sicker individuals enter the health plan, the money needed to cover their costs of care rise. In order to remain financially solvent, therefore, insurance premiums go up. Healthier individuals may leave the plan as a result of the rising costs and perception that they are unfairly paying for other people's treatments. With this exodus, the proportion of the insurance pool which is sick increases and initiates a cycle in which, ultimately, health care costs may exceed the insurance revenues or the insured's ability to pay, resulting in what insurers call a **death spiral**. The flip side of adverse selection is cream-skimming, or 'cherry picking,' which occurs when an insurance company selects healthier individuals for coverage through underwriting or through policy pricing mechanisms. Creating large risk pools, through voluntary or regulatory means, is a way in which adverse selection and cream-skimming may be negated (Schieber and Maeda 1997; Sered and Fernandopulle 2006). This can be achieved by assigning risk pools which are tied to geographic areas or large industries. Mandating the inclusion of people with pre-existing conditions is another way to impact cream-skimming (Schieber and Maeda 1997; Sered and Fernandopulle 2006).

Imperfect information surrounding different insurance plans is the final market failure. Economic theory operates based on the notion that suppliers and consumers have 'perfect information' about the options, implications, and short-comings of the products being considered. This information allows suppliers and consumers to signal each other through prices and magnitude of purchasing. However, in both health services and health insurance, the consumer has insufficient information to make truly informed choices. Decision-making is especially complex in insurance markets with numerous competitors (Raczynski 2001; Schieber and Maeda 1997; Sered and Fernandopulle 2006). Governments may regulate the type of information which companies must disclose, and may regulate how the information is disclosed.

In the latter part of the 20th century, both Sri Lanka and Chile adopted very different national policies with regards to development. They also experimented with a diverse mix of public and private resources in their health care systems. The next section explores the history, achievements, and failures of these two states.

3.3 Chile—Economic Growth Without Equity

From the 1960s to the 21st century, Chile rose from being a low income nation to being an upper middle income nation, and experienced attendant improvements in quality of life. Its GDP grew by an average of 7% per year throughout the 1990s, and today Chile has one of the highest GDPs per capita in Latin America (World Bank 2009b). As the macroeconomic indicators suggest, the standard of living in Chile is among the best in Latin America. Its health system covers greater than 90% of the population, and its human development indicators are enviable by the standards of highly developed nations. Life expectancy at birth is 78 years, the infant mortality rate per 1000 live births is 8, and the maternal mortality ratio per 100,000 live births is 18 (World Bank 2009b). These numbers belie the fact that Chile did not escape the Debt Crisis, which devastated low and middle income countries several decades ago. At that time, the country was spending more money than it was earning and, from 1981 to 1983, its economy contracted by 15% (Perry and Leipziger 1999). By implementing major reforms, Chile achieved outward oriented growth and fiscal balance and restructured the social services sector, an act that included transforming the health care system from a publicly funded model to a mixed public-private model. These reforms shifted part of the cost-burden of health to the private sector, but health provision continues to be financially unsustainable. Economic and social inequity remains a challenge. Further, equity in health care coverage and access to quality care has yet to be achieved. Despite these drawbacks, Chile is often cited as a successful model of economically-oriented development and implementation of market-oriented health care reform.

Chile's achievements in human and economic development reflect gains made over many decades against a backdrop of changing political and economic orientation. In fact, many of the gains in human health and welfare came about prior to economic liberalization. They were the product of decades of social investment that began in the 1920s. Under the Pinochet dictatorship, installed in 1973, neoliberal reforms contributed to economic diversification and revitalization. Health care reforms created some instances of economic efficiency but at the cost of growing inequity. With the return to democracy in the 1990s, economic growth continued and steps were taken to address the social costs of earlier reforms while trying to create a financially solvent health system.

The Chilean welfare state traces back to 1924 with the creation of a social insurance system. A **welfare state** is one in which the national government assumes responsibility for maintaining health and livelihood of its citizens through direct payments (pensions, etc.) and provision of social insurance. The Chilean system provided for military personnel and the working class in privileged sectors, including railroad workers and those who worked in nitrate and copper industries (Borzutsky 2002; Raczynski 2001). Separate social insurance funds[3] evolved based on special interest groups whose political power was not always proportional to the size of its membership or its economic importance (Borzutsky 2002). For example, the copper mining sector received social security benefits and was a powerful interest group both because of its high degree of organization and because of its economic importance (Borzutsky 2002). By 1970, the copper industry was responsible for 80% of the nation's foreign currency earning (Borzutsky 2002). One could argue that their political power was proportional to their economic importance. Not so the Race Track of Antofagasta workers who also received welfare benefits because of political patronage rather than economic import (Borzutsky 2002). Favored interest groups benefited from the patronage of ruling oligarchs.

[3]About 160 social insurance funds existed, each with different benefits (Borzutsky 2002).

The result was broad but fragmented coverage which favored organized labor and the urban workforce, a prejudice which continued throughout the 20th century.

Early social insurance included pensions, health insurance, family allowances and workers' compensation. Pensions and family allowances constituted cash allocations to assist with maintaining certain living standards. These benefits were not without problems. The pension systems were not adequately adjusted for inflation and lost their purchasing power over time (Borzutsky 2002). Thus, they created a financial drain without delivering the intended benefit of supporting livelihoods. Family allowances accounted for half of the social security expenses and covered 73% of the population (Borzutsky 2002). The family allowances were based on the number of dependents, with benefits increasing with more children as a way to incentivize large families (Borzutsky 2002). This notion was counter to modernization theory and concern with population demographics which dominated development discourse in the later part of the century. Still, in its early years, the Chilean state was concerned with increasing its population and supporting traditional family structures.

By 1925, health and maternity benefits provided access to curative and maternity care for the insured worker and his family, and expanded to include preventative care (Borzutsky 2002). Two components of these benefits were especially important for improving population health. The first aspect was that the insured population was obligated to receive an annual check-up which targeted specific diseases, such as tuberculosis and syphilis, that were of national concern (Borzutsky 2002). The second aspect was that anyone who was diagnosed with the specified illnesses was entitled to receive 100% of their wages for as long as necessary while undergoing therapy (Borzutsky 2002). Thus, certain diseases were prioritized but rather than being punished for being diagnosed as sick, such as through loss of work or income and associated stigma, the victims of such diseases were encouraged to be diagnosed and received such care as was available at the time. It is interesting to note that the early application of these public health laws was based on economic rather than humanitarian concerns (Borzutsky 2002). Whatever the motivation, the health system proved successful in improving various aspects of population health such as infant mortality rates which decreased from 21.2% in 1930 to 15.3% in 1947 (Borzutsky 2002).

Health care delivery was fragmented into five major funds until the 1950s, at which point the *Servicio Nacional de Salud* (SNS) was created to provide preventative care to the entire populace, and to provide comprehensive medical treatment to blue collar workers associated with the *Servicio de Seguro Social* and their dependents, as well as to indigent populations (Raczynski 2001). The SNS was co-funded by contributions to a blue-collar workers' fund and by state revenue; state funding accounted for 60% of the operating costs (Raczynski 2001). The *Servicio Médico Nacional de Empleados* (SERMENA) provided preventive care and, beginning in 1968, curative care, to white collar workers and civil service employees. Smaller funds also existed to provide medical care to specific groups, such as the military and police. In general, the funds were funded by a combination of employee, employer and state contributions. During the 1970s, SNS covered

Table 3.2 Health indicators in Chile, 1960–2005

Indicator	1960	1970	1980	1985	1990	1995	2000	2005
Life expectancy at birth	57	62	69	72	73	75	76	78
Maternal mortality ratio (per 100,000 live births	–	–	–	–	–	–	–	16
Infant mortality rate (per 1000 live births)	118	78	35	23.5	17.6	12.7	9.7	8.4

Data source World Bank (2009b)

approximately 60–65% of the population and SERMENA covered 25% (Raczynski 2001; Ewig and Kay 2008).

At a national level, these programs contributed to improved population health and improved access to care. Table 3.2 shows that the life expectancy at birth in 1960 was 57 years, and reached 62 years by 1970. Infant mortality rates fell from 118 per 1000 in 1960 to 56 by 1975 (World Bank 2009b). Ninety percent of the adult population had health care coverage in some form, and 90% of children under age six had access to health care programs (Raczynski 2001). The state also demonstrated high levels of achievement in primary education, which may have interacted positively with health outcomes. It is well understood that investment in early education, especially female education, contributes to improvement in health indicators (Caldwell 1986). By 1970, 94% of children aged 6–14 had access to primary education, with 90% enrolled in free public schools (Raczynski 2001). But these improving outcomes belie growing problems with social insurance.

The fragmented structure of the social insurance programs in general, and health care in particular, set up several problems which later reforms sought to address. The first issue was that of financial solvency, and the second, unequal coverage. Social insurance programs were paid for through a variety of mechanisms including employer and employee contributions from the private sector and public sector subsidies; the respective amount of contributions varied across the different social insurance funds. What was consistent, however, was that the multiple funds began running deficits that had to be covered by the federal government. Special taxes and monies from the central budget paid for the public portion of the social insurance programs (Borzutsky 2002). Direct state payments covered deficits as well as the scheduled contributions. The burden to the federal budget continued to grow such that by 1970 the social insurance programs covered approximately 70% of the population, and social spending accounted for 20% of the GDP (Raczynski 2001). By 1973, this proportion grew to 30% of the GDP, contributing to fiscal deficits, and was clearly unsustainable (Ewig and Kay 2008). Given that pensions proved unable to provide the intended financial security to retirees, and the inequity in coverage with health care, continuing such levels of funding was unjustifiable.

The SNS charter to provide public health services for the entire population, and curative care for specific working groups and the indigent population, proved to be too broad and financially difficult to manage. The very fact that the indigent population was forced into the public option set up a model in which those in worse health defaulted to the care of the public system skewing the risk pool and thereby driving up the costs of health care. Even with the existence of different health insurance funds, a portion of the public was left without ambulatory or in-patient treatment. Those who could afford to do so paid out-of-pocket. The SNS was revised in 1968 to provide subsidized care through a preferred provider system financed in part by out-of-pocket payments for health premiums and user fees that ranged from 30 to 50% of the cost of care (Raczynski 2001). This did not fix either problem of financial sustainability. The system operated at a deficit with 60% of its funding coming from the government (Ewig and Kay 2008), and contributed to the growing imbalance of state expenditures on social security.

Financial solvency was not the only problem. The state-subsidized system provided health insurance coverage to 80–90% of the Chilean population, but less than half of this number actually could access health services or have their health needs fully met (Raczynski 2001; Ewig and Kay 2008). The rural population received less insurance coverage and had poorer access to facilities than did the urban population. White collar workers could not afford to pay monthly premiums or user fees and blue collar workers and the indigent could not pay or physically access health facilities (Borzutsky 2002; Raczynski 2001).

Augusto Pinochet became president of Chile following a military coup in 1973. His government began nearly 20 years of dramatic political, social and economic change. The military dictatorship brokered no dissent and engaged in state-sponsored terror which led to the disappearance or execution of an estimated 3000 to 17,000 people (Ensalaco 1994; Graham 1990).[4] Among the enemies of the state were academics, intellectuals and school teachers. The politics of the regime were those of oppression and terror with no room for civil discourse or debate. The state became actively engaged in the politics of anti-communism and repression and its economic policy consisted of neoliberal reforms and withdrawal from state provision of social services.

Pinochet's regime embarked upon a program of market-oriented economic reform which fell into two periods. The initial phase focused on rapid economic growth and market liberalization as well as a weakening of protections for labor and social safety nets. The second phase came after the financial crisis of 1981–1983 when government spending outpaced earnings and caused severe economic contraction. With financial collapse imminent, the government received a bailout from the international financial institutions, but with the debt restructuring came tight fiscal constraints. Social policy became secondary to economic policy (Raczynski 2001). The period from 1973 to 1990 was marked by a development program which focused on outward oriented market growth rather than developing human

[4]Some sources place the estimate around 3000 (Ensalaco 1994). However, critics argue the numbers were not based on comprehensive assessments. Other sources place the number of those executed at 15,000 with an additional 2000 disappeared (Graham 1990).

capabilities, decentralization and privatization of enterprises including health and education, an end to redistributive welfare, and fiscal constraint (Ewig and Kay 2008; Raczynski 2001; Perry and Leipziger 1999).

The main health sector reforms of the 1980s entailed a separation of financing from provision, decentralization, and privatization. The SNS was dissolved. In its place came the *Fondo Nacional de Salud* (FONASA) which was charged with the collection, administration and distribution of financial resources for health care. FONASA also served as a public health insurance option. In this, its services paralleled the *Institutos de Salud Provisional* (ISAPRES)—a collection of private insurance companies formed in 1981. Both public and private insurance options were financed by a mandatory 7% income tax on formal sector employees. Workers chose which plan they preferred to pay into and received the attendant benefits (Titelman 1999; Larranñaga 1999). Indigents or those who could not pay insurance contributions fell under the umbrella of FONASA. In addition, FONASA provided all maternity coverage (Larranñaga 1999; Titelman 1999). Worker contributions did not fully cover the costs of the health care system. FONASA channeled additional public revenues to cover the differences in premiums collected and costs of services (Larranñaga 1999; Titelman 1999). Private insurance premiums and user fees provided a third source of financing for the Chilean health care system (Larranñaga 1999; Titelman 1999).

FONASA beneficiaries who contributed to the insurance funds could receive care through the public health system or through private health care providers(Larranñaga 1999). FONASA insurance provided all access to services under the public provider, the *Sistema Nacional de Servicios de Salud* (SNSS). Primary care was free. Tertiary care entailed co-payments (Larranñaga 1999). However, the Chilean system was marked by a free-choice modality which allowed FONASA beneficiaries to also access care through private providers for a fee (Titelman 1999). The services provided through FONASA were not tied to the actual contributions made. Every beneficiary could theoretically access the same package of care regardless of what s/he actually paid. Deficits in the FONASA operating system were paid for by general tax revenue (Larranñaga 1999; Titelman 1999). The FONASA system represented a **redistributive** or **progressive** tax system in that the wealthier sectors provided financing to cover the poorer sectors (Larranñaga 1999; Titelman 1999). It was applauded for being a system which built solidarity, but was challenged by the problems of risk pooling and financial sustainability, as we shall see.

ISAPRES was financed by a mandatory employee contribution and by market-determined premiums. Because of this co-financing mechanism, it tended to attract a smaller, wealthier portion of the population than did FONASA. The insurance premiums were adjusted by age, sex, the number of dependents, the types and limits of benefits provided, and by the range of choice in care facilities (Larranñaga 1999; Raczynski 2001). The insured paid variable user fees depending upon his/her specific policy and service received. Further, there was not a single standard of care package; the care one received under ISAPRES varied according to the premium s/he paid (Larranñaga 1999; Raczynski 2001). ISAPRES had coverage ceilings and time exclusions for pre-existing conditions (Larranñaga 1999; Raczynski 2001).

These pricing practices discriminated against the elderly and women, forcing them into the public option and distorting the risk pools of FONASA and ISAPRES. Under the differential pricing, the elderly and women paid premiums that were three or more times higher than the premium paid by a middle-aged male (Raczynski 2001; Larrañaga 1999; Ewig and Kay 2008). The system discriminated not only based on age and sex, but also against those involved in the informal sector who tended to have lower income. ISAPRES's ability to adjust premiums based on age and risk, along with lack of federal regulation governing the insurance market, forced the sicker population to the public sector while high income individuals are drawn to the public sector.

A dual system of health care evolved in which the wealthier, lower risk individuals entered into ISAPRES while the higher-risk, lower-income individuals fell under the care of the public system (Titelman 1999; Raczynski 2001; Ewig and Kay 2008; Larrañaga 1999). This not only created an adverse risk pool in the public system, while permitting cream-skimming in the private system, but also led to inefficient financing. ISAPRES received 65% of the resources paid for health care but delivered 25–27% of the services; FONASA delivered 100% of preventative services and 65% of the curative services while receiving only 35% of the contributions (Raczynski 2001).

In terms of administration and infrastructure, the Chilean model had a mixture of centralized and municipal level authorities. The Ministry of Health controlled national health care policy and maintained oversight of the health care system. FONASA, as mentioned, served as a mechanism to distribute state finances throughout the health care system. The SNSS, under the Ministry of Health, was responsible for the health provision infrastructure, including primary care clinics and health posts, secondary and tertiary care facilities throughout the 27 health areas in the nation.

State provided health and education were decentralized by 1989. Although decentralization began in the 1970s, it gained momentum, and indeed, became mandatory, following the financial crisis of the early 1980s. The idea was that local level administrators, the municipalities, would have better knowledge of local needs and be better suited to tailor the delivery of primary health care to suit the particular socioeconomic and cultural milieu in which they operated. Municipalities received cash transfers from the central government and could raise additional money for health care with some constraints (Raczynski 2001). Central government allocations were based on the number and type of services provided by the municipality per month, and based on the number and position of workers (Raczynski 2001). Ideally, this model would inspire competition among providers and transfer part of the financial burden away from the central government.

Some transfer of cost burden did occur, but it came at a price. The initial payment structure rewarded quantity over quality and higher cost services over lower cost ones (Raczynski 2001; Titelman 1999). The result was inefficient payment and corruption as some municipalities over-recorded higher paying services (Raczynski 2001; Titelman 1999). A second problem arose in that cash transfers from the central government did not cover all costs of care. Although municipalities were allowed to raise additional revenues, they were not always able to cover the funding gap (Larranñaga 1999; Raczynski 2001; Titelman 1999). Further, municipalities were prohibited by law from issuing debt instruments to cover the deficit and so had limited options (Larranñaga 1999). Under the Pinochet government, health workers lost their status as state employees and thereby lost state benefits, creating morale and staffing problems (Raczynski 2001). The initial period of decentralization resulted in deterioration of public health services. The real value of health subsidies decreased (Raczynski 2001). Medical infrastructure, medical inputs and overall quality of services decreased while waiting time to receive services increased (Raczynski 2001; Larranñaga 1999). Decentralization resulted in fragmentation of service delivery from primary through tertiary care as well as fragmentation across financial mechanisms resulting from limited ability to redistribute resources from wealthier to poorer municipalities (Raczynski 2001; Titelman 1999). Municipalities in which the majority of residents were either rural or of lower socioeconomic class were not particularly lucrative markets and so competition never materialized. Indeed, the sole public provider was not able to sufficiently address the health care needs in a timely manner (Perry and Leipziger 1999). Further, the small demand for certain services, and inability of municipalities to work together (based on the competitive financial mechanisms) meant that there were few opportunities to realize an economy of scale in purchasing health inputs or delivery of care (Perry and Leipziger 1999).

The impacts of this period of health care reform were mixed. No gains were made in terms of the percentage of the population covered by health insurance, but the cost burden of health care financing shifted slightly from the state to the private sector vis-à-vis the employee contributions. Fiscal contributions decreased from 1.2% of GDP in 1984 to 0.8% of GDP in 1990 (Titelman 1999). FONASA became less dependent upon fiscal contributions during this same period.[5] These small gains came at a cost in terms of equity and quality of care. ISAPRES covered high-income low-risk individuals whereas the low-income, high-risk population fell to FONASA (Titelman 1999; Raczynski 2001; Ewig and Kay 2008). The private insurance sector lacked transparency and regulation, and was allowed to cream-skim (Raczynski 2001; Larranñaga 1999). The public system had to stretch less money further as it became both a re-insurer and an insurer of last resort. In terms of health care delivery, decentralization of the public sector led to fragmentation in delivery, deterioration of service quality and infrastructure. By contrast, the private sector attracted greater wealth and built better facilities and provided high quality services with a preference for wealthy, urban areas.

The return to democracy in 1990 provided an opportunity for the government to address issues of solidarity, equality and reconciliation that festered under Pinochet. The nation achieved remarkable economic success with economic growth averaging 7% per year from 1985 through the late 1990s, well above the regional average,

[5]In 1984 fiscal contributions accounted for 42.6% of FONASA's financial base; this decreased to 37.8% in 1990 (Titelman 1999).

and decreasing levels of inflation (Perry and Leipziger 1999). The government maintained tight fiscal control, a policy which resulted in favorable balance of payments and budgetary surplus. The government also increased trade openness and attracted high levels of FDI while regulating credit and financial markets that have strengthened and stabilized the economy (Perry and Leipziger 1999). Despite the growth, the issues of inequity and injustice that arose or grew under the military dictatorship still needed to be addressed. In terms of social policy, this meant reincorporating those groups which the dictatorship terrorized through national policies of reconciliation. The inequalities in the health care system warranted further policy revision but not policy reversal.

A clear area for policy intervention was the establishment of greater regulation and oversight of ISAPRES. The government passed the *Plan de Acceso Universal con Garantías Explícitas* (Plan AUGE) that established a universal package of care which all insurers had to offer (Ewig and Kay 2008). This forced ISAPRES plans to provide reproductive health care for women and alleviated some of the push factors which forced certain populations to seek coverage under the public plan (Ewig and Kay 2008). Several other laws regulating ISAPRES were passed, including regulating information that the insurance companies had to disclose to users, regulating pricing for certain populations such as the elderly, and regulating coverage exclusions (Ewig and Kay 2008; Titelman 1999). The hope was that these reforms would equalize the appeal of ISAPRES and provide better risk pooling and resource allocation between the public and private insurance schemes. The gap between per capita expenses in FONASA as opposed to ISAPRES has since decreased by half (Titelman 1999). None-the-less, issues of cream-skimming and efficiency remain today (Titelman 1999).

Decentralization revealed a number of problems, some of which were addressed through additional government investment in infrastructure, in both health and education, and changes in reimbursement mechanisms (Raczynski 2001; Titelman 1999). From the 1990s forward, payments have shifted towards **capitation** at the municipal level, that is a certain fee paid per person who is covered by the provider for a specific period of time regardless of whether or not s/he seeks care, and **diagnostic-related payments** (DRP) which pay for a group of treatments associated with specific diagnoses at secondary and tertiary levels of care (Raczynski 2001; Titelman 1999). Health care wages accounted for 40% of total public health expenditures but remain tied to seniority rather than performance (Titelman 1999). Hospitals were also granted greater autonomy in personnel and operations decisions (Ewig and Kay 2008).

The results continue to be mixed. Capitation increased the amount of money available for low income municipalities outside of the city, but inequity within the urban areas remains (Raczynski 2001). Referral coordination in the public health delivery system improved, but both primary and secondary tiers of care suffer from insufficient human and resource capacity (Raczynski 2001).

Health care spending increased throughout the 1990s in both the public and private sectors. Government spending on health care was six times higher in the 1990s than in the 1980s; public health expenditure doubled in real terms from 1990 to 1997 (Titelman 1999). These data reflect both a concerted effort by the government to redress the inequity of care that resulted from earlier reforms and cost escalation in medical care. The lack of economic incentives to control supply side costs contributes to the rising expenses (Larranñaga 1999), as does a changing epidemiological profile (Ewig and Kay 2008). Non-communicable disease, increased longevity, and increased prevalence of HIV/AIDS add to long-term, costly medical care. The public system continues to struggle with increased demand for care and shrinking finances. So, too, does the private sector. Real taxable income for members of ISAPRES dropped by more than 30% since the mid-1980s, a trend which does not bode well for the future (Titelman 1999). Current levels of health care spending are not considered sustainable (Titelman 1999).

Chile successfully opened its economy, achieved economic growth and realized improvements in quality of life but saw only marginal gains in terms of health care outcomes during reforms over thirty years. Such change did not occur smoothly. The reform period of the 1980s was marked by extraordinary debt, economic contraction, social hardships, and radical reforms to the social insurance. Pensions, health care and education were at least partially privatized with the result that private actors are now powerful forces in policy formulation. While there has been some shift of cost burden of health care to the private sector, the mixed public-private system cannot adequately respond to escalating health care costs. Further, despite considerable efforts to reform and better target resources, inequity in health care access and coverage remains.

3.4 Sri Lanka—Equity Without Growth

Sri Lanka stands in stark contrast to Chile in terms of economic growth, but proves to be equal when considering achievements in human development. Despite the fact that Sri Lanka experienced an average annual growth rate of 5% during the past decade, its GNI per capita is a mere US$1540 (World Bank 2009b). The country has diversified its economy over the course of some 30 years, but it remains largely rural (World Bank 2009a). Despite this, the average life expectancy at birth is 72 years, infant mortality rates per 1000 live births are 17, maternal deaths are 58 per 100,000 births, and there is nearly universal literacy (World Bank 2009b). These figures belie the idea that growing the national income is a necessary precursor to human development. Sri Lanka's achievements in human development have allowed the country to become an important study of human development, democratization and rural development along with other countries/regions such as Costa Rica, Cuba, China and Kerala, India. These achievements are even more astonishing when one considers the fact that Sri Lanka ended 26 years of bloody internal conflict in May, 2009.

The Sri Lankan success story is frequently analyzed by experts in the fields of development, economics, political science, sociology and global health. Collectively, these studies attribute the nation's remarkable achievements in human development to early investment in human capital (health and education), early and persistent female empowerment, democratization, political will, investment in public health, government-supported nutrition programs, widespread education, rural development and universal access to health care (Caldwell 1986; Aturupane 1994; Anand and Ravi Kanbur 1991; Sanderatne 2000; Bjorkman 1985; Osmani 1994; Rannan-Eliya and Sikurajapathy 2009). To this extensive list, the elements of which interact with and support each other, can be added comparatively early and equal access to family planning and contraception and long-term maint enance of government investment in the social sector (Anand and Ravi Kanbur 1991; Aturupane 1994; Johnson and Samarasinghe 2008; UNICEF n.d. a and n.d. b). Although there is debate as to the relative importance of each of the above-mentioned variables, the results cannot be denied.

One of the more heavily debated aspects of Sri Lanka's success has been the relative contribution of government investment in social services as compared to economic investment with respect to furthering gains in social development, particularly after 1977 when the nation undertook economic liberalization. Prior to the liberalization, the average life expectancy was 65 years of age and infant mortality rates were 45 per 1000 live births; these numbers are indicative of a population that had already transformed demographically and in terms of health (Central Bank of Sri Lanka 2009). Various analyses show that economic growth did contribute to some marginal gains and longer-term sustainability of basic needs outcomes, but government commitment and investment in social goods were central to the nation's development success (Anand and Ravi Kanbur 1991; Aturupane 1994). This is not to say, however, that the Sri Lankan experience can easily be replicated in another cultural or political context. As we shall see in this case study, there were several fortunate convergences that allowed for mutually re-enforcing policies and actions to be undertaken. A critical question for policy makers is which of the variables associated with Sri Lanka's success is most important to realizing positive gains in human development and population health at the national level, and whether or not the short term opportunity costs would allow for such policies to be implemented and persist in different historical and cultural contexts.

Sri Lanka's successes in human development owe a great deal to historical trajectories that began in the late 19th and early 20th century. Ceylon, as Sri Lanka was previously known, was a British colony dominated by a plantation economy. Colonial medicine focused on maintaining the health and welfare of the British military, civil servants, and the plantation workers who were so critical to the economy of the island and empire. As a result, medical care was concentrated in urban areas, the seat of the British administration, and in plantations, the seat of colonial wealth (Bjorkman 1985). None-the-less, a number of early innovations and investments in health care primed Sri Lanka for its transformation. The first medical college opened in Colombo in the 1870s, and the first sanitary corps was established in 1913 (Anand and Ravi Kanbur 1991). This latter event marked the separation of public sanitation and hygiene from general health services. The early period of expansion of health infrastructure culminated in 1926 with the creation of the first Health Units, responsible for primary care and control of infectious disease (Anand and Ravi Kanbur 1991).

The year 1931 marked the beginning of a great social experiment with democratization, and the start of Sri Lanka's expansive commitment to health care for all. This was the year the British government gave self-rule to the citizens of Ceylon. This action was taken in response to recommendations made by the Donoughmore Commission, a committee formed in 1928 under the aegis of the British government to study and recommend appropriate constitutional and governmental structures for the colony. The committee recommended self-rule, and in 1931 the citizens of Ceylon received universal suffrage. Men and women across the island received the right to vote. With participatory governance came government accountability in that politicians needed to please constituents across the island in order to remain in power. This enfranchisement gave rural areas a powerful voice shaping in government, and it is a voice which remains strong to this day.

Government accountability to men and women throughout the island entailed responding to demands for public investment in social services and for equalizing access to the same. Perhaps the most successful rallying of public resources to expand health programs came in response to a single disease, malaria. A malaria epidemic struck the island in 1934–1935 and killed as many as 80,000 people (Silva 2009). The government failed to respond to the first wave of malaria. Such apathy would not stand as public pressure required government intervention lest elected officials be voted out of office. The government therefore increased its involvement in disease control by establishing rural dispensaries and by providing supplementary health and social services targeted to families in the districts most heavily hit by the epidemic (Silva 2009; Sanderatne 2000). The supplemental services included nutritional and financial support (Silva 2009; Sanderatne 2000). Although efforts to control malaria were not truly successful until after the Second World War and the introduction of DDT, the anti-malaria campaign spurred expansion of health care to previously neglected, largely rural areas, and expanded the definition of health to include protection of nutritional intake and modest access to material goods. Between 1931 and 1947, the government of Sri Lanka committed 2.5% of its GDP, or 12–16% of its total budget, to health, nutrition, water and sanitation, and education (Sanderatne 2000). The combined efforts of disease prevention and expansion of social services contributed to increasing longevity; life expectancy increased from 30 to 45 by the start of WWII (Bjorkman 1985; Caldwell 1986). Control of this one disease accounted for a significant reduction in the disease burden of the island (Caldwell 1986; Sanderatne 2000).

Ceylon gained full independence from Britain in 1948. It changed its name to Sri Lanka in 1972. The democratic government not only maintained but also expanded state investment in social services with the goal of providing universal access to health, education, and nutrition. The period following WWII through the early 1960s was a golden age for Sri Lankan social welfare. The economy, driven by tea, rubber and coconut exports, was thriving, balance of payments were strong and foreign reserves were high (Sanderatne 2000). As a result, the government was able to invest heavily in social services and allocated as much as 7% of GDP to this end

(Sanderatne 2000). Military spending was inconsequential. Education became a pillar of social services with the state committing to free primary through tertiary education and expanding primary and secondary school infrastructure throughout the island (Bjorkman 1985). A second pillar of social investment came in the form of nutritional supports. During WWII, food had been rationed throughout the island. At the end of the war, rationing was replaced by a universal food subsidy. The subsidy was supplemented by maternal/child health programs which included food supplements and school-based programs (Sanderatne 2000). These programs continued to expand through the 1960s, and were responsible for increasing caloric intake throughout the country (Sanderatne 2000). The health care infrastructure, the third pillar for building human capital, continued to expand with extensive construction and improved staffing of rural clinics under the administration of the central government. The number of hospital beds available throughout the nation nearly doubled, the number of doctors increased by 75%, and the number of trained nurses grew by more than 200% (Sanderatne 2000).

But paradise was soon lost. The economy began a downward spiral in the 1960s, a trend that continued until the end of the 1970s. Commodity prices fell, leaving the government with few resources to pay for its fiscal obligations (Osmani 1994). The Sri Lankan economy relied on the export of raw goods which no longer earned competitive prices. Protectionist barriers limited international trade and hampered economic diversification. As import prices increased, the balance of payments shifted from a surplus to a deficit; the once strong foreign reserves dried up (Osmani 1994). Expenses for the food subsidies and education reached an all-time high in the mid-1960s, straining the state's limited (and decreasing) financial resources (Rannan-Eliya and Sikurajapathy 2009; Sanderatne 2000). During the same period, population growth was at its highest. Demand for medical care increased with this growth. Despite the gains made in health care personnel during the 1950s, these gains failed to keep pace with population growth and demand (Rannan-Eliya and Sikurajapathy 2009). Further, the economic contraction forced the government to decrease spending in health and education (Sanderatne 2000). This, coupled with the population growth, began to erode the quality of public services as demand outpaced supply (Rannan-Eliya and Sikurajapathy 2009; Sanderatne 2000). An exodus of medical personnel, driven by political instability, low pay and rising cost of living, worsened the situation (Sanderatne 2000). The fiscal difficulties which began in the 1960s deteriorated with the fuel crisis of the 1970s and the continuing trade stagnation. The government of Sri Lanka faced a structural deficit and rising foreign debt. It could not pay for food and fuel imports, let alone the entitlement programs. The decade was marked by food shortages, high unemployment, and rising incidence of acute malnutrition (Sanderatne 2000). Deteriorating social conditions gave rise to discontent, and a growing youth insurgency. This in turn demanded greater national investment in defense and created competition for declining fiscal resources between state security and human security needs. Health and education were cut and spending in these sectors reached an all time low (Sanderatne 2000), but the reduced fiscal expenditures were not sufficient to stabilize the economy. The government needed to change the way it did business.

Table 3.3 Select health indicators for Sri Lanka, 1960–2007

	1960	1965	1970	1975	1980	1985	1990	1995	2000	2005	2007
Life expectancy at birth, total (years)	62	64	65	66	68	69	70	71	71	72	72
Mortality rate, infant (per 1000 live births)	83	77	65	47	36	30.3	25.6	20.4	18.3	16.9	16.5
Maternal mortality ratio (modeled estimate, per 100,000 live births)	–	–	–	–	–	–	–	–	–	58	–

Data source World Bank (2009b)

The government began a program of economic liberalization in 1977. This program included trade liberalization, economic diversification, and a reduction of public subsidies. The macroeconomic restructuring proved successful in terms of spurring economic growth and decreasing the balance of payment deficit.[6] The economy grew by 6% from 1978–1982 due in part to foreign aid and loans which flooded in following the economic liberalization (Sanderatne 2000). Social spending decreased in the early 1980s, then gradually rose, but never again reached the levels seen prior to 1970. The impact these spending reforms had on human development is difficult to discern; prior to implementation of these reforms, life expectancy was already so high (65 years) that any gains made or lost would be marginal barring complete social collapse. The more sensitive infant mortality rate continued to improve during this period, suggesting that despite the decrease in perceived quality, the basic infrastructure and public expectation of maternal/child care were being met and that the service infrastructure remained intact (see Table 3.3). Reports of acute malnutrition continued to rise through the early 1980s but then decreased (Osmani 1994). Of particular import to rising malnutrition was food policy.

Trade liberalization entailed the elimination of export taxes on cash crops, reduction of various other taxes, and removal of price controls, most importantly on food (Osmani 1994). At the same time that food prices were rising, the government needed to cut fiscal expenditures. Food subsidies were a logical target, but care was needed in reducing spending on these subsidies given the historical commitment to this program, the wide-spread food shortages and the increasing amount of money

[6]Annual GDP growth rates ranged from 4 to 6% through the 1980s; BOP deficits as % of GDP declined from double to single digits by 1984 (World Bank 2009a; Central Bank of Sri Lanka 2008, 2009).

households needed to spend on food.[7] At the time of reform, food subsidies had nearly universal coverage to the point that the program was regressive; the non-poor benefited as much if not more than the poor. The government replaced the universal subsidy with means-tested food stamps that initially had low qualifying limits (Sanderatne 2000). Public pressure soon forced the government to raise the limits to the point where some 40% of the population remained covered by the subsidy (Sanderatne 2000). Other problems persisted. The price of food stamps was held constant but food prices continued to escalate such that the buying power of the foods stamps quickly eroded thereby necessitating further reform (Osmani 1994; Sanderatne 2000). The food subsidy program was restructured twice in the 1990s, and again in the 21st century. Today it constitutes a welfare program, *samurdhi* ('prosperity' in English), that provides food stamps, free school books and uniforms, and mid-day meals to children of qualified families. Although the government's commitment to nutritional support was able to decrease chronic malnutrition throughout the country, the problem was never entirely eliminated.

In 1983, a new element entered the Sri Lankan policy hierarchy and remained entrenched for nearly three decades. That element was one of death and deprivation in the form of civil war. What began as a conflict over structural inequities and demands for justice by the Tamil minority grew into a 26 year war which cost more than 60,000 lives (Renner 2007).[8] The war between the Government of Sri Lanka (GoSL) and the Liberation Tigers of Tamil Eelam (LTTE) ended with defeat of the LTTE in May 2009. War meant growing military expenditures, destruction of infrastructure, and diversion of resources to fight and to rebuild, and countless opportunity costs. Figure 3.1 shows the proportion of government spending allocated to military, health, and education. Military demands ebbed and flowed with intensification and de-escalation of battle, but consistently placed a high demand on government coffers. The war resulted in internal and external migration. The number of internally displaced people (IDPs) likewise waxed and waned, with peaks of 800,000 in 2003/2004 and 300,000 in 2009 (UNHCR 2002).

Gauging the true effects of war is difficult. Data gathered by the central government has excluded the northern and eastern provinces, the site of the conflict, since the 1980s. As a result, the national indicators show small but steady gains in terms of human development with no indication that the war disrupted human development. However, the war resulted in both direct and indirect loss of life. We will further explore the impacts of conflict on health and development in Chap. 5. What is important to note is that Sri Lankan society as a whole did not experience the downward spiral of human security typically associated with protracted conflict. Many believe that human capital had been raised to such a point that the early gains could not easily be eroded by war. Further, the nation remained a constitutional democracy. Throughout the conflict the public expected and demanded a certain

[7]By 1978, households spent approximately 11% of their income on food, up from 8% in previous years. (Central Bank of Sri Lanka 2008, 2009).

[8]Other reports estimate more than 70,000 casualties (Gardner 2007).

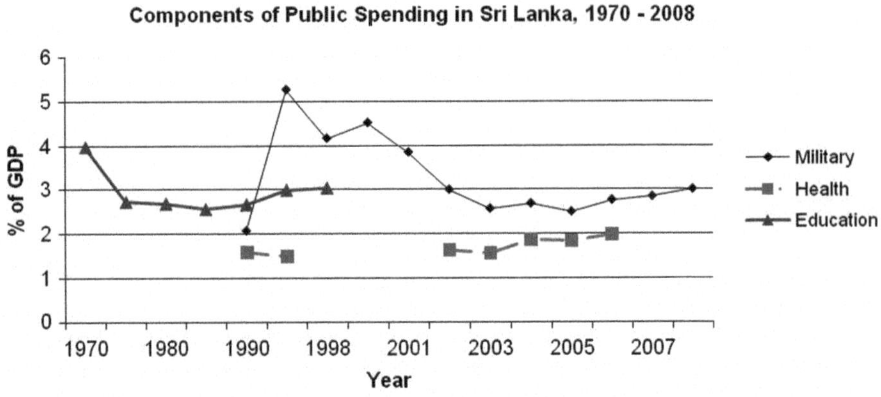

Fig. 3.1 Components of government spending in Sri Lanka, 1970–2008. *Data sources* World Bank (2009a, b); Sanderatne (2000)

standard of social services which politicians would not easily or readily deny their constituents if they wished to remain in office (Rannan-Eliya and Sikurajapathy 2009). On December 26, 2004, a tsunami struck Sri Lanka. It impacted an estimated 2/3rd of the country's coastline, killed more than 35,000 people and displaced an estimated 443,000 people (Asian Development Bank 2005). The scale of the tragedy was great, and impacted economic and human development in the coastal provinces, and frayed a fragile peace process (Fig. 3.1).

There were three separate ceasefires prior to the end of the war in 2009. The most important was that of 1987 (the Indo-Lanka accord) in which the government agreed to devolve certain powers to provinces. Among these was a degree of autonomy in administering health care. Such local oversight, however, came at a price in that provinces and local governments had to assume a portion of health care financing. As of 2002–2003, provinces covered an average of 14% of public health care costs, whereas local government covered approximately 1% of such costs (Ministry of Healthcare and Nutrition 2005). Today, provincial and district-level facilities therefore remain largely dependent upon financing from the central government. Allocation of personnel likewise remains centralized, and the government experienced significant problems staffing posts in the war-torn northern and eastern provinces, and several other rural provinces.

By the 21st century, Sri Lanka continued to see economic growth, but also incurred increasing debt along with a seemingly endless war. The nation achieved replacement level population growth in the 1990s. It also experienced the epidemiological transition. With a quarter of the population aged 55 or older, this translated into increased demand for curative health services and their attendant high costs (Central Bank of Sri Lanka 2009). Public resources were more and more being directed away from public health and primary care to curative services and tertiary care while private actors were being asked to cover costs of the more elementary services. The future direction of health care in Sri Lanka is under debate. The current system is criticized for fragmentation, decreased quality of care and increased inequity brought about by the growing burden being placed upon consumers to pay for their own ambulatory care, and poor quality/inequity in provision of medications (Rannan-Eliya and Sikurajapathy 2009). A central debate focuses on how much can be spent on traditional health care services given the marginal gains in health outcomes, and how to best address new threats to health including chronic disease and re-emergent/new diseases such as malaria and dengue.

A long-standing goal of Sri Lankan society was universal access to health care, a goal that was realized shortly after independence, and has been maintained through the present. Health care, public education and nutrition together formed three pillars of Sri Lanka's social investment. The health care system placed an early emphasis on government provision of primary health through state-run clinics. This system morphed into a system of mixed public and private financing and provision. It is notable that there is no national insurance program. Rather, citizens of the state are guaranteed access to any public medical facility. This right dates back to pre-WWII. Medical personnel are state employees. Government services include both preventative and curative services which are delivered through an extensive network of government-funded primary care centers, secondary and tertiary care facilities (Institute for Policy Studies 2002). Most residents live within three kilometers of a health care facility both because of the extent of the care network and because of the comparatively modest size of the island (Bjorkman 1985; Institute for Policy Studies 2002). Public financing comes almost exclusively from general tax revenue with international development assistance amounting to less than 5% (Rannan-Eliya and Sikurajapathy 2009). Public funds account for a decreasing portion of overall health costs; funding was 48% in 1999 and fell to 43% in 2002 (Institute for Policy Studies 2002). Public funds primarily pay for hospital costs and public health programs. A growing private sector provides approximately 76% of the ambulatory services and is paid for out of pocket by the individual recipient of care or employment-based insurance (Institute for Policy Studies 2002). Although mixed funding goes back decades, in recent years private funding has grown increasingly more important because of rising medical costs, increased availability of private providers with perceived increase in service quality and convenience, declining availability of public fiscal resources, and rising demands of an increasingly affluent population (Institute for Policy Studies 2002; Rannan-Eliya and Sikurajapathy 2009). It is notable, however, that the majority of out-of-pocket payments is made for comparatively low cost ambulatory care (Institute for Policy Studies 2002). The public relies on public provision for higher cost curative treatment and hospitalization. The rising costs of care, from increased input prices and increased demands for a population experiencing epidemiological and demographic transitions, suggest that the sustainability of the current health care system structure is in jeopardy. Health care outcomes, however, are the product of decades of social investment and will likely be maintained (Table 3.4).

Sri Lanka has shown the world that a dedicated and coordinated government program to improve human welfare can indeed achieve improvements in the quality

Table 3.4 Percentage of health care service by funding source, Sri Lanka 1997

Service	Public	Private
Hospital services	81	19
Ambulatory care	39	61
Medical goods dispenses	5	95
Public health and preventative	87	13

Data source Ministry of Healthcare and Nutrition (2002). *Sri Lanka National Heath Accounts*. Colombo: Ministry of Health and Nutrition

of life with comparatively low absolute investment and low economic growth. It must be remembered that political development, education, health, nutrition and female empowerment came together in this unique island country. It must also be remembered the payoff developed over the course of decades, not years, and that despite changes in government political parties, public officials stayed the course in terms of a continued commitment to and investment in social services. Sri Lanka also showed that such investment could not be sustainable without economic growth. The economic contraction of the 1960s–1970s proved that social investment could not continue without income growth, and that external and internal economic shocks threatened health gains and the stability of a carefully crafted system. It would not matter that a clinic was within three kilometers of any citizen if there was neither trained staff nor medicines available at that clinic. Changing demographics and epidemiological profile, increased costs for the inputs necessary to health and well-being, and decades of conflict are eroding the quality of social services and the ability of the government to provide the services in an equitable manner. Increased economic activity and centralization around Colombo is resulting in increasing inequity. Although not yet at the levels one sees in more unequal parts of the world such as Latin America and Africa, this is cause for concern. With the end of the war, many questions arise as to what development will look like in the short and long runs. In 2009, the GOSL received an IMF loan because of continued balance of payment deficits. Rising fuel costs and global economic instability took their toll, as did the military escalation which preceded the GOSL's ultimate military victory. The government is now faced with rebuilding the savaged Northern and Eastern provinces, but has limited fiscal resources with which to proceed. The hope offered by foreign aid has yet to materialize, with donors citing human rights abuses, increasing militarism, decreasing democracy, and the global economic crisis as causes for concern. The lack of a clear map to re-integrate the people who lost their homes and livelihoods in the war back into broad national society and lack of a clear plan to re-integrate the conflict area into the broader nation are worrisome both in terms of maintaining peace and ensuring that the benefits of Sri Lanka's remarkable successes in human development accrue to all.

3.5 Conclusion

Context matters. Chile and Sri Lanka began with different natural endowments. Both countries were colonized by European powers, and both gained their independence, although there was nearly a century between the two. In the 20th century, each nation adopted a political system that was unique to its cultural, political and economic features. Chile developed a political system and welfare state driven by a largely formal and urban worker base. Sri Lanka developed a political system driven by a largely rural population, a system expected to decrease inequities across rural-urban boundaries. One nation developed a thriving international economy, the other maintained a modest economy which is only now becoming more diverse. Yet both nations stand out in terms of achievements in human development with exceptional health outcomes and high levels of educational obtainment. One fights to gain greater equity across class and gender, the other struggles to maintain high levels of equity and coverage. Both, however, must confront the new frontier of caring for an aging population, rising medical costs and a decreasing ability of the government to pay for these services.

One lesson which can be learned is that policy consistency pays off in the long term. The Sri Lankan political system has been marked by a rotation of power between two dominant parties that the public votes out and then back in on a regular basis. Despite this, and despite a civil war, the government has continued investment in health, education, and nutrition and has been responsive to a public possessed of universal suffrage. Chile's social insurance was restructured, but not entirely eliminated, by a military dictatorship. Abrupt economic change and fiscal restructuring created short-term losses in terms of health and education. However, with the return to democracy, policy changes which relied upon the creation of both a public and private market continued but with a role for government intervention in the interest of promoting equity and protecting the most marginal populations.

Neither system proved to be perfect, nor perhaps can any system ever be. With increasing life expectancy, the gains from higher investment in health care become more and more marginal and pursuing the goal of continuing gains seems quixotic at best. Immortality, as of yet, continues to elude us. Therefore an appropriate focus for understanding human heath becomes tied less to longevity, in nations where the life expectancy is in the 60s and 70s, and more to improving the quality of life. But what constitutes quality of life varies across cultures. While the policy-maker or economist concerned with macro-level outcomes would argue that the gain of a single year in life expectancy may not be worth investing an additional $8000 per person, an individual facing death may argue that it would be worth $8 million dollars to have an extra hour to bid loved ones farewell. It is with this idea, that the macro gaze that focuses on the needs of the many may obscure the individual lived experience and cannot do justice to culture and norms which vary from individuals to households, that we turn our attention to communities and community-based programming that allow for the variation of smaller scale collectives to become a strength when setting goals for improving health, wealth, and human capability.

Discussion Questions

1. How does the health of a nation-state differ from the health of individuals residing within a nation-state? How are the two connected?
2. Think of a country that has recently been in the news because of either economic or political instability. Describe some of the policy options the country has to either stabilize economically or stabilize socially. What factors need to be in place domestically for the country to take these actions? What factors need to be in place internationally? How much control over domestic policy do you believe policy-makers in this country have?
3. How did Chile's early investment in health impact its macro-economic stability? What about Sri Lanka's investment in health?
4. Describe the economic reforms that occurred in Chile in the 1980s. How did these reforms impact equity in healthcare?
5. What reforms would you propose to correct the inequity of the 1980s healthcare system in Chile?
6. How did Sri Lanka's achievements in health care differ from those in Chile prior to economic liberalization? How did the economic reforms impact Sri Lanka's healthcare?
7. Which country was more successful in terms of building a healthy state, Chile or Sri Lanka? Why do you believe this?

References

Anand, S., & Ravi Kanbur, S. M. (1991). Public policy and basic needs provision: Intervention and achievement in Sri Lanka. In J. Dreze & A. Sen (Eds.), *The political ecology of hunger* (Vol. 3, pp. 59–92). Oxford: Claredon.

Anderson, B. (2001). *Imagined communities: Reflections on the origin and spread of nationalism*. London, New York: Verso.

Asian Development Bank. (8 December 2005). *Sri Lanka: Tsunami summary*. http://www.adb.org/media/Articles/2005/6619_tsunami_impact_Sri_Lanka/default.asp. Accessed June 9, 2010.

Aturupane, H. (1994). Poverty, human development, and growth: An emerging concensus? *The American Economic Review, 84*(2), 244–246.

Berkman, L., & Kawachi, I. (Eds.). (2000). *Social epidemiology*. New York: Oxford University Press.

Bjorkman, J. W. (1985). Health policy and politics in Sri Lanka: Developments in the South Asian welfare state. *Asian Survey, 25*(5), 537–552.

Borzutsky, S. (2002). *Vital connections: Politics, social security, and inequality in Chile*. Notre Dame, Indiana: University of Notre Dame Press.

Brown, G. (2005). Protecting workers' health and safety in the globalizing economy through international trade treaties. *International Journal of Occupational and Environmental Health, 11*(2), 207–209.

Caldwell, J. C. (1986). Routes to low mortality in low income countries. *Population and Development Review, 12*(2), 171–220.

Central Bank of Sri Lanka. (2008). *Economic and social statistics for Sri Lanka*. Colombo, Sri Lanka: Central Bank.

Central Bank of Sri Lanka. (2009). *Statistical Annex*. Colombo, Sri Lanka: Central Bank.

Clemens, H., & de Groot, J. (1988). Agrarian labor market and technology under different regimes: A comparison of Cuba and the Dominican Republic. *Social Science and Medicine, 27*(12), 1357–1368.

Eller, J. (1999). *From culture to ethnicity to conflict: An anthropological perspective on international ethnic conflict*. Ann Arbor: University of Michigan Press.

Ensalaco, M. (1994). Truth commissions for Chile and El Salvador: A report and assessment. *Human Rights Quarterly, 16*(4), 656–675.

Espinal, R. (1995). Economic restructuring, social protest, and democratization in the Dominican Republic. *Latin American Perspectives, 22*(3), 63–79.

Esty, D., & Geradin, D. (1997). Market access, competitiveness, and harmonization: Environmental protection in regional trade agreements. *Harvard Environmental Law Review, 21*, 265–336.

Ewig, C., & Kay, S. J. (2008). New political legacies and the politics of health and pension re-reforms in Chile. In D. Beland & B. Gran (Eds.), *Public and private social policy: Health and pension policies in a new era* (pp. 249–268). Houndsmills, UK: Palgrave Macmillan.

Frenk, J., Gómez-Dantés, O., Cruz, C., Chacón, F., Hernández, P., & Freeman, P. (1994). *American Journal of Public Health, 84*(10), 1591–1597.

Gardner, S. (23 May 2007). Red cross quits Sri Lanka war front, death toll mounts. http://www.alertnet.org/thenews/newsdesk/L23654919.htm. Accessed June 13, 2010.

Gladwell, M. (29 August 2005). The moral-hazard myth: The bad idea behind our failed health-care system. *The New Yorker*.

Graham, C. (1990). Chile's return to democracy. *The brookings review, 8*, 39–41.

Institute for Policy Studies. (2002). *Sri Lanka national health expenditures 1990–1999*. Colombo, Sri Lanka: Author.

Johnson, S., & Samarasinghe, S. (2008). *Violent conflict, health and well-being*. Paper presented at the "State Security, Conflict and Terrorism" Conference, International Centre for Ethnic Studies, Kandy, Sri Lanka, August 11–13, 2007.

Kawachi, I., Kennedy, B., & Wilkenson, R. (Eds.). (1999). *The society and population health reader: Income inequality and health*. New York: The New Press.

Kunitz, S. J. (2007). *The health of populations: General theories and particular realities*. Oxford: Oxford University.

Larrañaga, O. (1999). Health sector reforms in Chile. In G. Perry & D. M. Leipziger (Eds.), *Chile: Recent policy lessons and emerging challenges* (pp. 189–226). Washington, DC: World Bank.

Martinussen, J. (1995). *Society, state and market: A guide to competing theories of development*. Atlantic Heights (NJ): Zed Books.

Ministry of Healthcare and Nutrition (2002). *Sri Lanka National Heath Accounts*. Colombo: Ministry of Health and Nutrition.

Ministry of Healthcare and Nutrition. (2005). *Sri Lanka national health accounts 2000–2002*. Colombo, Sri Lanka: Ministry of Healthcare and Nutrition.

Moya Pons, F. (1995). *The dominican republic: A national history*. New Rochelle, NY: Hispaniola Books.

Moya Pons, F. (1999). *Breve historia contemporiana de la republica dominicana*. Mexico: Fondo de Cultura Económico.

NAFTA Secretariate. (2010). *North American free trade agreement*. http://www.nafta-sec-alena.org/en/view.aspx?conID=590. Accessed November 02, 2011.

Osmani, S. R. (1994). Economic reform and social welfare: The case of nutrition in Sri Lanka. *American Economic Review, 84*(2), 291–296.

Perry, G., & Leipziger, D. M. (1999). Introduction. In G. Perry & D. M. Leipziger (Eds.), *Chile: Recent policy lessons and emerging challenges* (pp. 1–22). Washington, DC: World Bank.

Raczynski, G. (2001). Provision of social services in Chile: A search for a new model. In G. Mwabu, C. Ugaz, & G. White (Eds.), *Social provision in low-income countries: New patterns and emerging trends* (pp. 211–227). Oxford: Oxford University Press.

Rannan-Eliya, R. P., & Sikurajapathy, L. (2009). *Sri Lanka: "Good Practice" in expanding health care coverage*. Colombo, Sri Lanka: Institute for Health Policy.

Renner, M. (18 July 2007). The casualties of Sri Lanka's intensifying war. *Natural Disasters & Peacemaking*. http://www.worldwatch.org/node/5184. Accessed June 13, 2010.

Ruiz-Beltran, M., & Kamau, J. (2001). The socio-economic and cultural impediments to well-being along the US-Mexico border. *Journal of Community Health, 26*(2), 123–132.

Sanderatne, N. (2000). *Economic growth and social transformations: Five lectures on Sri Lanka*. Colombo, Sri Lanka: Tamarind Publications.

Schieber, G., & Maeda, A. (1997). A curmudgeon's guide to financing health care in developing countries. In George Schieber (Ed.), *Innovations in health care financing: Proceedings from a world bank conference, March 10–11, 1997* (pp. 1–38). Washington DC: World Bank. Discussion Paper No. 365.

Sered, S. S., & Fernandopulle, R. (2006). *Uninsured in America: Life and death in the land of opportunity*. Berkeley, CA: University of California Press.

Silva, K. T. (2009). 'Tsunami third wave' and the politics of disaster management in Sri Lanka. *Norwegian Journal of Geography, 63*(1), 61–72.

Titelman, D. (1999). *Reforms to health system financing in Chile, CEPAL/ECLA* (Vol. 69). Santiago, Chile: United Nations.

United Nations Children's Fund (UNICEF). (n.d. a). *Sri Lanka—Overview—Nutrition Status of children*. http://www.unicef.org/srilanka/overview_1646.htm. Accessed July 26, 2007.

United Nations Children's Fund (UNICEF). (n.d. b). *Sri Lanka—Overview—Regional disparities*. http://www.unicef.org/srilanka/overview_1645.htm. Accessed July 26, 2007.

United Nations Conference on Trade and Development. (2009). *World investment report*. New York, Geneva: Author.

United Nations Conference on Trade and Development. (1 August 2008). *Foreign direct investment reached new record in 2007*. http://www.unctad.org/templates/webflyer.asp?docid=9439&intItemID=1528&lang=1. Accessed June 13, 2010.

United Nations High Commissioner on Refugees. (2002). *UNHCR's programme for internally displaced persons in Sri Lanka*. http://www.chs.ubc.ca/srilanka/PDFs/UNHCR%20programme%20for%20IDPs%20in%20Sri%20Lanka.pdf. Accessed July 15, 2007.

Vedovato, C. (1986). *Politics, foreign trade and economic development: A study of the dominican republic*. London: Croom Helm.

World Bank. (2009a). *Sri Lanka at a glance*. http://devdata.worldbank.org/AAG/lka_aag.pdf. Accessed November 14, 2009.

World Bank. (2009b). *World development indicators*. http://databank.worldbank.org/ddp/homedo?Step12&id=4&CNO=2. Accessed November 12, 2009.

Chapter 4
Community-Based Interventions

Abstract National programs create materials for and interest in health and development, but the benefits of such programs are not equally distributed across geographic territories or across sub-populations. The poor, minorities, women and those living in rural areas tend to receive fewer benefits and experience large differentials in terms of overall development and health outcomes. Non-governmental organizations, civil society, and parastatal organizations can address the gaps in services and resources. They do this through small-scale enterprises and locally-based investment in individuals and households. One such community-based program is the Grameen Bank, an NGO that provides microcredit to poor, rural, women. It has been successful in raising household income and improving human capital in Bangladesh, but it has had mixed results in terms of scaling up for broader-scale poverty alleviation and social impact. Gonoshasthaya Kendra is an NGO that provides community-based health care in Bangladesh using allopathic and traditional means. It has been successful in reducing maternal mortality in the regions it serves by understanding and using resources at the local level. Although this NGO provides evidence that community-based health programs can be successful in delivering appropriate and acceptable health care to select communities, difficulty remains in scaling to national levels. A final example of community development is found in the Millennium Villages Project which addresses multi-faceted poverty through coordinated efforts by local, national and international actors to address development across economic, health and social sectors. The Project proved successful in improving livelihoods and health at the community level but has yet to prove either scalable or sustainable.

As we learned in Chap. 3, cookie-cutter programs that appeal at a macro level do not account for the variation in experiences which occur across the heterogeneous cultural, economic, political, and social landscape of a nation-state. Further, national measures and the macro-focus obscure variation in the health and development status and needs of distinct regions, communities and households. Consider the cases of Chile and Sri Lanka. Both nations have a life expectancy of 72 or higher. On average, 90% or more of the adult population is literate in both

S.A. Johnson, *Challenges in Health and Development*,
DOI 10.1007/978-3-319-53204-2_4

countries. Over the last decade, both countries saw their average GDP per capita grow 3% or more (World Bank 2009a, b). But, as we learned in Chap. 3, development and health programs did not provide equal coverage to all citizens and were failing to reach certain populations in these countries. In Chile, health care reforms failed to reach the very poor and those living in rural areas. In Sri Lanka, there were broad health care coverage failings in the provision of nutritional and economic support as well as education for plantation workers and those in the conflict areas.

Disaggregated data provide further evidence of the disconnect between what is occurring in specific populations and communities as opposed to what is happening in the nation as a whole. **Quintile distribution** shows the proportion of certain goods, such as income or access to food, that is controlled by the poorest 20% of the population, the second poorest 20%, and so forth through the wealthiest 20% of the population. The **gini coefficient** measures how equally certain goods are distributed across income groups within a country. It is typically given as a number between 0.0 and 1.0, with values closer to zero reflecting a more equal distribution across the different income levels of a population. At times, the gini coefficient is converted to whole numbers in which numbers closer to 100 indicate less equality than numbers closer to zero. Coefficients over 60 (0.6) are considered to be highly unequal and suggest that a social schism exists and is approaching a critical level, which could result in open conflict (UNHABITAT 2008). The country with the highest gini coefficient is currently Seychelles, with a gini coefficient of 65.8 (UNDP 2015). Chile has a gini coefficient of 50.8, symptomatic of a highly unequal country, whereas Sri Lanka has a gini of 36.4 suggesting a somewhat more equal country. When we look at the quintile distribution of income (Table 4.1), we see that the top 20% of Chile controls nearly 57% of the wealth. In Sri Lanka, the poorest 20% control a little more than 7% of the national income (only slightly better than the 4% the poor control in Chile), and the wealthiest quintile controls 46% of the wealth. There is somewhat more equal distribution among the middle quintiles in Sri Lanka than in Chile. While the gini coefficient only shows inequities bounded by social class, inequities also exist along geographic and cultural boundaries. In Chile, it was noted that the rural population suffers from economic exclusion and has less access to health services. Clearly, the advantages and disadvantages are not equally distributed.

Based on the gini coefficient and the historical emphasis on rural development in Sri Lanka, Sri Lanka should have a more equal distribution of health outcomes. But Table 4.2 shows that several districts suffer from health outcomes well below national averages. The highest MMR, 80.2 per 100,000 live births, is found in Jaffna, is well above the national rate of 22.0. Several other districts, Trincomalee and Batticaloa, all former conflict zones, also suffer from high MMRs. The worst IMRs are found in Mullaitivu and Batticaloa (Sri Lanka Ministry of Health, Nutrition and Indigenous Medicine 2016).

These data show that there are clear disparities with fault lines along regional geography, political ecology, ethnicity and concentration of minorities, and culture. During the period represented by these data, Mullaitivu was largely held by the LTTE and was the site of extensive fighting in the ethnic conflict between the

Table 4.1 Quintile distribution of income in Chile and Sri Lanka

% income by quintile					
	Lowest 20%	Second 20%	Third 20%	Fourth 20%	Highest 20%
Chile (2013)	4.63	8.29	12.05	18.33	56.69
Sri Lanka (2012)	7.27	11	14.66	20.57	46.49

Data source World Bank (2015)

Table 4.2 District-level health indicators in Sri Lanka

District	Crude death rate, 2014, per 1000 population	Maternal mortality rate, 2010, per 100,000 live births	Infant mortality rate, 2010, per 1000 population
Colombo	6.8	7.2	15.6
Gampaha	6.0	18.6	3.9
Kalutara	6.5	24.7	5.6
Kandy	7.2	20.4	16.6
Matale	6.5	20.0	7.6
Nuwara Eliya	6.2	20.4	12.1
Galle	7.3	31.9	8.6
Matara	6.3	–	10.3
Hambantota	5.4	11.4	5.4
Jaffna	7.1	80.2	13.0
Kilinochchi	2.9	26.2	0.3
Mannar	3.7	–	–
Vavuniya	4.9	31.5	8.2
Mullaitivu	4.2	–	26.0
Batticaloa	4.8	48.9	19.2
Ampara	4.6	21.3	4.3
Trincomalee	4.1	49.3	3.0
Kurunegala	6.6	34.3	9.6
Puttalam	5.4	7.1	6.7
Anuradhapura	5.5	43.7	16.7
Polonnaruwa	5.5	–	2.7
Badulla	6.4	28.5	8.3
Moneragala	4.7	14.6	2.8
Ratnapura	6.1	5.0	7.2
Kegalle	6.9	27.5	6.1
Sri Lanka	6.2	22.0	9.9

Data source Sri Lanka Ministry of Healthcare, Nutrition and Indigenous Medicine. 2016. *Annual Health Statistics: Sri Lanka 2015*. Colombo (Sri Lanka)

Government of Sri Lanka and the LTTE. It is an historically underdeveloped area, and so one might expect poorer health and higher death rates. These rates emphasize, however, that human development is not equally distributed.[1] Jaffna and Batticaloa are also districts in the conflict zone. Jaffna was once a political seat of power known for comparatively high levels of development. The tremendous gap between its MMR and the national average emphasizes the point that there has been inequity in health associated with war. The political disintegration and conflict, concentrated along ethnic lines, may account for the high death rate. If one were to consider only national level data, which show CDR is 6.2, MMR is 22.0 and IMR is 9.9, the extensive differences in health at the local level would never be seen.

This chapter will examine community-based programs which target poverty alleviation and health. The advantage of looking at community is that it allows for a more detailed understanding of the causal network of poverty and poor health, and highlights how individuals, households and groups interact with each other and interact with the broader socioeconomic and political context. Diverse definitions of community exist; community can be defined by geographic scale and by cultural boundaries. For the purpose of the exploration herein, we will use community synonymously with local in that we will examine the operations of several agencies which work in a local context as opposed to regional or national. Exploration of community entails looking at the small scale populace as well as the operations of households and the individuals within each household. It is hoped that through this exploration of community and its constituent parts, one is better able to appreciate that agency, abilities, and constraints are defined by social networks, age, sex, and type of household. These factors are ill-defined and poorly understood when considering a larger geographic or institutional perspective. In looking at trends and generalities, national-level analysis reduces individual stories and details into more manageable data, but data which tell of the many rather than the individual. Community-level work attempts to understand and utilize the distinct characteristics of the local in program.

4.1 The Importance of Community

The impact of policies and programs is felt at the local, regional, national and global levels. Whether looking at health or poverty, such impact can be discussed in terms of substance as well as reach (Zohir and Matin 2004). Substantive impact may be seen in social, economic, political or cultural spheres and may be felt by program stakeholders or institutions (Zohir and Matin 2004). This section will examine the outcomes of community health and micro-finance programs, and a multisectoral

[1]These data reflect conditions from 2005, a period when the district was under LTTE control (albeit during a ceasefire). This speaks to the difficulty of gauging development during war, and to the difficulties in realizing equity in development during conflict.

intervention at the community level. In all cases, there is a symbiotic relationship between health and economic development that, while distinct, resonates within the national landscape.

When examining the local domain, attention must be paid to feedback loops between local actors, across programming sectors, and the synergies between local networks and change therein, and national/international networks. In terms of community health, local feedbacks define disease causation and treatment. Causes and cures entail physical, social and economic risks and tools that increase or decrease agency. Health is a product of exposure and risk, as well as interpersonal processes including engagement, communication, transactions and negotiation which intermingle and mediate biomedical and socio-political influences (Kleinman and Kleinman 1997). Such processes can create physical and psychological symptoms that may result in disease, abnormalities in the structure and function of biological systems, or illness, a perception or experience of socially devalued states (Kleinman and Kleinman 1997). The individual and the local world are catchments areas for, respectively, allopathic and traditional medicine. The clinical gaze of allopathic medicine looks at the individual, whereas the healing gaze looks at the individual within a web of interpersonal and communal relations (Kleinman and Kleinman 1997; Young 1982). Although a division exists between these approaches to disease, illness, and healing, these ways of understanding health are not mutually exclusive as the individual can be examined alone or embedded within a larger context. Both perspectives offer a counter to the macro- and meso-perspectives of population and global health. Disease and illness are used by anthropologists to differentiate biomedically recognized conditions—diseases—and socially recognized or culturally-bounded illnesses and speak to what is perceived to be causes, and cures, for the un-natural state.

Failed interpersonal processes may create illness or disease (Janzen and Arkinstall 1978; Scheper-Hughes 1992; Kleinman and Kleinman 1997; Farmer 1992). Antagonism between broader society and the individual or community may also result in illness. Just as interpersonal interaction can create illness through physical and psychological channels, interpersonal interaction is also necessary for healing. For example, in their early work on illness and healing among the BaKongo in Zaire, Janzen and Arkinstall (1978) found that interpersonal conflict led to illness. The BaKongo sought healing through western and traditional medicine. Part of the healing involved confrontation and resolution between the afflicted and their kin or other community members. The phenomena of social causation of illness, and the importance of social networks in healing are widely observed in ethnographic studies. These observations are not limited to any particular culture or group. Rather, individuals are embedded within local and broader networks which may cause and cure illness and disease.

The idea of a healing network is intuitive. Think about who was involved and what supports were brought to bear the last time you were sick with the flu. Perhaps friends or relatives brought you food or entertainment? If so, you and they were part of a healing network. Consider a growing corpus of research on cancer survival and social networks in high income countries. Studies find that in addition to physical and psychosocial support, the availability of social and spiritual supports from family, friends and the broader community reduces mortality and improves survivorship (Antman et al. 2002; Cartwright-Alcarese et al. 2003; Braun et al. 2002; Ashing-Giwa and Lim 2009; Bloom 2008; Ka'opua et al. 2007; Berkman and Kawachi 2000).

Feedbacks in health extend beyond the direct interactions with causation and cure. There are feedbacks within the household, across labor markets and, potentially, within the national macro-economic sphere. Work on household economics demonstrates that when a single member of the household becomes ill, household assets may be used in seeking treatment. With savings depleted, the capabilities and agencies of other household members are limited, and intergenerational transfers of wealth are threatened. Consider a poor farmer who succumbs to AIDS. The family may deplete their savings and perhaps sell household goods or livestock in order to obtain medical care. With no savings left, there is no money to guard against other calamities, no money to invest in child health and education (Berman et al. 1994). If the parent dies, children may need to leave school to support the family. This is a familiar scenario in low income households. Such loss is not limited to the very poor in developing countries. Fifty to sixty percent of the personal bankruptcies in the United States are filed due to medical causes (Himmelstein et al. 2005, 2009). Household illness also entails broader economic impacts. Individuals may miss work or die, causing loss of productivity to businesses and creating additional costs for temporary help or training of new employees. As labor markets suffer, so too do industries. Such labor losses may feed back into macro economic performance, and may be deleterious to attracting both domestic and foreign investment (World Health Organization 2001).

Economic development for the individual and within a local setting likewise have theoretical feedbacks which impact individual, household and broader society. Local poverty alleviation efforts seek to raise individuals out of poverty. These efforts are expected to produce incremental results—no project seeks to create millionaires. Rather, minimal economic and/or capital inputs are provided to individuals and households existing at a subsistence level. The idea is, with the modest input, the individual may invest in livestock or in technologies such as fertilizers or a three-wheeler. This would allow him or her to produce enough goods, or earn enough income, to move beyond the subsistence level. For example, a farmer may be able to plant additional land such that the harvest provides for the household needs plus a little extra which can be sold in the open market. This surplus contributes to continued capital accumulation by the individual or household. At the village level, if multiple individuals are producing surplus, then a communal food bank or such can be created, producing public goods and communal gains. Surplus can be sold in national markets, or international markets, producing economic gains for the community and nation. Accumulated capital may also be invested in growing a business enterprise and hiring additional labor (Islam 2007; Mosley and Rock 2004). As entrepreneurs leave one business sector for another, the decrease in labor supply may result in an increase in wages as industries attempt to attract workers from competing interests (Islam 2007). As households move above subsistent levels, the savings and capital may be invested in better nutrition, education and health, improving current and future economic and health prospects for the household, and feeding back into the community and nation with a healthier, better educated and therefore more desirable workforce and populace (Islam 2007; Chowdhury and Mosley 2004; World Health Organization 2001).

Theory suggests that a variety of goods will accumulate across local, national, and even international levels through local efforts to improve health and economic opportunities. Community-based work is therefore a worthy endeavor for the development-minded. Such programs are delivered by a variety of actors including those from the public sector, commercial enterprises, and not-for-profit NGOs, charities, or missions. The success of community-based work depends upon institutional goals, methods, resources and behaviors, as well as the program design, and the local and national context. Many of the more successful projects engage in a constant process of monitoring, evaluation, quality improvement, and re-evaluation to ensure that their intended clients are indeed realizing positive and desired outcomes for "(t)he ultimate test of any institution is not whether it merely exists or sustains itself, but whether it manages to do something useful for its members" (Islam 2007, p. 93). Monitoring and evaluation as a best practice is now incorporated into the SDG structure. Good practice dictates that community-based projects work with existing national and local institutions and frameworks. With this in mind, we will now turn our attention to case studies in the community from the health and economic development sectors.

4.1.1 Community-Based Health Care

Community-based health care has proven to be a successful, if sometimes ignored, model for delivering health care and improving health outcomes at the local level. Although there is no single definition of community-based care, in its most basic form, community-based health care refers to health delivery in the local context be it of a town, village or neighborhood, or delivery of care within an ethnically- or culturally-defined population. A more comprehensive notion of community-based health care is that of applied social medicine in which health care and delivery strive to incorporate individual medical diagnoses and analyses of the communal environment in order to treat and prevent social and medical ills that inform an unhealthy nexus. What differentiates community-based care from other health delivery systems is that the foci for intervention are determined by the epidemiological profile of the relevant community and delivered through local offices and staff. The interventions themselves are tailored to the sociocultural milieu in order to garner local acceptance.

Although the idea of community-based care seems to continually be rediscovered and reinvented, it is tied to traditional practices of care-giving found in many cultures around the world. At its heart, it is nothing more than people taking care of those they know and are in close contact with. For centuries, when an individual became sick, his or her family provided care. Sometimes, neighbors would assist in care-giving, perhaps by bringing over food or other supplies. Caring for members of a religious community is a long-standing tradition in Christianity, Islam, Buddhism and other religions. By extension, invoking a social network or communal network seems to be a reasonable up-scaling of historical practices.

Many community-based health programs are staffed by residents of the community being served and/or incorporate community members into accountability mechanisms. For example, community leaders or representatives of different clients/stakeholders may serve on a board of directors. Local residents and clientele may be involved in identifying health priorities and in developing culturally-appropriate interventions. This collaborative process is commonly associated with **community-based participatory research (CBPR)**, an approach to health research and programming that has gained popularity in the late 20th century. CBPR attempts to bring the lay community and topical experts and technocrats together to exchange knowledge and build collaboration in order to bring positive change to participating communities.[2] Community care may be delivered by public or private organizations, through domestic or international actors.

Community-based care offers a number of advantages to centrally-planned care. First, by looking at the local epidemiological profile, community health allows for effective and efficient service provision. Because they are concerned with local health problems, providers examine the local environment in order to identify risks and points of intervention that often only those living and working in the community understand. Centralized medical planning, which often takes place in a distant city, is divorced from the everyday realities which shape diseases and responses at the local level. Second, health interventions are unrolled within the community by workers who have knowledge of community practices, norms, and networks. The staff know their patients and can incorporate this knowledge into modifying or creating interventions which are culturally acceptable and likely to be adopted. They can incorporate local explanatory models for illnesses and their respective cures into their conversations with clients. A third advantage of this model of care is that staff are often recruited from within the neighborhood or village. This adds legitimacy to the enterprise in that, by hiring locals, the staff are no longer viewed as outside agents descending upon a community for their own purpose. Local staff help build trust between local residents and workers from other areas. Further, local staff bring intimate knowledge of the community and social networks. They may be better able to help identify people and households in the community who are in need.

Community-based care also has a cost advantage. As we saw in both Sri Lanka and Chile, central governments are challenged by the rising cost of care. The

[2]See http://depts.washington.edu/ccph/index.html, http://www.ncbi.nlm.nih.gov/bookshelf/br.fcgi?book=hserta&part=A148846, and http://www.press.jhu.edu/journals/progress_in_community_health_partnerships/ for details on this type of research.

governments in both cases witnessed difficulties in deploying central health staff to distant or rural areas both because of poor pay in locations where opportunities to earn additional income via private practice were limited, and the perception that living standards in such areas were poor, which created staffing disincentives. Recruiting local staff eliminates the issue of desirability. In many cases, local medical needs can be met by assistants with specialized training, but without complete medical education. These are **community health workers (CHW)**. Such training is available at a comparatively low cost. These assistants can operate independently or under the supervision of a medical officer. The salary requirements for local staff may also be lower than those required by individuals who have higher levels of training or who are used to incomes which match higher costs of living in urban areas. The availability of local jobs contributes to employment and earnings and may even provide social mobility for staff, thereby contributing to improved livelihoods and increased local development. Community-based programs, such as Gonoshasthaya Kendra, incorporate biomedical training with traditional practice in areas such as maternal care. This method keeps the cost of training relatively low and validates different ways of knowing and understanding illness. The wave of professionalization that occurred in biomedicine had many benefits, including minimizing exploitative, dangerous practices of the untrained, but it also delegitimized beneficial knowledge and services used by traditional healers. By providing appropriate training to village members already recognized for their healing roles, community-based organizations honor the heritage of those they purport to serve. Through cooperation, they may better be able to improve allopathic and traditional practices.

4.1.2 Pholela Health Center—An Early Innovator

The Pholela Health Center, founded in South Africa in 1940, was an early success in community-based health care. In 1938, Dr. Sidney Kark, a South African born and trained medical doctor, was part of a national health survey team that concluded that poor nutrition and infectious disease interactively created poor overall health and a plague upon the nation (Tollman 1994). The survey also concluded that these conditions were preventable. In response to the survey, the Health Ministry established the Pholela Health Unit, in rural Natal Province, as a model for a planned country-wide network of health centers that would target under-nutrition and disease (Brown 2002; Tollman 1994). The unit was to combine curative and preventative medicine to prevent and treat specific diseases (among them typhoid, typhus, malaria, syphilis, TB, scabies and impetigo), provide health education with a special focus on maternal and child care, and build local cooperation and community responsibility through coordinated local and national action (Tollman 1994). Dr. Kark was appointed to head the unit. He, along with his wife Emily, also a physician, moved to Pholela and there developed the community-oriented primary health care (COPC) model that later came to define community health.

The Pholela model of COPC linked clinical and epidemiological perspectives on health with clinical diagnoses, analyses of the distribution of illness throughout the community, and investigation into what accounted for the distribution. This approach connected individual diagnoses and treatment with the community as a patient, and recognized that disease clustering created a 'community syndrome' (Tollman 1994, p. 657). In the case of Pholela, this syndrome was "malnutrition, communicable diseases and mental ill-health in a poor rural community undergoing rapid change" (Kark as cited in Tollman 1994, p. 658). The COPC model utilized cyclical planning with assessment, individual/community diagnosis, program planning and implementation, monitoring, re-assessment and evaluation (Tollman 1994).

To implement this model, the health center provided general services and a Family Health and Medical Care Program. The general services included outpatient services that were available to anyone who presented at the center regardless of his/her place of residence, as well as controlling disease outbreaks in the Pholela and neighboring districts (Kark and Cassel 1952). The Family Health and Medical Care Program provided intensive services, including health education, to a limited number of families in the Pholela district. The initial program reached 900 persons; by 1951 it covered 8500 people (Kark and Cassel 1952). The center was staffed by medical officers who provided treatment for the sick, direct preventive services (including giving periodic health exams), and directing nursing services. Nurses engaged in curative and preventative services with a primary focus on maternal and child care. Health assistants formed the base of the service pyramid. Their main focus was health education, and they were charged with home visits, leading group discussions, and carrying out demonstrations (Kark and Cassel 1952). The health assistants were largely local residents hired for their knowledge of the community and to build trust between the Center and the Community. Dr. Kark wrote of the health center's success in controlling typhoid and typhus epidemics:

> Patients suffering from typhus, typhoid fever or diphtheria have come to live in homes in this area, in order to get treatment from the Health Centre. In no case has there been any spread of the disease. The health assistant has not only proved a most useful health educator but, by his knowledge of the community, has been able to report on the arrival of a sick person to a particular home. This has led to early recognition of such cases by the medical officers and medical aides, with consequent early treatment and preventive measures (Kark and Cassel 1952: 102–103).

Another innovation of the Pholela Health Center was that Dr. Kark encouraged staff to work with local beliefs rather than to belittle them.

> Maladjusted and unhappy relationships with emotional tension and neurotic conflicts are major features of the various illnesses believed to be due to witchcraft. Clinical practice and health education require an understanding of these processes if the needs of the people are to be met by the Health Centre (Kark and Cassel 1952: 102).

The Center achieved remarkable results. Infant mortality rates dropped from 256 per 1000 in 1940–1942 to 86 per 1000 in 1955–1956 (Tollman 1994). Weight gains in infants showed statistically significant improvement (Tollman 1994). Epidemics of typhoid and typhus were eliminated within the defined coverage area (Kark and Cassel 1952). Syphilis incidence declined from 13.5 per 1000 in 1943 to 0.79 per 1000 in 1957, and stillbirths to syphilitic mothers declined from 15% in 1949 to 1.9% in 1953 (Tollman 1994). Scabies and impetigo, immunizable disease, sexually transmitted infections, and tuberculosis also declined over time in the service area.

Despite the Center's remarkable health achievements, political will was necessary to keep the center going and such will ultimately evaporated. General elections in 1948 heralded the rise of a socially conservative government. In the 1950s, the political climate changed and racial divisions in the country again became stark and violent. The end result was apartheid. The brief period of liberal policy came to an end and Dr. Kark and colleagues left the country (Tollman 1994; Brown 2002). The COPC model was dismantled in South Africa, but not before it spread to other countries. Israel, the United States, Canada, Spain, the UK and countries in Asia and Latin America adopted this model of community-based health (Tollman 1994).

The Pholela Health Center demonstrated what could be accomplished with community-based health care, but ultimately, the grand experiment came to an end as financial and political support from the government disappeared. This program reflected the strengths of local and national integration, but also showed one of the problems which consistently confronts public health care—dependence upon fiscal resources which are not always available. Resources are tied to policy and political will both of which change along with political systems, ruling parties, social pressures and power hierarchies. Where there is a dearth of public allocations for health care, other organizations, such as charitable organizations, mission-based groups, and NGOs may step in.

4.1.3 Gonoshasthaya Kendra—A Continuing Success

Gonoshasthaya Kendra (GK), which is Bengla for "the people's health center," is an NGO which stepped into deliver health care where there was such a dearth of state resources. This organization grew out of the operation of several doctors working on the frontlines of war as Bangladesh fought for and won independence from Pakistan (Gonoshasthaya Kendra, n.d.). In 1972, GK organized to provide affordable health services in the Dhaka district with a focus on basic health care including maternal and child health (Chaudhury and Chowdhury 2008). From its humble beginning of 22 volunteers and doctors, GK has grown to serve one million people in 592 villages and 11 districts throughout Bangladesh, making it one of the largest health care providers in the country outside of the Ministry of Health Care and Nutrition (Chaudhury and Chowdhury 2008). GK began its work, as many NGOs do, in the post-conflict context of nation-building. It operated on the principle that health care must be integrated with other development activities, and so worked in collaboration with the government (Chaudhury and Chowdhury 2008; Gonoshasthaya Kendra, n.d.). When Bangladesh marked its independence in December, 1971, the country was not an easy place to begin a health care

Table 4.3 Select indicators for Bangladesh, 1972–2014

Indicator	1972	2014
GDP per capita (constant US$ 2010)	318	924
Crude birth rate (per 1000)	47	20
Crude death rate (per 1000)	19	5
Total fertility (births per woman)	7	2
Life expectancy at birth	47	71
MMR per 100,000 live births		210[a]
IMR per 1000 live births	148	32

[a]Data from 2011

Data source World Bank (2015). *World Development Indicators*

revolution. Bangladesh was recovering from a genocide in which between 200,000 and 3,000,000 people were killed and another 10 million became refugees.[3] The nation was poor, the people were poor, and so too was population health (Table 4.3).

In the early 1970s, GK established village-level services throughout Dhaka. Reproductive and child health (RCH) was a central component. The RCH activities included registration of and follow-up with pregnant women, maternal tetanus immunization, childhood immunization, nutritional education and promotion, family planning services, pro-poor health insurance schemes, mobile maternal care clinics, and, in the case of maternal or infant deaths, follow-up meetings with family and community (Chaudhury and Chowdhury 2008). Many of the services were provided by a network of village-based trained health workers, most of whom were female. Today, these health workers undergo a six-month foundational training program, followed by a 12-month supervised training (Chaudhury and Chowdhury 2008).

Traditional birth attendants (TBAs) were and continue to be an important part of the GK network. The TBAs receive training on the scientific basis of pregnancy and procedures for handling normal deliveries, with a focus on home delivery (Chaudhury and Chowdhury 2008). The TBAs and health workers can refer complicated pregnancies to appropriate care through clinics or hospitals operated by GK, the government, or other NGOs depending upon the specific circumstance. In many ways, this program parallels and complements the government's initiative to increase the number of skilled birth attendants (SBAs) through recruitment and provision of an 18-month training program (Chaudhury and Chowdhury 2008). The GK's use of TBAs taps into an existing cultural network of individuals whose role is already understood by the communities the program hopes to serve, thereby legitimizing GK services and staff, honoring local knowledge and, given that

[3]The official death toll according to the government of Bangladesh is 3 million; Harff and Gurr (1988) estimate 1250 to 3,000,000. Matthew White (2005) provides a well documented list of deaths associated with various wars at his website http://users.erols.com/mwhite28/warstat2.htm
.

doctors or nurses attend only 6% of rural births, efficiently using existing resources with relatively small input for training (and retraining).

The GK methodology includes forming village health committees in order to build participation and accountability. These goals are further enhanced through "death meetings" at which GK health workers meet with community representatives and family members to discuss possible causes of maternal or neonatal deaths and whether or not the deaths were preventable (Chaudhury and Chowdhury 2008). These meetings not only provide accountability, but they also have a social awakening impact in that participants come to realize that some factors that contributed to the deaths may be controlled (Chaudhury and Chowdhury 2008). Village-level audits are complemented by regional review by GK doctors.

As a result of the GK community-based care, maternal health has improved both in terms of inputs to health and outcomes. The national MMR in 1990 was 574 per 100,000 live births. This rate was 299 per 100,000 in the villages being served by GK (Chaudhury and Chowdhury 2008). This number dropped to 186 for the period of 2000–2005 (Chaudhury and Chowdhury 2008). Between 2002 and 2005, 80% of births in GK villages were attended by TBAs as opposed to 12% nationally (NIPORT 2003; Chaudhury and Chowdhury 2008). Antenatal services were accessed more in GK areas than in the nation as a whole. On average, women received five antenatal care (ANC) service visits in GK villages; 97% of the women received a tetanus shot as opposed to 85% nationally, and 100% of pregnant women in GK areas received ANC during their pregnancy compared to 47.6% nationally (NIPORT 2003; Chaudhury and Chowdhury 2008). Only 12% of the births in GK areas were attended by untrained birth attendants as opposed to 74% nationally, and 90% of home deliveries were attended by medically trained personnel versus 24% for the nation (NIPORT 2003; Chaudhury and Chowdhury 2008). Evidence also suggests that the referral system GK uses for more complicated pregnancies worked, albeit imperfectly.[4]

While the impact of low cost investment in health workers, and utilization of village-based health care has been impressive, a number of obstacles remain. Many maternal deaths continue to occur because of a delay in seeking care, which is partially related to a dearth of resources for staffing local clinics (Chaudhury and Chowdhury 2008). In some cases of maternal death, women called upon multiple providers for care after being referred by a TBA. However, the search for open or staffed facilities took precious time. Facilities were either closed or not staffed during operating hours (Chaudhury and Chowdhury 2008). This speaks to management, training, and financial problems. Resources at the individual level also impacted the number of deaths. Lack of transportation, and/or the time required to arrange adequate transport, was a contributing factor to timely receipt of care (Chaudhury and Chowdhury 2008). Other factors included the need for continued training for health technicians, differential perception of pregnancy-related risk

[4]This is based on data as to where deliveries occurred, who was in attendance and where and with whom maternal deaths occurred.

among different members of the community, continued need for community education and behavioral change, and the need for improved negotiating power for women (Chaudhury and Chowdhury 2008). Many of these factors require change at the regional and national levels in order to complement change at the community level.

4.1.4 Implications for Local Health and National Development

These cases demonstrate that community-based care, from public or private actors, can improve health outcomes at the local level. The interactive impacts of improved health on household and community behaviors and activities are not fully understood, nor are they easy to measure. It is also difficult to quantify the specific impact of prevention programs, which are key components to community-based care. How does one measure something which might have happened, but did not? Further, health programming frequently has a lag effect with significant changes in health measures coming only over a long period of time.

The ability of researchers to quantify the interaction of local health and national/international development may be weak, but it is comparatively easy to hypothesize the potential mechanisms of interaction. Evidence suggests that positive impacts from community-based care are accrued at the individual, household, and community levels. At the individual and household level, the elimination of epidemics of typhoid and typhus by the Pholela Center clearly contributed to individual health and longevity. Maternal care provided by GK reduced the likelihood of a woman dying during pregnancy in the service provision areas. The achievements implicitly reduced the need for family and friends to dedicate time, energy and resources to care-giving and living mothers could continue to care for infants and children within their households. Reduction of negative health sequelae frees up household resources, including human energy and labor, to be dedicated to other activities. Reduced mortality means families need not deplete their savings to cover funerary costs and that resources may be invested intergenerationally for health and education. Children need not drop out of school to work and earn wages to replace lost parental income, or drop out of school to assume the care-giving role of dead mothers.

The control of individual health and household health contributes to a change in community health most notably in decreases of infectious disease. As witnessed at the Pholela Center, epidemic disease disappeared from the service area thanks to treatment, early detection and prevention. Even those not treated directly by the program receive a public good as the likelihood of transmission decreased in the community. The GK programs likewise impacted community health through programs of education and participation. The death meetings contributed to community understanding and ownership of preventable maternal and child deaths. Education about maternal and child health provides better skills in assessing and responding to risks. Education also enables the network of formal and informal caregivers to cooperatively share information and resources. Social change in the GK areas did not occur quickly, but the results of such change are visible with decreased mortality, increased rates of family planning, and decreased fertility rates as reported above. The community-level change may resound in broader national society via improved capabilities and productivity.

4.2 Microcredit and Microfinance

Microfinance and microcredit by definition target individuals or specific sub-populations. To differentiate, **microfinance** refers to a range of financial products and services for poor or low-income clients who typically cannot access traditional financial products such as savings accounts and credit. **Microcredit** is a sub-sector of microfinance and refers to the provision of non-collateralized loans to low-income or poor clientele. Microcredit loans are for small amounts, with global averages around US$350, but many less than US$100 (Mosley and Rock 2004; Islam 2007). This may seem like a very small amount of money, but consider that microcredit targets the poor and very poor, whose annual household income may be less than $US365 per year for very poor. Male loanees of the Grameen Bank in Bangladesh, for instance, have a gross family income of US$322; female members report an average annual income of US$280.[5] With so little income, the poor live a life that is little more than subsistent. There are no additional monies or assets available to insure against catastrophic events, let alone provide even minimal investment funds for business or family development, or collateral to procure a traditional loan. Yet, sometimes minimal investment is all that is necessary to invest in better crop inputs, in transportation such as a three-wheeler, or even a cell phone to 'rent'.[6]

Given that microfinance and microcredit typically target the poor, it may be useful to understand who the poor are. Unfortunately, there is no single standard for defining this term. The Copenhagen Declaration of the World Summit for Social Development defined absolute poverty as "… a condition characterized as severe deprivation of basic human needs, including food, safe drinking water, sanitation facilities, health, shelter, education and information. It depends not only on income but also on access to social services" (United Nations 2005). Poverty is typically measured in terms of income or consumption. Experts argue that measures of

[5]Calculated from income levels in Islam (2007). Taka converted to US dollars based on Jan. 2010 international exchange rates.

[6]See NPR (2010) for several stories on the enterprises financed by microcredit, including Bangladesh's "phone ladies."

consumption more accurately gauge well-being.[7] Many countries set a **national poverty line** which is based on the minimal amount of income deemed necessary for basic survival. This line is not calculated in any one way and so national poverty lines are not readily comparable across nation-states. Other methods for assessing poverty include establishing an essential bundle of goods such as food, clothing and housing, and using the ability to access these goods as a means to assess who is poor or not poor (UNDP 2003). A measure used internationally is the global poverty line defined as $1.90 (PPP). The World Bank adjusted this line to the current level in October 2015. Previously, the line was $1.25 (PPP). The PPP refers to purchasing power parity which adjusts monetary units based on the goods the money can buy within the local economy rather than based on the international exchange rate.

Formal and informal sources of credit exist around the world, but may not be accessible to the poor. Informal sources include loans from families, friends and usurers or "loan sharks" who charge inordinate interest rates. The family and friend network is by no means universally available nor is it universally capable of making loans. The very poor cannot afford the high interest rates in the informal sector and so may not seek loans there (Islam 2007). Formal credit sources include commercial banks, government programs, and non-governmental organizations. The lending practices and lending criteria of commercial banks often preclude the poor. Further, social stigma and self-perception may prevent the poor from seeking loans through commercial institutions (Islam 2007). For better or worse, commercial institutions, attracted by the success of some microcredit programs and the allure of new markets, are now entering the microfinance market. Some government programs target individuals who may not otherwise be able to access financial products, but such programs are dependent upon fiscal resources and political will. NGOs also provide services to fill the gap between what is provided by formal and informal channels, and what is actually accessible to the poor.

The Grameen Bank is one such organization which pioneered microcredit financing in Bangladesh. The bank began operating in 1976 as an NGO. It became a formal banking institution in 1983 with majority ownership by borrowers and by the government of Bangladesh (Grameen Bank 2010). This change shows not only that the institution evolved over time, but also that its goals worked in conjunction with national goals—an important factor when considering development. The bank, and its founder Professor Muhammad Yunus, won the Nobel Peace Prize in 2006 for their achievements in bottom-up, rural development. It is to this institution we now turn our focus.

---

[7] For resources on measuring poverty, see: http://web.worldbank.org/WBSITE/EXTERNAL/TOPICS/EXTPOVERTY/EXTPA/0,,contentMDK:20202198~menuPK:435055~pagePK:148956~piPK:216618~theSitePK:430367,00.html.

4.2.1 *Grameen Bank—Early Innovator and Continuing Success*

A founding principle of the Grameen Bank is to create a 'virtuous circle' in which individuals with low income receive money on credit, which is invested in small scale enterprise, that in turn yields increased income for further investment and by which to receive more credit, which leads to further investment, and so forth. The objective of the Grameen Bank is to target credit programs for the rural poor in order to create opportunities for self-employment and thereby alleviate poverty (Islam 2007; Grameen Bank 2010). It does this through community-based micro-credit lending in which solidarity groups form a central component. The Grameen Bank operates by establishing bank branches which are responsible for delivering services to 15–22 villages (Grameen Bank 2010). Preliminary work includes bank staff familiarizing themselves with the local communities, and identifying potential clientele (Grameen Bank 2010). Once potential clients are identified, they are formed into groups of five who will qualify for loans. These are the solidarity groups. Initially, only two of the five group members will receive loans for a micro-enterprise. Only when these members have demonstrated their ability to repay the principal and interest are other group members eligible to receive a loan (Grameen Bank 2010). In this way, group members become invested in one another's success. By drawing upon members of a community to form a cooperative enterprise, the solidarity groups draw upon personal and communal knowledge, about individuals and business opportunities, and build social networks which can enhance professional and personal communication channels. Social pressure is brought to bear on loan recipients, and there is individual and group accountability. Collateral is not required and no legal instruments are used in Bank activities with its clientele (Grameen Bank 2010). Ninety-seven percent of the borrowers are women (Grameen Bank 2010).

The Grameen Bank is pro-poor in that it espouses the philosophy that the poor are able to help themselves, and that change begins with individuals and households. This is a perspective of empowerment in which the poor do not suffer from a dearth of morality or abilities as stereotypes would suggest,[8] but rather are highly capable but disarticulated from institutions, tools and power hierarchies which are necessary for them to translate their labor and knowledge into wealth. Credit is seen as a right, not a privilege. Grameen Bank strives to change the links between credit power-hierarchies and recipients. The bank bases its success on the success of its borrowers. The loan repayment rate is 97% (Grameen Bank 2010). By comparison, loan default rates for U.S. banks between 1984 and 2001 ranged from 5 to 25%, with an average of 15% (Farrer 2008). The profits generated through

---

[8] *A Framework for Understanding Poverty* by Ruby K. Payne (2005) and *An African Centered Response to Ruby Payne's Poverty Theory* (2006) by Jawanza Kunjufu provide interesting cross-cultural discussion of causes, and (mis)perceptions of poverty.

interest and loan repayment now fund Grameen Bank activities.[9] From its inception through 2008, Grameen Bank lent US$6.85 billion and generated US$174 million in profit (Grameen Bank 2010). In addition to poverty alleviation, the Grameen Bank attempts to engage in social development by encouraging female empowerment and social/political engagement as reflected in the 'Sixteen Decisions' Grameen borrowers adopt. These include building/maintaining adequate housing, maintaining appropriate diets, and limiting a family size (Grameen Bank 1998). It should be noted that while this is an admirable tangent, the bank remains focused on microfinance activities and does not engage in technical training or capacity building outside of financial management (Islam 2007). The bank publishes annual reports and audits (available at www.grameen.com) and engages in self-analysis as part of its goals for transparency and improvement. As a result of the continuing process of evaluation, the bank initiated Phase II in 2002. This phase extends the focus of the bank from microcredit to include a broad range of microfinance products, such as savings accounts, and a wider variety of loan products such as loans for improved housing, sanitation and hygiene, and scholarships and loans for education (Islam 2007; Grameen Bank 2010).

The institution has proven successful in terms of finances, evaluation and operation, but the question remains as to how it has performed in terms of its goal of poverty alleviation at the individual and broader societal levels. The Grameen Bank states that it is interested in targeting the very poor. The bank has proven successful at increasing household income, building household working capital and assets, increasing productivity, and improving female participation in the workforce among its members (Islam 2007). However, the benefits have not accrued equally across membership with the extreme poor not realizing the same magnitude of gains as did the poor (Islam 2007). This is one of the more well known problems with microcredit programs in general; they tend to be well suited to reach the poor but often fail to reach the extremely poor in any given society (Chowdhury and Mosley 2004; Mosley and Rock 2004; Woller 2002). A study conducted in Bangladesh found that the average household income of Grameen Bank members was significantly higher than that of non-members, but that the extremely poor did not experience significant gains in income as a result of the microcredit program (Islam 2007). The gains that were made in household income were associated with increased self-employment and new employment, especially for previously unemployed women. Data indicated that male loan recipients tended to move from wage labor to trading and transportation. Female recipients entered the work force, and increased participation in manufacturing and trading/shop keeping. Both increased livestock ownership (Islam 2007). Evidence suggests that many households experienced an improved standard of living as a result of receiving Grameen Bank loans (Islam 2007).

[9]Grameen Bank stopped accepting donations in 1995 and adopted a stance in which it will not take out loans.

To the extent that improved living standards and raised income levels help smooth consumption, which is a central concern for reducing the vulnerability of the poor to external shocks (Dréze and Sen 1991; Sen 2000), then the program can be deemed successful in reducing the vulnerability of the poor. However, the risk of catastrophic occurrence remains. Grameen Bank, while improving the income of households, has not been universally successful in lifting its clientele out of poverty. There is little difference in terms of household food security, a primary concern for household vulnerability, between Grameen Bank members and non-members based on minimal divergence in food expenditure between the two (Islam 2007). While there is variation in consumption of non-food items, particularly in housing (Islam 2007), the degree to which investment in non-food items provides extra security for households cannot be determined from the available data.

Program impact on the economic and social position of participating individuals is unclear. One study found that only 23% of the Grameen Bank members experienced significant improvement in their economic position (Islam 2007). Other studies have shown that the bank did little more that help members to “keep one’s head above water” (Sobhan as cited in Islam 2007: 132–134). The program reduced the likelihood that the poor would experience downward mobility, but the poor remain subject to the economic stressors of a rural economy, such as agricultural cycles, natural calamity and sudden crises, over which they have little control (Islam 2007). Upward social mobility associated with this specific microcredit program appears to be limited (Islam 2007). While Sobhan’s statement suggests that members experienced little in the way of lifestyle improvement, we cannot know if without the loan a household would have been able to stave off a catastrophic loss. One could imagine that the loan had important meaning to an individual whose income increased even marginally, even though such an increase may not register in the research-based assessment, nor might such symbolic or real impact be in line with institutional goals.

In terms of human capital impacts, members of the bank demonstrated gains. It is worth re-emphasizing that the program was successful at raising the income of women, and bringing women into the workforce. Although women did not achieve the same productivity gains as did men, the successes were not easily won given the social and cultural milieu (Islam 2007). Thus, without broader structural change, the benefits accrued to the women count for only so much. Other changes in social capital came within the household due to investment in household health and nutrition, children’s health and education. Investment in these items rose with participation in the Grameen Bank microcredit program, with women investing more in human capital than either non-member or male members (Islam 2007). A study undertaken on 300 households between 1998 and 1999 found that for every 1% increase in Grameen Bank credit received by female members, the probability of school enrollment for girls in the household increased by 1.9% and by 2.4% for boys (Islam 2007). A similar increase in loans to men found that the likelihood of male child school enrollment went up by 2.8% but that there was no impact on the education of girls (Islam 2007).

4.2.2 Implications for Development and Well-Being

The success of the Grameen Bank helped to initiate interest in and growth of microfinance. Today, microcredit and microfinance programs exist throughout the world and have demonstrated various degrees of success. Microfinance programs raised income and helped to smooth consumption of individual recipients and the households in which they reside (Islam 2007; Chowdhury and Mosley 2004; Mosley and Rock 2004; Velasco and Marconi 2004). Microfinance increased savings, via income and material wealth, among its members (Islam 2007; Mosley and Rock 2004; Velasco and Marconi 2004) and beneficiaries increased their productive capital (Islam 2007). Microfinance thereby has had a profound impact on economic development of individuals and households.

Microfinance has also contributed to increased social development. Households that received microfinancing have experienced improved nutritional status and child survival due to better nutrition, through the purchase of more nutritious food, and increased spending on health (Chowdhury and Bhuiya 2004; Chowdhury and Mosley 2004; Islam 2007; Mosley and Rock 2004). This was especially true in female-headed households. Changes in family planning, with a preference for fewer children, also occurred (Chowdhury and Mosley 2004). Intergenerational transfers vis-à-vis child education and investment in child health increased (Islam 2007; Mosley and Rock 2004; Chowdhury and Bhuiya 2004; Velasco and Marconi 2004).

Female empowerment is another outcome of microfinance seen across various cultural settings (Islam 2007; Mosley and Rock 2004; Velasco and Marconi 2004). Further investment in girls occurred where recipients were women, creating cross-generational female empowerment and contributing to an environment where social and political change is possible. Micro-enterprises increased education not only of female children but of women themselves through formal schooling and classes and informal, information exchange with other women in the community. Increased female health was both an independent impact of microfinance programs, and an interactive result of the program with education (Rodriguez-Garcia et al. 2001; Velasco and Marconi 2004). The links between female education and improved health are well known and consistent across different countries and regions (Cleland and Van Ginneken 1988). The potential for broader societal impact in terms of declining fertility rates exists where microfinance programs are tied to increased knowledge about family planning.

Household and productivity improvements helped to stabilize the availability of basic goods and creating a modicum of economic stability within the local context (Velasco and Marconi 2004). Surplus food production has provided for a community food bank and has been made available for school feeding programs, which strengthen the local safety net (Sanchez et al. 2007; Islam 2007). In their study of Bolivia, Velasco and Marconi (2004) found that the continuance of high repayment rates among members of the microfinance organization, *ProMujer*, contributed to macroeconomic stability during the recession beginning in 1999.

This should not be taken to mean that microfinance is the great panacea for poverty alleviation which some perceive it to be. Success is very much dependent upon the structure of the particular program, the local socio-economic context, and the ability of a program to monitor and adjust to the particular operating context. A standing critique of microfinance is that it fails to reach the very poor and does little to reduce client poverty let alone alleviate broader societal poverty (Islam 2007; Chowdhury and Mosley 2004; Mosley and Rock 2004). Microcredit, in fact, proved better able to raise the income of those who were comparatively better off to begin with. A critique associated with the problem of targeting and outcomes is that poverty alleviation will not happen through the force of microfinance alone. Institutional and policy contexts matter (Chowdhury and Mosley 2004; Mosley and Rock 2004). Program and policy direction needs to focus on improved targeting for the poor as well as improve integration into a broader development framework. But caution is warranted in using this particular failure, that of not better raising the income of poor, as an excuse to detract from a financial operation which reaches the poor, for what is meaningful programmatically is often very different from what is meaningful to an individual (Hulme and Mosley 1996, 1998; Islam 2007; Karnani 2007). Another failure of microcredit has to do with loan fungibility. Since the fungibility of a loan makes it difficult to attach to a specific use, one cannot guarantee the money will be used for the stated purpose of the loan. This weakness may also be a strength in that the money is available for household uses and may perhaps prove to be a fail-safe which does not register in improved income, but does impact quality of life and affords protection from calamity (Islam 2007).

Although the intent of microfinance is to produce change in the individual and household as well as the broader community, measuring the wider societal impact is problematic, in part because of the difficulty of demonstrating association or causation between individual change and national change. For example, in terms of economic impact, it is hypothesized that microcredit will have a multiplier effect within a community in that recipients will build businesses and therefore be able to hire other community members. However, evidence on this is mixed. Cases from Bangladesh show that few microcredit entrepreneurs hired members outside of the household (Islam 2007). Evidence from several African nations suggests only limited success in expanding employment opportunities and providing for local social mobility (Mosley and Rock 2004).

Even when human capital and community coping capacity are increased vis-à-vis improved household health and education, the link to broader social improvement is largely theoretical. To the extent that improved utilization of health care results in improved vaccination rates and the potential for herd-immunity, and better control of infectious disease, even those households which did not receive a microcredit loan may benefit as the likelihood of exposure to infection decreases. Microfinance may improve community health by assisting with household access to health care (via such means as provision of money for user fees), which will thereby increase demand for health services such that provider incentives exist to establish new or expand existing health services, and/or bring about health care reform (Rodriguez-Garcia et al. 2001). However, exploring the links between micro-enterprise and health is a relatively new avenue of research which, as of yet, has poorly defined methods and tools, and few comprehensive studies (Rodriguez-Garcia et al. 2001).

Microfinancing schemes raise social capital in part by enhancing the skills of the recipients and in part through the growth of social networks which can share information, pool resources, etc. (Chowdhury and Bhuiya 2004; Chowdhury and Mosley 2004). The Grameen Bank solidarity loan groups demonstrate small level impact on social capital in that five individuals become linked with their individual success depending upon the success of others in the group. At a broader level, membership within a microfinance community has led to the sharing of resources, such as transportation costs, and the formation of interest groups to lobby for public change (Chowdhury and Bhuiya 2004; Sanchez et al. 2007; Velasco and Marconi 2004). Increased political participation, social mobilization, diffusion of ideas and social awareness are associated with some, but not all, microfinance programs (Chowdhury and Mosley 2004; Chowdhury and Bhuiya 2004; Mosley and Rock 2004; Rodriguez-Garcia et al. 2001). Much is dependent upon the specific geographic context and the operating structure of the specific microfinance institution (MFI).

As with many NGOs and INGOs, there is a lack of regulation of MFIs, leading to problems of legitimacy and exploitation. Given the transnational reach of some MFIs, the different abilities of nation-states to regulate financial systems, decreased regulation of international finances, and lack of information to help potential clients determine which MFIs are legitimate, a framework for regulation, monitoring and dissemination of information is warranted (Van Greuning et al. 1998a, b). The guidelines that currently exist are not enforceable (Microfinance Regulation and Supervision Resource Center 2010). In some cases, institutions that engage in microfinance may hurt rather than help broader programs of development, or may harm the reputation and acceptability of microfinance in general. For example, commercial bank entry into the Bolivian and Kenyan microfinance market destabilized financial discipline, increasingly excluded the poor from microfinance opportunities, and proved harmful to the legitimacy of microfinance enterprises (Velasco and Marconi 2004). The title of microfinance has, in some cases, been co-opted by groups that, at best, use some principles of microfinance to exploit money-making opportunities without relating the program to human or social development and, at worst, prove to be scams designed solely to make money through illegitimate and exploitative means (Mulama 2009). Thus, institutional behavior matters.

4.3 Millennium Villages—A Multisectoral Intervention

Community health programs and microfinance programs both seek to improve human development, and create ‘virtuous cycles’ at the local level with the hope that the outcomes will resonate beyond the local. They do this through a targeted intervention. Health is the primary target of the community health programs we examined, but the underlying belief is that healthy people make healthy communities and create public and private goods. The idea of micro credit is that provision of the means to earn a livelihood will impact individual wealth and resonate into household security, improved community investment, and investment in future generations resulting in overall improvement in well-being. These strategies have been shown to positively impact the outcomes of primary interest, health and household income, but the indirect effects are not clear. Given that development is a multi-faceted process, it was only a matter of time before someone realized the value in concurrently addressing multiple aspects of poverty. The Millennium Villages Project (MVP) seeks to do just that.

MVP attempts to jump start development in areas of extreme poverty by providing a staged package of interventions to address agricultural productivity, health, education, empowerment, market access and infrastructure. The project is guided by the Earth Institute at Colombia University, Millennium Promise and the United Nations. The project is a demonstration project that seeks to test outcomes and scalability of a low-cost package of interventions on alleviating extreme poverty and fostering sustainable development (Millennium Villages 2016).

The project is guided by the principle that poverty traps are created in areas of 'extreme shortage' in terms of natural, human and financial capital (Sanchez et al. 2007, p. 16775). In order to address the multitude of deficits, a multitude of interventions are necessary. Investment in economic development is not sufficient in communities of extreme poverty as the health deficit will decrease productive opportunities. Health must therefore be stabilized in order to jumpstart labor, livelihoods, savings and investment. These projects embody the principle of a cyclic relationship between health and development as espoused by the Committee on Macroeconomic and Health, but implement these ideals at the community level. That the Millennium Villages share this philosophy with the CMH is no surprise as Jeffrey Sachs chaired the CMH, is director of the Earth Institute, and is co-founder of the Millennium Promise Alliance.

The project identified development deserts, communities in a number of African nations which were unlikely to achieve the MDGs (Sanchez et al. 2007; Pronyk et al. 2012). The sites were similar in that they suffered from multi-dimensional poverty in terms of income, productivity, health and infrastructure, but varied across other characteristics including existing healthcare resources and agricultural zone (Sanchez et al. 2007; Pronyk et al. 2012; Tozan et al. 2011). The MVP identified 14 sites in 10 countries (MillenniumVillages.org). The first millennium village is Sauri, Kenya which entered into the MVP in December 2004. Koraro, Ethiopia followed shortly in February 2005 with other sites coming on line in Ethiopia, Ghana, Malawi, Mali, Nigeria, Rwanda, Senegal, Tanzania and Uganda in later years (Sanchez et al. 2007). The MVP goal was to begin with a village in each study site and gradually scale-up the intervention to other villages within the site.

The MVP's focuses on improving agricultural productivity, health, education, infrastructure and capacity building through a five to ten-year package of interventions which are implemented in partnership with local, national and international partners (Sanchez et al. 2007; Tozan et al. 2011). The intervention package is guided by the principle of evidence-based practice (Millennium Village 2016; Sanchez et al. 2007). Further, the interventions are staged. The first phase addresses basic needs in terms of agricultural production, health, access to safe water, and community education and empowerment (Sanchez et al. 2007). The second phase entails expansion and diversification of agricultural production, expanded health services, improved water and sanitation programs, and primary education (Sanchez et al. 2007).

A primary component of the MVP is to provide agricultural subsidies for improved seed-stocks and fertilizers along with technical training (Sanchez et al. 2007). In theory, the amount of the subsidy would decrease over time as households build wealth and/or local communities take on a larger share of investment (Millennium Villages 2016). The goal of the agricultural intervention is to raise household income and food security, with a long-term goal of increased market participation, private savings and investment (Millennium Villages 2016). As food productivity rises, households will turn from subsistence agriculture to producing surplus which can be sold in the market. The increased productivity will also allow households to increase their savings, be it in kind or cash, to protect from external shock or catastrophe. Further, as savings accrue, households will reinvest in new crops or techniques thus diversifying their assets. As household incomes rise, so too with community income. Thus, the 'virtuous cycle' is obtained at a household and community level.

Health interventions focus on the provision of primary health care at an accessible level. MVP has a goal of ensuring a clinic was available for every 5000 people (Tozan et al. 2011). To this end, the MVP partners worked to establish, appropriately staff and supply clinics in the villages. The needs of each village differed. Sauri had neither clinic nor staff. The MVP opened the Sauri Community Dispensary in July 2005 with staffing paid for in part by the Ministry of Health and in part by the MVP (Sanchez et al. 2007; Tozan et al. 2011). Koraro has a clinic but neither staff nor medication (Sanchez et al. 2007). The Ministry of Health provided clinic staffing (Sanchez et al. 2007). Infectious disease, primarily malaria and diarrheal disease, were of specific concern in the areas. Anti-malaria measures, including distribution of mosquito nets and provision of anti-malaria medication, were included in the first wave intervention (Sanchez et al. 2007). The clinical care was free for residents of the village (Sanchez et al. 2007; Pronyk et al. 2012). In the second phase, health provision are scaled-up to include family planning, nutritional security, HIV/AIDS and TB prevention and treatment and implementation of continuum-of-care referrals with other facilities.

The MVP set an investment level of $110 per person per year which would be shared by the various partners. Of this, $10 was expected to come from the household or local community through in-kind contributions such as contributing harvest surplus to a community food bank (Sanchez et al. 2007). Thirty dollars was to come from the government, and the remaining $70 would come from a variety of donors (Sanchez et al. 2007). To this was added $10 management cost (from donor) so the total investment level reached $120 (Tozan et al. 2011). The model assumed that both the household/community and national government contribution would increase over time. As crop productivity yielded surplus and savings, community investment is expected to increase. National governments are expected to take up full investment in health care facilities, staff, and educational costs as the MVP phases out. The assumption is that the government will be able to cover these costs partially through increased ODA (Millennium Village 2016; Tozan et al. 2011).

To date, the MVP has succeeded in producing immediate results speaking to singular goals, such as reducing malaria, and has shown promise in achieving more complex outcomes, like fostering entry into the market. What remains to be seen is whether or not the MVP will result in a sustainability. Immediate wins occurred through the provision of goods and services where previously there were none. For example, where previously there had been no malaria control, the provision of bednets, detection and treatment facilitated a decrease in prevalence by 51–66% within one year (Sanchez et al. 2007). Over three years, prevalence decreased 79–89% in MVP villages (Tozan et al. 2011). At the start of the project, Sauri residents had no access to anti-retroviral treatment (ART), prevention of mother to child transmission, or HIV testing. The MVP worked with the Ministry of Health and Centers for Disease Control and Prevention (CDC) to provide these services first at the district hospital and later at village level clinics (Tozan et al. 2011).

Agricultural productivity and household security increased, although not without a few missteps. The original plan called for the MVP agricultural subsidies to phase out over five years, but villagers believed there would be a five year subsidy (Tozan et al. 2011). The conflict was resolved by the MVP agreeing to fully subsidize the poorest households for the extent of the program (Tozan et al. 2011). Subsidies could be repaid in kind with donation of crop surplus to school meal programs, a community food bank or such (Sanchez 2007; Tozan et al. 2011). Crop yields increased two to three times (Nziguheba et al. 2010). The new crops and new techniques yielded surplus which farmers were able to sell and thereby increase household income and market participation (Tozan et al. 2011). Farmers also diversified crops. There was an attendant decrease in food insecurity (Pronyk et al. 2012; Tozan et al. 2011). Poverty, measured by an asset index, also decreased (Pronyk et al. 2012).

Access to primary care and other health outcomes improved across the Millennium Villages. Under 5 mortality rates decreased by 22% compared to baseline, and decreased at a rate faster than observed at the national level (Pronyk et al. 2012). Access to immunization, and postnatal checks, and a decrease of diarrheal disease were noted and may have contributed to this outcome. Skilled birth attendance improved, as did access to improved water and sanitation, and stunting decreased (Pronyk et al. 2012; Tozan et al. 2011). The MVP also successfully introduce CHWs.

With the MVP winding down in 2015, it remains to be seen how sustainable the intervention and outcomes will prove to be, and whether or not scaling up is feasible. While the MVP did lead to accelerated progress towards the MDGs, in is not clear what portion of the observed improvements in health and well-being stem directly from the MVP, resulted from coordinated efforts of governments and donors to stimulate development as a result of the MDGS, or were produced from a combination of both. There is clear evidence that the agricultural interventions directly affected food productivity and food security (Nziguheba et al. 2010; Pronyk et al. 2012; Tozan et al. 2011). Further, there were clear improvements across baseline measures. Whether or not the Program actually decreased poverty is unclear. One study that compared MVP sites to non-MVP sites found no significant difference in poverty levels between experiment and non-experimental sites, but found significant differences in food security (Pronyk et al. 2012). A final evaluation of the MVP impact is expected in late 2016 (Millennium Village 2016).

Continued government or outside funding will be necessary to maintain the health, education and infrastructure facilities, inputs and staff (Sanchez et al. 2007; Tozan et al. 2011). For example, in Kenya a modified intervention included full agricultural subsidies for the most vulnerable populations for the extent of the project. What will happen to these farmers when the project ends? Programmers tried to encourage education on microfinance programs but the reported uptake was low (Tozan et al. 2011). The retention of health staff and CHWs is a foreseeable challenge, the success of which will depend upon remuneration and whether or not staff become part of the government work force (Tozan et al. 2011). One possible mechanism for the continued support if for the government to direct ODA into the established supports (Millennium Village 2016; Tozan et al. 2011). Given that communities do not have the resources to assume full program costs, it will be critical for there to be agreement between local priorities and national and donor funding. This is dependent in part upon donors meeting set targets for ODA and partially on government priorities. If national governments are able to sustain funding vis-à-vis a combination of domestic and international sources, then there may be gains in sustainability at the local level. However, that a government will need ODA to continue to pay for the facilities does little to decrease dependency and build national sustainability.

4.4 Conclusion

Community and household level programs demonstrate important albeit small-scale impact at the local level, but have mixed results on a regional, national or global scale. They none-the-less form an important tool in the toolkit for international health and development because local programming is better able to identify the needs and abilities of marginal communities, such as excluded minorities, rural communities, women and the poor than are centralized operations. Community-level programming is delivered through a variety of public and private agencies. One trend identified in terms of successes with the programs discussed in this chapter is the integration of services and/or priorities between the local operatives and national development agendas. Organizations such as GK, Grameen Bank and MVP built missions designed to enhance national development efforts—a strategy which speaks to the interconnectedness of economic, health, social, and political aspects of human and state well-being. Community-based health programs demonstrated positive impacts on local health. Logically such improvement feeds back into national health, but efforts to show the impact improved health has on economic progress either locally or nationally remain minimal. Microfinance has proven successful at changing household incomes and human capital, but wider impacts, while suggested, remain inconclusive. As Chowdhury and Mosley (2004, p. 298) astutely observe, "… markets will not produce assessments of social impact, because they are not profitable to any individual." The MVP embedded local needs within an international development agenda and targeted multiple interventions to achieve synchronous results, but whether or not these result resonate across a broader geographic scale and are sustainable remains in question.

These programs demonstrate that the links between local, national, and even international levels exist but the strength of the links, particularly when considering upward pressures of local change impacting the state, are not easily accounted for. Although individuals are acted upon by national forces, individual change seldom registers at the national or global level. A change in one person's health is unlikely to cause a major shift in population health. An increase in one person's wealth is unlikely to reduce national poverty levels. But our inability to account for individual or local change at broader spatial or institutional scales should by no means diminish the import of realizing such change—although it may not change the wealth of a nation it does change an individual life.

Appreciating and prioritizing the realm of the individual remains one of the challenges in health and development. Clinicians diagnose disease based on the details of individual cases. Ethnographies of the poor or the sick have humanized macro-level forces and impacts. Community workers live with the triumphs and tragedies of individuals. The lived experience is appreciated in a way no trend line, national average or summary report of annual activities can capture. These stories put a face on policies that are created in locations and circumstances far removed from the individual lives that will be affected. These small but important details may not lend themselves to number crunching, but provide new and useful insight into needs, wants, and (un)intended consequences of policies. Such details are needed to understand and diagnose development from the bottom up as well as the top down.

In this chapter, we looked at the relative successes of GK, and the Grameen Bank, two entities that arose in the context of post-conflict nation-building. Both organizations started out as NGOs whose missions included integration into broader national development. In these instances, the results were positive co-existence between the NGOs and state ministries, and mutual re-enforcement of their respective missions. But such is not always the case. Indeed, one can ask if in the case of a failed state, where a government is making no effort to care for its citizens (or a select population therein), is it just or appropriate for an NGO to even attempt to work with the government? What if the government is engaged in genocide? How should an NGO operate? In Chapter Five we will more closely examine the challenges of scaling up and down-scaling health and development activities in the context of failed states and conflict. We will also look at the special challenges these fragile states must confront.

Discussion Questions

1. Use the World Development Indicators or Human Development Statistics to look up the GDP/capita for a low income and a middle income country. Now look up the gini coefficient and quintile distribution of income for each of these countries. What do you think this means in terms of equity and distribution of wealth? Now look up the income distribution for your country of residence. Do think this accurately depicts the distribution of wealth where you live?
2. What are some of the positive aspects of community-based health care? Which of these do you see in the examples of the Pholela Center and Gonoshasthaya Kendra?
3. Gonoshasthaya Kendra employs a method of holding 'death meetings' to debrief various parties in the case of maternal or early child death. How might these meetings contribute to the organization's goal of improving maternal and child health in the community?
4. How do the Grameen Bank's solidarity groups contribute to the goal of household poverty alleviation?
5. Describe how any one of the strategies used by the MPV embody the 'virtuous circle'?
6. What is the most common measure of poverty used in your country of residence? Do you think this is an appropriate way to measure poverty based on the Copenhagen Declaration's definition of poverty?
7. Do you consider improving household wealth or household health to be a more difficult challenge? What evidence of this do you see in the case studies? Based on the household level evidence, do you belief investment in income-earning opportunities, or in health is the most direct route to improving household level development? Development in the community?

References

Antman, K., Abraido-Lanza, A. F., Blum, D., Brownfield, E., Cicatelli, B., Debor, M. D., et al. (2002). Reducing disparities in breast cancer survival: A Columbia University and Avon Breast Cancer Research and Care Network Symposium. *Breast Cancer Research and Treatment, 75,* 269–280.

Ashing-Giwa, K. T., & Lim, J. W. (2009). *Psychooncology* (Epub ahead of print).

Berkman, L., & Kawachi, I. (Eds.). (2000). *Social epidemiology*. New York: Oxford University Press.

Berman, P., Kendall, C., & Bhattacharyya, K. (1994). The household production of health: Integrating social science perspectives on micro-level health determinants. *Social Science and Medicine, 38*(2), 205–215.

Bloom, J. R. (2008). Improving the health and well-being of cancer survivors: Past as prologue. *Psychooncology, 17,* 525–532.

Braun, K. L., Mokuau, N., Hunt, G. H., Kaanoi, M., & Gotay, C. C. (2002). Supports and obstacles to cancer survival for Hawaii's native people. *Cancer Practice, 10,* 192–200.
Brown, T. M. (2002). Voices from the past: Sidney Kark and John Cassel: Social medicine pioneers and South African émigrés. *American Journal of Public Health, 92,* 1744–1745.
Cartwright-Alcarese, F., Sung, M. W., Brenner, B., Zambodla, A., Geduld, A., & Desjardins, L. (2003). An interdisciplinary approach to the provision of patient support resources across the oncology care continuum: Description of a performance improvement project. *Journal of Nursing Care Quality, 18,* 61–72.
Chaudhury, R. H., & Chowdhury, Z. (2008). Maternal mortality in Rural Bangladesh: Lessons learned from Gonoshasthaya Kendra Programme Villages. *Asian-Pacific Population Journal, 23,* 55–78.
Chowdhury, A. M. R., & Bhuiya, A. (2004). The wider impacts of BRAC poverty alleviation programme in Bangladesh. *Journal of International Development, 16,* 369–386.
Chowdhury, A. M. R., & Mosley, P. (2004). The social impact of microfinance: Introduction. *Journal of International Development, 16,* 291–300.
Cleland, J. G., & Van Ginneken, J. K. (1988). Maternal education and child survival in developing countries: The search for pathways of influence. *Social Science and Medicine, 27,* 1357–1368.
Dréze, J., & Sen, A. (1991). *Hunger and public action*. Oxford: Oxford University Press.
Farmer, P. (1992). *Aids and accusation: Haiti and the geography of blame*. Berkeley, CA: University of California Press.
Farrer, R. (2008). Exploring the human rights implications of microfinance initiatives. *International Journal of Legal Information, 36*(3), 447–489.
Gonoshasthaya Kendra: People's Health Centre. (n.d.). http://www.gkbd.org/aboutus.htm. Accessed December 12, 2009.
Grameen Bank. (1998). *16 decisions*. http://www.grameen-info.org/index.php?option=com_content&task=view&id=22&Itemid=109. Accessed June 10, 2010.
Grameen Bank. (2010). *Grameen Bank at a glance: April, 2010*. Grameen Bank: Banking for the Poor. http://www.grameen-info.org/index.php?option=com_content&task=view&id=26&Itemid=175. Accessed January 3, 2010.
Harff, B., & Gurr, T. R. (1988). Toward an empirical theory of genocides and politicides: Identification and measurement of cases since 1945. *International Studies Quarterly, 32*(3), 359–371.
Himmelstein, D., Thorne, D., Warrne, E., & Woolhandler, S. (2009). Medical bankruptcy in the United States, 2007: Results of a national study. *American Journal of Medicine, 122*(8), 741–746.
Himmelstein, D., Warren, E., Thorne, D., & Woolhandler, S. (2005). Illness and injury as contributors to bankruptcy. *Health Affairs—Web Exclusive, 5,* 63–73.
Hulme, D., & Mosley, P. (1996). *Finance against poverty*. London, UK: Routledge.
Hulme, D., & Mosley, P. (1998). Microenterprise credit programmes: Is there a conflict between growth and poverty reduction. *World Development, 26,* 783–790.
Islam, T. (2007). *Microcredit and poverty alleviation*. Burlington, VT: Ashgate Publishing.
Janzen, J., & Arkinstall, W. (1978). *The quest for therapy in lower zaire*. Berkeley, CA: University of California Press.
Ka'opua, L. S., Gotay, C. C., & Boehm, P. S. (2007). Spiritually based resources in adaptation to long-term prostate cancer survival: Perspectives of elderly wives. *Health and Social Work, 32,* 29–39.
Kark, S., & Cassel, J. (1952). The Pholela Health Centre: A progress report. *South African Medical Journal, 26*(6), 101–104.
Karnani, A. (2007). Microfinance misses its mark. *Stanford Social Innovations Review*. http://www.ssireview.org/articles/entry/microfinance_misses_its_mark/. Accessed June 13, 2010.
Kleinman, A., & Kleinman, J. (1997). Moral transformations of health and suffering in Chinese Society. In A. Brandt & P. Rozin (Eds.), *Morality and health*. London, UK: Routledge Inc.
Kunjufu, J. (2006). *An African centered response to Ruby Payne's poverty theory*. United States of America: African American Images.

Microfinance Regulation and Supervision Resource Center. (2010). http://www.microfinanceregulation center.org/resource_centers/reg_sup. Accessed January 3, 2010.
Millenium Villages. (2016). http://millenniumvillages.org. Accessed July 18, 2016.
Mosley, P., & Rock, J. (2004). Microfinance, labor markets and poverty in Africa: A study of six institutions. *Journal of International Development, 16*, 467–500.
Mulama, J. (2009). *Economy-Kenya: Microfinance, major problems*. http://ipsnews.net/news.asp?idnews=31010. Accessed January 4, 2010.
National Institute of Population Research and Training (NIPORT), ORC Macro and Johns Hopkins University. (2003). *Bangladesh maternal health services and maternal mortality survey* 2001. Dhaka: NIPORT.
NPR. (2010). *The economic fruits of a 'Microcredit' laureate*. http://www.npr.org/templates/story/story.php?storyId=6260981. Accessed June 14, 2010.
Nziguheba, G., Palm, C. A., Berhe, T., Denning, G., Dicko, A., Diouf, O., … Sanchez, P. A. (2010). Chapter three—The African Green Revolution: Results from the Millennium Villages Project. In L. S. Donald (Ed.), *Advances in agronomy* (Vol. 109, pp. 75–115). London: Academic Press.
Payne, R. K. (2005). *A framework for understanding poverty*. Highlands, TX: aha! Process, Inc.
Pronyk, P. M., Muniz, M., Nemser, B., Somers, M. A., McClellan, L., Palm, C. A., et al. (2012). The effect of an integrated multisector model for achieving the Millennium Development Goals and improving child survival in rural sub-Saharan Africa: A non-randomised controlled assessment. *Lancet, 379*(9832), 2179–2188.
Rodriguez-Garcia, R., Macinko, J., & Waters, W. (2001). *Microenterprise development for better health outcomes*. Westport, CT: Greenwood Press.
Sanchez, P., Palm, C., Sachs, J., Denning, G., et al. (2007). The African Millennium Villages. *Proceedings of the National Academy of Sciences, 104*(43), 16775–16780.
Scheper-Hughes, N. (1992). *Death without weeping: The violence of everyday life in Brazil*. Berkeley, CA: University of California Press.
Sen, A. (2000). *Development as freedom*. New York: Anchor Books.
Sri Lanka Ministry of Health, Nutrition and Indigenous Medicine. (2016). *Annual Health Statistics: Sri Lanka 2014*. Colombo, Sri Lanka.
The World Bank. (2009a). *Chile at a glance*. http://devdata.worldbank.org/AAG/chl_aag.pdf. Accessed November 14, 2009.
The World Bank. (2009b). *Sri Lanka at a glance*. http://devdata.worldbank.org/AAG/lka_aag.pdf. Accessed November 14, 2009.
The World Bank. (2015). *World development indicators*. http://databank.worldbank.org/data/reports.aspx?source=world-development-indicators. Accessed August 25, 2016.
Tollman, S. M. (1994). The Pholela Health Centre—the origins of community—oriented primary care (COPC): An appreciation of the work of Sidney and Emily Kark. *South African Medical Journal, 84*(10), 653–658.
Tozan, Y., Negin, J., & Ogola Wariero, J. (2011). The Millennium Villages Project: Improving health and eliminating extreme poverty in rural African communities. In E. Blas, J. Sommerfeld, A. Sivasankara Kurup, & C. Ebooks (Eds.), *Social determinants approaches to public health from concept to practice* (pp. 91–104). Geneva: World Health Organization.
UNHABITAT. (2008). *State of the World's Cities 2008/2009*. London: Earthscan.
United Nations Development Programme. (2003). *UNDP Practice Area: Poverty Reduction Synthesis of Lessons Learned. Essentials 10*. United Nations. http://www.undp.org/evaluation/documents/essentials/MonitoringPoverty.pdf. Accessed May 4, 2010.
United Nations Development Programme. (2005). *Millennium Development Goals Country Report 2005—Sri Lanka*.
United Nations Development Programme. (2015). *Human Development Report 2015: Work for human development*. New York: UNDP.
Van Greuning, H., Gallardo, J., & Randhawa, B. (1998a). *A framework for Regulating Microfinance Institutes*. The World Bank. http://www.microfinancegateway.org/gm/document-1.9.25003/2293_file_02293.pdf. Accessed June 14, 2010.

Van Greuning, H. Gallardo, J., & Randhawa, B. (1998b) *A framework for regulating microfinance institutes*, report to the Financial Sector Development Program at the World Bank. http://www.microfinancegateway.org/gm/document-1.9.25003/2293_file_02293.pdf. Accessed October 25, 2009.

Velasco, C., & Marconi, R. (2004). Group dynamics, gender, and microfinance in Bolivia. *Journal of International Development, 16*, 519–528.

White, M. (2005). *Death tolls for the major wars and atrocities of the twentieth century*. http://users.erols.com/mwhite28/warstat2.htm. Accessed June 14, 2010.

Woller, G. (2002). From market failure to marketing failure: Market orientation as the key to deep outreach in microfinance. *Journal of International Development, 14*(3), 305–324.

World Health Organization. (2001). *Macroeconomics and health: Investing in health for economic development. A report of the Commission on Macroeconomics and Health*. Geneva: Author.

Young, A. (1982). The anthropologies of illness and sickness. *Annual Review of Anthropology, 11*, 257–285.

Zohir, S., & Matin, I. (2004). Wider impacts of microfinance institutions: Issues and concepts. *Journal of International Development, 16*, 301–330.

Chapter 5
Development in Failed and Fragile States

Abstract Failed states and states in conflict are special cases in terms of health and development in that the national government, the main party responsible for directing policy to improve national well-being, may lack the resources, will or legitimacy to provide health infrastructure or opportunities for economic development. Although NGOs can fill the power and resource vacuum in these states in the short term, they may not contribute to sustainable health care delivery or development. A main policy challenge in failed and conflict-ridden states is how best to scale up programs offered by diverse actors targeting health and/or development. A second challenge is building resources and capacity to transform fragility into stability and achieving an adequate level of sectoral development in order to be able to respond to extraordinary threats to national and human security. The first two case studies examined in this chapter are Partners-in-Health/Zanmi LaSante in Haiti, which serves as a model for up-scaling, and the Government of Rwanda, which worked to consolidate and direct the resources of disparate non-governmental actors in order to meet national development and health goals. The final case study explores the Ebola outbreak in Western Africa, which took hold in three fragile states where it grew to unprecedented levels.

Gains in economic and human well-being at the individual level do not always translate into shifts at the sub-national and national scale, and yet one can argue that improvement at the micro level is a worthy goal for those working in health and development. As we saw in Chap. 4, community-based programming can have dramatic and positive effects on the lives of individuals whether or not such improvements alter the national profile. Part of the success seen in Bangladesh was realized by linking local and national actors and directing disparate resources towards a common goal. Government programs, NGOs, and the public-private partnerships evolved and formed successful working relationships over the course of some 30 years. That this occurred in the context of nation-building following a violent conflict suggests that Bangladesh is a unique example of growth and stabilization emerging from conflict. By way of contrast, the Pholela Center in South Africa was dismantled under faltering political support, growing social

S.A. Johnson, *Challenges in Health and Development*,
DOI 10.1007/978-3-319-53204-2_5

fragmentation and government repression. These cases beg the question as to how and when to either up-scale programs or centralize program authority.

Failed states and states in conflict present similar challenges to increasing economic growth and improving human development and well-being. These challenges are often more acute in conflict or post-conflict settings. In a failed state, for example, one might expect to see increased deaths related to acute and chronic malnutrition, as well as other preventable causes. The failure of a state to provide for basic needs, including nutrition and health care, contributes to an increased burden of disease and increased mortality. In the case of conflict, however, the chronic issues of failing health are amplified through an acute rise in death and injury that occur as a result of warfare.

This chapter will examine the difficulties in linking macro- and micro-level programming in the context of failed and conflict-ridden states characterized by weak governments, poor health and development status, and social distrust. Human and economic development are especially difficult to maintain or improve in the context of failed states and conflict because the financial and human resources necessary for investment in the inputs, structure and institutions of development and health are scarce. The hierarchy of needs places basic security ahead of economic growth and health promotion. Enforcing basic security and rule of law becomes the dominant policy focus during social upheavals, with little credence or resources given to more abstract programs such as investing in education or health care 'for the future'. In the vacuum of government services, people are left to fend for themselves, or NGOs step in. Such resources are delivered in local, geographically disparate centers through a smattering of often uncoordinated programs in which competing mandates, mismatched scales of operation and a failure of integration between public and private actors may actually undermine human development. In the aftermath of war, or where states are weak, state needs are high, resources are sparse and the threat of descent into war or falling even deeper into the poverty spiral remains. It takes but a small perturbation to bring the fragile system to the brink of collapse.

5.1 Development, Failed States and States in Conflict

Failed states and conflict-ridden states are not mutually exclusive; rather, they form a continuum. Conflict is itself not a discrete event, but rather a cycle (Gurr and Harff 1994; Zartman 1995). In the landscape of "new wars", conflicts are usually intra-state rather than inter-state (Gurr and Harff 1994; Münkler 2009). Such conflict frequently begins with political upheaval or state failure (Esty et al. 1995; Zartman 1995). In the political, social and economic insecurity that accompanies state collapse, social disadvantages and cleavages are exacerbated and violence emerges as a means for diverse actors to express grievances and attempt to (re)gain control (Esty et al. 1995; Zartman 1995). In cases of protracted conflict, violence waxes and wanes. Periods of conflict may lead to humanitarian emergencies in which a large number of people are in need of sustenance and/or physical protection and safety. In states recovering from conflict, (re)building state institutions may take time; resources are not readily available and so tensions may rise and lead yet again to open conflict.

State failure occurs when a government can no longer carry out the basic functions of a government (Zartman 1995). These functions include exercising sovereign authority—in which a state provides a cohesive national identity, decision-making and governing powers, functioning institutions that organize policies and services, and policing in which the state uses its power to enforce rules and to provide physical security for its citizens (Zartman 1995). Government breakdown may be partial or total. Under the principle of **sovereignty**, the state has the sole legitimate authority to use violence. This monopoly is theoretically utilized to uphold the rule of law. But as state institutions weaken, this authority may also weaken, such that a state cannot enforce the rule of law, or abuses it as in the case of state-sponsored terror. Where laws are not transparent or not enforced, corruption follows. State failure is also manifest when the economic, human, managerial, or technical capacity of a state to deliver basic goods such as health care and food to its populace diminishes or is non-existent. These stoppages and inadequacies result in a crisis of legitimacy in which the state is no longer viewed as an effective or just provider of basic needs and protections. Widespread government corruption further erodes legitimacy.

Institutional failures of the state correlate to and in some cases couple with a variety of social, economic, and political indicators that can drive a state from collapse to conflict (Foreign Policy 2009; Goldstone et al. 2010; Esty et al. 1995). These variables include: demographic pressures such as dense populations and a '**youth bulge**' in which a large percentage of the population consists of young adults from age 14 into the early 20s; movement of refugees/internally displaced persons (IDPs); social and economic inequity; history of blame and violence between different cultural groups; consistent human flight such as occurs with **brain drain**—when individuals in the professional classes migrate to other countries; severe economic decline; rise of paramilitary forces; rise of factionalized elites; and intervention by international actors (Fund for Peace 2007).

Institutional failures inform a rupture of the social contract that exists between the governing body and the governed. In the case of ruptured social contract, investment in human capital is often weak or unequal (Collier et al. 2003; Murshed 2002). This may be because of a lack of resources to provide for all parts of society, or lack of political will to distribute goods in an equitable manner. The lack of investment exacerbates cleavages and is detrimental to building human and economic capacity across different sectors of society (Collier et al. 2003; Murshed 2002). Dissolution of the social contract may begin a cycle in which the lack of resources and government failures to provide for social needs, be they physical or symbolic, detract from state legitimacy and deteriorate the ability of state actors to govern (Hansch and Burkholder 1996; Macrae 1994). Economic and human development cannot occur where society is unstable (Collier et al. 2003; Murshed 2002).

State failure and conflict cause economic harm in the short and long term. War reduces income by as much as 15% of what would have been earned without conflict, and heightens vulnerability to external economic shocks even after the conclusion of the conflict (Collier et al. 2003). Resources are not available to develop human or physical capital. Wartime spending often diverts state resources away from development enterprises, such as the provision of education, in order to maintain troops and purchase weapons (Collier et al. 2003). In conflict and failed states, foreign investment is pulled out and can be difficult to attract even after the state has stabilized. The perception of investment risk can remain high and, without insurance or guarantees of return on investment, companies may choose to invest in more stable territories. Even though a key to peace-building and transforming a conflicted society to a stable one entails addressing the structural issues that led to the disrupted social order, resources are often directed to address the immediate post-war needs rather than the underlying causes of conflict and state failure. Rebuilding any of the components of the failed system is further complicated because state (re)building occurs in a context of limited physical and capital resources, and infrastructure and capacity must be rebuilt while addressing the grievances that led to conflict. Deprivation and conflict feed each other and can lead to a seemingly intractable cycle of underdevelopment and war.

5.1.1 Issues of Health

Loss of life and protracted suffering accompany state failure and conflict. Conflict ruptures the physical and social frameworks in a state, often causing a dramatic downward spiral in health of which short-term losses are but one part. Acute health shocks can lead to protracted health crises because few healthcare structures that can mitigate vulnerability remain intact. As population health declines, so too do opportunities for human and economic advancement. In areas of humanitarian crises, providing for immediate needs to ensure population survival can overwhelm domestic and international resources such that little attention is paid to longer-term structural issues that may contribute to national stability and improved, sustainable welfare.

The direct impacts of war include loss of life and injury as a direct result of violence. Acute loss of life is suffered by combatants and by civilian targets of violence. Civilians are increasingly the targets of violent attacks and murder in conflict areas (Münkler 2009). Reports on the wars in Sudan, Rwanda, Bosnia-Herzegovina, and the Democratic Republic of Congo decried the murder, rape and terrorizing of civilians perpetrated by armed combatants. But direct violence is not the only tactic used to harm the populace. Health becomes a weapon of war as inputs to health are disrupted and manipulated by combatants. For example, food is a necessary input for human survival. In conflicts around the world, food shipments are hijacked by combatants with the purpose of terrorizing and starving people, and/or forcing the populace into dependency and allegiance to the warlords who control access to food (Kennedy et al. 1998; Messer 1993). One estimate shows that food deprivation was used as a weapon of war in 29 nations in 1993 alone (Messer 1993). Interruption of the food supply causes acute and chronic malnutrition and attendant health sequelae. Food deprivation is especially problematic for children whose mental and physical development is dependent upon a minimum caloric and nutrient intake. Health is held hostage in other ways during and in the aftermath of war. Combatants may bar, delay or hijack shipments of medical goods (Bossert 1984; Brentlinger 1996; Williams 1984).

Health care can also be offered to legitimize a party and gain adherents to a particular side of the conflict. Nicaragua serves as an example of this. Social justice and equity were ideals espoused by the Sandinista National Liberation Front (FSLN) forces during the rebellion against the Somoza regime in the late 1970s. Upon their victory, the Sandinistas established health as a national priority couched in terms of social justice (Bossert 1984; Williams 1984). The new government established a national health plan, the National Unified Health System (SNUS) that focused on the delivery of primary care through local health posts and health centers (Garfield 1984). These actions helped to legitimize the Sandinista cause and government at the end of the war (Bossert 1984; Donahue 1984). But peace proved to be of short duration. Hostilities broke out between the remnants of the Somoza National Guard (the *Contras*), who were supported by the U.S., and the Sandinista government. The gains in primary health care obtained under the Sandinistas were not easily abandoned. During the *contra* war, vaccination rates were noted to be higher in the territory controlled by the Sandinistas than in other areas of conflict because of the high levels of commitment by local health brigades to maintain such services (Donahue 1984). But, as discussed previously, preservation of health in conflict areas is not typical.

The acute phase of conflict destroys healthcare infrastructure thereby removing vital care from people who are most in need (Macrae 1994). Primary care programs and health networks fall apart with the loss of infrastructure. Roads and other transportation networks are diminished or destroyed such that essential medications and vaccines can no longer be shipped to or made available in conflict areas. The roads become impassible because of destruction, the placement of mines, or military roadblocks, all of which make it difficult, if not impossible, for those in need of medical care to seek it. Curfews implemented in conflict areas create further obstacles for those seeking care, even if such care is locally available. Access to the populations most in need of medical care, those in conflict zones, is often restricted (Hansch and Burkholder 1996). As if bad roads and travel restrictions were not a significant enough challenge for noncombatants in conflict-ridden areas, transportation is also scarce. Walking, riding animals, riding bicycles or motorbikes may be the only options available to residents of conflict areas. This combination of poor roads, curfews, checkpoints, and reliance on suboptimal transportation contributes to increased maternal mortality in conflict areas as women are not able to get to care centers, or maternal caregivers are not allowed to access women in their homes during complicated deliveries (Johnson and Samarasinghe 2008). If pregnant women can find transportation, they still may die a preventable death due to being badly jostled during their trip along the rutted roads, or to being turned back at a checkpoint before reaching a clinic (Johnson and Samarasinghe 2008). As infrastructure is destroyed, the ability of clinics to maintain cold chain or even engage in essential sterilization and sanitation practices dissolves, if indeed medical personnel even remain to provide care. Vaccination programs, a cost-effective pillar of primary health care, erode or collapse through intentional disruption or through neglect (Hansch and Burkholder 1996; Lee et al. 1997; WHO 2009a).

Harassment and human rights abuses directed against both those seeking and giving care are reported in conflict zones, adding further barriers to health care delivery (Brentlinger 1996; Rubardt 1985). Medical posts are destroyed by combatants. Medical personnel are deliberately targeted and killed (Brentlinger 1996; Rubardt 1985). Given the lack of personal security and the poor living conditions, it is not surprising that maintaining medical staff in unstable regions of nations with low or high intensity conflict is difficult (Brentlinger 1996; Donahue 1984; Hansch and Burkholder 1996; Rubardt 1985). Medical personnel may flee the conflict zones or may leave the conflict-ridden country as social and economic conditions decline (Hansch and Burkholder 1996; Institute of Policy Studies 2002). It can be equally challenging to re-staff the regions even after open hostilities have ceased. Social chaos and lawlessness add to the heightened insecurity.

5.1.2 Refugees and IDPs

War forces people out of their homes and communities and, many times, across international boundaries. When the population movement occurs within the boundaries of the nation-state, the displaced population is referred to as **internally displaced persons** (IDPs). When people are forced to relocate across national boundaries, they become **refugees**. These groups face particular problems in terms of health and development. There were 19.5 million refugees and 38.2 million IDPs worldwide at the end of 2014 (UNHCR 2009). Displaced populations have high mortality and morbidity rates. Women and children are especially hard hit (Connolly et al. 2004; Hansch and Burkholder 1996; Toole and Waldman 1993). The primary causes of death and sickness are malnourishment, measles, diarrheal disease, pneumonia and location-specific diseases such as malaria (Van Hear and Harrell-Bond 1991). The living conditions found in IDP and refugee camps are a primary risk factor for disease. People live in crowded camps, residing in substandard shelters with limited access to clean water, sanitary facilities, and food supplies (Van Hear and Harrell-Bond 1991). Although the health status of the camp populations may not be qualitatively different than that of neighbors in the surrounding communities, quantitatively the health outcomes are much poorer as they are exacerbated by the camp living conditions and inability of camp authorities to adequately monitor health and quickly respond to health crisis (Connolly et al. 2004; Van Hear and Harrell-Bond 1991). The resources of host-nation governments and aid organizations can become strained with increased flow of refugees and IDPs

Table 5.1 Refugee population by region, end of 2014 (UNHCR 2015)

UNHCR region	Refugees
Central Africa and Great Lakes	662,600
East and Horn of Africa	2,601,400
Southern Africa	174,700
West Africa	252,000
Americas	769,000
Asia and Pacific	3,848,600
Europe	3,112,800
Middle East and North Africa	2,963,900
Total	14,385,000

and the need to provide aid. In many cases, these organizations and governments already face resource constraints, constraints that become more acute when faced with long-term refugee crises. Consider, for instance, that developing countries host 86% of the world's refugees (UNHCR 2015, p. 9) (Table 5.1).

5.1.3 Long Term Impacts

The residual impact of conflict is felt in health and development for many years after war's end. The loss of life due to death and disability following war is massive and sustained across years if not decades (Connolly et al. 2004; Ghobarah et al. 2004; Hansch and Burkholder 1996; IRC 2007; Macrae 1994; Toole and Waldman 1993). The long-term losses are estimated to be nearly double the losses attributed directly to war (Ghobarah et al. 2004). Life expectancy decreases in war-torn countries, and infant mortality rates rise (Davis and Kuritsky 2002). The most common causes of death and disability after war's end are from infectious diseases, most of which were present in-country prior to the war (Ghobarah et al. 2004; IRC 2007). The largest decreases in health occur in women and children (Ghobarah et al. 2004; IRC 2007). The impact is felt in both the conflict countries and neighboring countries (Ghobarah et al. 2004; Hansch and Burkholder 1996; Toole and Waldman 1993; Van Hear and Harrell-Bond 1991). A 2004 study on the long term impacts of war on health estimated that 15 million DALYs were lost in 1999 due to wars that occurred between 1991 and 1997 (Ghobarah et al. 2004). This estimate included 12 million DALYs lost in countries which experienced war directly, and an additional 3 million suffered by neighboring countries (Ghobarah et al. 2004).

In countries which experience war, the loss of life and well-being are often associated with the collapse of infrastructure and loss of medical personnel and supplies which occur during a war. War-time deprivation causes increased vulnerability. At the local level, livelihoods are lost, houses destroyed, and access to basic necessities is limited. People may be injured, become ill, and/or suffer from malnutrition. These factors may interact separately or cumulatively to increase susceptibility to illness. With neither the biological resources necessary to adequately fight off infections, nor the financial or material resources to mitigate the risk or impact of infection, vulnerability becomes illness. These losses in health and social welfare occur at a time when the national institutions are least able to provide services, social assistance or deliver care. As a result, health problems that may have been controlled during peacetime prior to war erupt into epidemics and public health crises during the post-war period.

In states experiencing complex emergencies, the death rate may be 60 times higher than the baseline rate (Connolly et al. 2004). Infectious disease, malnutrition, neonatal and pregnancy-related conditions and homicide are among the most common causes of death (Connolly et al. 2004; Ghobarah et al. 2004; IRC 2007). Loss of life stems from systemic collapse as well as a change in the epidemiological profile that results from disease resurgence, or (re)introduction of contagious disease through population movement (Connolly et al. 2004). IDP and refugee populations are highly vulnerable to the ravages of contagious disease and malnutrition and present special health care challenges to the nation-states receiving them.

An example of the long-term toll war has on health is seen the Democratic Republic of Congo (DRC). An estimated 2.1 million excess deaths occurred in the DRC since the official end of the war in 2002. The crude mortality rates were 57% higher than the average in Sub-Saharan Africa (IRC 2007). Only 0.4% of the deaths were attributed to on-going violence. Where cause of death was available, the main causes in those five years of age or older included fever/malaria (26.3–27.7%), diarrhea (8.9–9.1%), tuberculosis (6.6–6.8%), acute respiratory-tract infections (5.5–7.5%), neo-natal causes (6.5–7.1%), measles (2.9–5.5%), malnutrition (4.0–4.3%), anemia (3.2–4.3%), meningitis (2.8–3.2%, accident/injury (2.4–3.4%), maternal death (2.3–2.8%), and AIDS (0.8–1.2%) (IRC 2007: 10). Fever and malaria accounted for more than one third of the deaths in children under age five, and approximately 14% of the deaths were from neo-natal causes (IRC 2007). A study by the International Rescue Committee noted that the majority of these deaths were preventable and came about due to a "crisis of neglect" from conflict and historical abandonment in the political and socioeconomic spheres (IRC 2007).

5.2 The Challenge of Rebuilding

Governments face multiple priorities when attempting to stabilize or recover from conflict. Foremost among these is the provision of physical security. Without rule of law, there is no stable political, social or economic space for recovery and growth. However, the provision of security itself is challenging, especially in regions that have experienced intense conflict because the motives of national police or military may be doubted by the citizenry and trust may be hard to come by. In some cases, the presence of international peacekeepers, be they from regional organizations such as the African Union, or global organizations such as the UN, may provide for a period of transition and trust-building.

In many cases, governments are not able to deliver the services one would expect in order to be deemed fully functional and responsible. Given that such inability may be what led to political and social break-down in the first place, there is a special challenge in terms of staging resumption of services and authority, communicating with the public in a manner that (re)legitimizes the government and increases public buy-in and support.

Even if the government prioritizes rebuilding the health sector, this presents several challenges. In the aftermath of conflict, health system capacity is greatly reduced. The availability of finance, staff, equipment, medicines and infrastructure, decimated by the war, is not easily or quickly rebuilt (Connolly et al. 2004; Macrae 1994). Despite the urgent need to re-establish health services, governments recovering from war face difficult financial restraints as public source funding is reduced and international aid revenues change (Macrae 1994). For example, the tax revenue available to the Ugandan government following the end of conflict amounted to only 6% of GDP as opposed to its more typical average of 20% in the years prior to the war (Macrae 1994). Even when some resources are available, governments may rebuild major infrastructures, such as roads, or invest in military and police operations to maintain rule of law, while neglecting primary and secondary health centers. Resources are also often centralized in urban areas (Macrae 1994).

Staffing of health care facilities remains challenging after the termination of fighting. Healthcare staff who left the public sector during conflict may have little motivation to return to public practice due to poor working conditions, inadequate supplies, and lack of financial incentives (IPS 2002; Macrae 1994). Competition from private-sector actors such as INGOs, which are able to pay better wages, pose further difficulties to staffing public sector health facilities (Garrett 2007). In some cases, the wages paid by international actors may not be consistent with local market forces thereby inflating the cost of medical inputs. Health-seeking behavior also alters in the aftermath of war. Social networks and referral networks are broken up (Hansch and Burkholder 1996). As health structure falls apart, health care may be privatized or people may seek increasing amounts of care from traditional practitioners (Hansch and Burkholder 1996; Macrae 1994). When the new structures of healthcare fall into place, patterns of informal social supports and referrals through both formal and informal systems need to be relearned.

Governments are also challenged to address what reconstruction should look like (Macrae 1994). Does one rebuild the infrastructure and institutions to resemble what they were prior to social dissolution or conflict, or does one attempt to construct something new? If, in fact, inequities in previous structures contributed to social cleavage, where does one start to rebuild in a manner which addresses the underlying causes of conflict while speaking to shorter-term population needs? How a government addresses these issues will contribute to or detract from its legitimacy and prospects for sustainable development.

Given the aforementioned fiscal, physical, and human constraints, as well as the dearth of political capital, the challenge is considerable. Success may depend upon a combination of public and private actors and resources. In the wake of state failure, new actors enter the scene. IGOs, NGOs and INGOs with greater fiscal and human resources and mandates that speak to humanitarian assistance and to development arrive to fill the gaps in service provision, to serve their organizational principles and, increasingly, to realize profit (Economist 2000; Council on Foreign Relations 2009). Within this group of actors, international humanitarian aid (HA) agencies operate under mandates that call for the provision of emergency services to be delivered in independent, impartial, neutral ways in order to decrease human suffering (ICRC 1996). Such ideals are coupled with the notion that humanistic principles require action to preserve human life and mitigate suffering (Anderson 1996). Delivery of service should be guided by need, not politics or notions of 'right' and 'wrong', 'good' or 'bad'.

With numerous actors operating with different goals and timelines, a challenge for long-term recovery and development becomes providing logistical support and coordination (Connolly et al. 2004; Hansch and Burkholder 1996; Macrae 1994; Van Hear and Harrell-Bond 1991). NGOs work within what Macrae (1994) calls 'micro policy domains', with goals defined by the individual project rather than national needs or guidelines. Coordinating the different mandates and scope of services, with an eye towards building domestic capacity and sustainability, is of critical import for the rebuilding the nation, but is not always achieved.

How public and private entities will operate is a concern. Numerous recommendations have been made as to how to do this in a manner that will increase the legitimacy of national governments, when such legitimacy is warranted, and that address sustainability (ICRC 2010; Macrae 1994; Van Hear and Harrell-Bond 1991). In some cases, donors and NGOs provide money for staff salaries, and the purchase of essential drugs as a type of bridge loan to maintain critical services. This is done with an understanding that the government will eventually take over these services and expenses (Macrae 1994). Community participation is recommended as another avenue to building sustainable care (Macrae 1994; Van Hear and Harrell-Bond 1991).

5.2.1 Building Dependency

The short-term time horizon of many NGOs is at odds with the longer term vision and strategies necessary for sustained improvement and development. This is not to say that NGOs are the only source of failure in long-term planning and coordination. Many governments, which should have longer term vision, focus on short-term goals rather than longer term structural needs (Macrae 1994). Given the immediate needs of citizens in failed or post-conflict nations, such prioritization is not unwarranted.

Tensions exist between public and private actors over operational timelines. When a nation is failed or in conflict, providing for the basic needs necessary for survival is the pre-emanate concern. Longer term projects fall to the wayside. This can become problematic in that services and resources may be directed to immediate care, providing food and water for displaced or disrupted populations, without allocating resources to address underlying inequities or social disorders which contributed to state failure. In keeping the population alive without addressing underlying tensions or increasing state legitimacy and capabilities, one could say the population is being kept alive to continue to suffer.

Humanitarian aid missions were initially envisioned as short-term operations—to provide emergency resources to see a population through during a crisis—and were not charged with long-term development. Since protracted intrastate conflict has become more common, a number of HA missions around the world have become long-term efforts to provide life support to populations experiencing complex emergencies. Amid this change, the appropriate role of humanitarian assistance, with its stricture to "first do no harm" is debated.

The provision of critical services to populations in need is an ethical, humanitarian imperative, but humanitarian aid is criticized for contributing to protracted conflict and creating dependency (Curtis and ODI 2001). It is argued that if institutions other than those of the state continue to provide for the care of the civilian population, then the state will never feel the pressure or need to assume provision of such services. Indeed, such service provision by humanitarian aid agencies allows state actors to continue to divert resources to other sectors such as military, thereby prolonging conflict. If aid continues after conflict ends and the government is not able or willing to assume responsibility for such care, then an important avenue to building legitimacy and stability is lost. The state is relieved of its responsibility by well-intentioned actions which may prove to be detrimental. Critics further argue that aid does not always decrease vulnerability (Curtis and ODI 2001). The independence in humanitarian aid is also questioned given that humanitarian aid organizations depend upon the support of donors, including donor nations, to maintain organizational operations. Thus, humanitarian aid is increasingly becoming politicized (Curtis and ODI 2001; ICRC 2010).

When humanitarian crises occur or are imminent, a further issue can arise in terms of how to address and stage interventions. Does an actor adopt an approach that promotes providing for basic needs or protecting basic rights? If the former, then distribution of food and water may be the operating mandate; if the latter, seeking legal and structural changes becomes an operating principle. Immediate and long term requirements, whether needs or rights driven, return to the ideal that a state must be rebuilt or strengthened and a government must engage in aspects of nation building or protection. To do so, it needs not only fiscal and human resources, but also management capabilities and legitimacy. Obtaining such is a long term process. Within the transformation, there will need to be stages and, potentially, cooperation between state and non-state actors. With this, the question of scaling up or downscaling arises again.

5.3 The Pros and Cons of Scaled Approaches

In an ideal situation, development programs and health care are delivered across local, regional and national levels with coordination across agencies. This coordination allows for efficient utilization of resources and cohesiveness in actions and goals that will hopefully lead to a pathway for sustainable development which is responsive to population needs and health trends. Arguments can be made for scaling up programs that prove successful in a local context, and for downscaling through centralized goal setting, resource distribution and coordination.

There are several advantages to **scaling up**, an approach that seeks to translate small-scale success into a replicable model that can be implemented in a larger geographic territory or with an expanded scope of operations. The first advantage is that in a localized setting there are multiple actors operating with a diverse set of approaches and resources. Second, there may be more money available in the private sector than in the public sector. Not only is there more money available from the private sector, but it may be easier for donor nations to fund NGOs or private actors than it is for them to fund states. Funding for nation-states is tied to foreign policy and many governments have restrictions as to what states they may fund, and for what purposes the money may be used. Such limitations do not necessarily apply to funding of non-state actors. Third, operations that are limited to a small area, or are confined in scope of operation, provide greater ability to identify context-specific needs and capabilities, and to engage participation from the local community. Fourth, operations with small, specific missions can provide a basic human support structure or management structure that can be adopted for various purposes, such as we observed in Chap. 2 in how the structure of vaccination campaigns was transformed to also provide health monitoring and surveillance. Fifth, the localized perspective can allow for better communication among residents, staff, and program managers such that programs can be adopted to incorporate local priorities and sensibilities. Activities and communications can be constructed to show mutual respect across stake-holders and thereby build trust. Health facilities and local health systems can also incorporate pluralistic medical practices to achieve broader and more acceptable coverage. Many of the lessons and best practices that are defined at the local level can inform up-scaling.

Scaling up, however, presents numerous challenges and is not always successful. INGs/NGOs function on individual mandates that are driven by donors and the individual organization's structure rather than by the needs or goals of the host government. The result is that NGOs may not be addressing the primary development or health concerns of either the local community or of the host government (Garrett 2007). The sheer number of NGOs operating can also tax the government's ability to track operations thereby hindering their capacity to coordinate different groups. This leads to one of the most significant difficulties of scaling up: coordination of NGOs is so complex and time consuming that such activities may overwhelm governmental capacity. NGOs tend to function with short-term horizons, often with single-year missions (Economist 2000; Garrett 2007). Short-term goals may be very different from long-term needs to create truly sustainable programs, and organizations begin in-country operations with no true exit strategy or way in which to ensure continuity of services upon their withdrawal (Garrett 2007). Many NGOs are short-term, mission-specific; such missions seldom include an assessment of program efficacy, impact, or sustainability (Garrett 2007). Many programs do not have a true participatory process for the local community. Further, the NGO operations create market distortions by paying well over the going rate for wages or materials, and by providing higher levels of investment from external funds than from domestic funds. This can lead to inflation. The wage inflation may prohibit domestic or public enterprises from successfully competing for or maintaining skilled local workers. This problem can be exacerbated, especially in health, as skilled personnel leave the developing world for the developed world creating a drain of personnel (Garrett 2007).

Many organizations that provide services in conflict or failed states function on a for-profit basis; their mandates are dictated by donor interests rather than local needs, and many have constraints on uses of funds (Economist 2000, 2010; Garrett 2007). In cases where primary donors are other nation-states, politically driven motivation may supersede true humanitarian or humanist interests, and may infringe upon sovereign rights. Administrative overhead and bureaucratic labyrinths divert funds from field operations. A World Bank study estimated that only half of the funds for health operations in Sub-Saharan Africa are ever used for medicines and delivery of care in the field (Garrett 2007). The lack of international and domestic regulation for these non-state actors contributes to the sense of a *laissez faire* environment in which the NGOs profit economically but fail to contribute to local or national development efforts; in some cases their operations cause outright harm, particularly in the context of failed states, humanitarian assistance and conflict/post-conflict settings (Economist 2000; Matul and Tsilikounas 2004).

Ultimately, rehabilitation of the state is dependent upon context-specific factors. Arguments are made both in favor of scaling up and in favor of centralization. The following case studies explore different approaches to the question of rehabilitation, and challenges of fragile states. Haiti serves as a case study of a failed state in which government legitimacy and will to deliver health care were questionable. Despite this, strides were made in controlling HIV/AIDS and tuberculosis through localized efforts that were successfully being scaled up until the January 2010 earthquake. Rwanda provides an example of rebuilding in the wake of war and genocide in which the government set forth a plan to coordinate and up-scale resources from disparate actors in a bid to make economic and social factors better than they were prior to the war, and, in so doing, help legitimize the new government and policies of social solidarity. Our final case looks at the Ebola epidemic which began in 2013 in West Africa. The epidemic proved to be devastating to both human and state well-being in part because of the virus erupted in post-conflict states. Guinea, Liberia and Sierra Leone suffered from fragile governments and weak healthcare systems which proved unable to respond to the 'black swan' crisis of the Ebola virus disease.

5.4 Haiti—Partners in Health/Zanmi Lasante

Although it is the poorest state in the Western hemisphere, Haiti is also the site of pioneering work and success in community-based HIV prevention and treatment and demonstrates that scaling up can be achieved even in the most unstable and chaotic of situations. Haiti itself has suffered a violent and turbulent history that began in conquest and continues with violence and underdevelopment. It is the most under-developed country in the Americas, and is one of the poorest in the world. Haiti became the first nation of freed slaves following a successful rebellion against France in 1804, but the hope that liberty would bring prosperity never materialized. Violent changes in national leadership and foreign intervention dominated the Haitian political landscape for many years. In the late 20th century, the nation languished under the corrupt dictatorship of François "Papa Doc" Duvalier and his son Jean-Claude Duvalier from 1957 to 1986. When the Duvaliers were ousted, political instability followed until the democratic election of Jean Bertrand Aristide in December, 1990. But stability was short-lived. Aristide was overthrown in a military coup in 1991, only to be re-instated through international peace-keeping efforts in 1994. In 2004 another rebellion occurred, again ousting Mr. Aristide. An interim government was in place until 2006, at which point the nation returned to a procedural democracy with the election of Andre Préval.

The momentary stability ended in 2010 when a 7.0 earthquake leveled the capital city and surrounding area. On January 12, 2010, a 7.0 magnitude earthquake struck Haiti. It leveled cities, towns and villages. In a few short seconds, it undid the small gains in development that had taken years to achieve. An estimated 230,000 people were killed in the quake, another 1.5 million lost their homes and were displaced, and infrastructure was reduced to rubble (CDC 2015a; Lacey and Thompson 2010). Recovery is expected to cost between US$7.2 billion and US$13.2 billion dollars (New York Times 2010). A cholera epidemic took hold in the country ten months after the earthquake and continues in sporadic outbreaks. Since that time there have been an estimated 739,000 cholera cases and 8,900 deaths (Partners in Health 2015). Recovery since the earthquake has been poor with a loss of state legitimacy, lack of coordination among diverse actors, and little progress towards restarting development.

The earthquake occurred shortly before presidential elections. As a result, the 2010 elections were briefly postponed. Michel Martelly was elected president in a run-off in 2011. A political crisis ensued when the Martelly government failed to hold elections for four years. When Martelly stepped down in 2016 there was no elected successor due to protests and charges of election fraud in the 2015 election. Jocelerme Privert was appointed the interim president until elections were held in October 2016. Jovenel Moise won the election and was sworn in as Haiti's president in February, 2017.

In the last 30 years, Haiti has been marked by political instability, a weak economy, high levels of national debt, and under-development. The national economy took a downward turn in the early 1980s and has yet to fully recover (See Fig. 5.1). Economic decline also followed the coups in 1991 and 2004. By 2005,

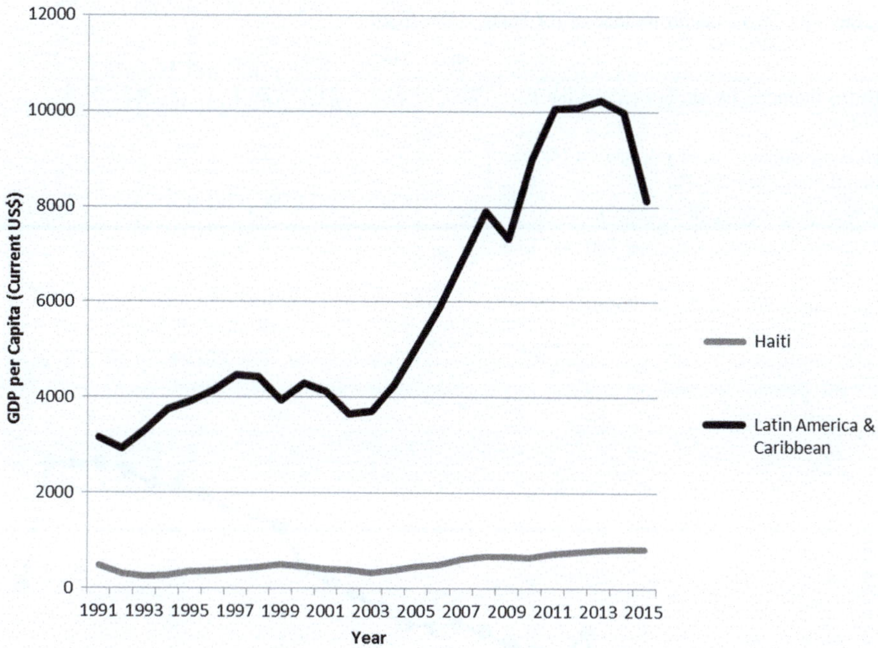

Fig. 5.1 GDP per capita for Haiti versus Latin America and the Caribbean. Data source: World Bank (2016a)

the GDP per capita was less than what it had been in 1990 (World Bank 2016a). Haiti's GDP per capita in 2010 stood at US$662, well below the regional average of US$4301 (World Bank 2016a). In the five years following the earthquake, the GDP per capita rose to only $828 (World Bank 2016a).

The moderate gains made by the country prior to 2010 have been lost and the country and its health system remain decimated. Poverty rates in the country remain high with more than half of the population living on less than US$1.90 per day (WHO 2016a). While poverty increased, health and social services deteriorated. Primary care decreased as noted by precipitous drop in vaccination rates and an increase in infant mortality (World Bank 2016a). At 62 years, life expectancy at birth is much lower than the regional average of 72 years. Haiti suffers from the highest HIV prevalence rate in the Caribbean, estimated to be 2% of the population, and adult literacy remains low (World Bank 2016a).

Despite these poor health and social indicators, some gradual improvements occurred prior to the earthquake. For example, IMR per 1000 live births was 101 in 1990 and decreased to 60 in 2009 (WHO 2016a). Although the rate soared to 85 per 1000 following the earthquake, it was down to 52.2 by 2014 (World Bank 2016a). Childhood immunization rates show marked improvement through 2010, as did maternal health services reflected in the number of births at which a skilled attendant was present (Table 5.2 and Fig. 5.2). Figure 5.3 shows small but

Table 5.2 Select health indicators for Haiti, 1989–2014

	1989	1995	2000	2006	2010	2012	2014
Births attended by skilled technician (% of total)	23	20.6	23.8	26.1		37.3	
HIV prevalence, adult population (% of population ages 15–49)		3.3	3.2	2.3	2.1	2.0	
Life expectancy at birth (total)	54	57	57	60	61	62	63
Maternal mortality ratio per 100,000 live births			523	630			

Data source: World Bank (2016a)

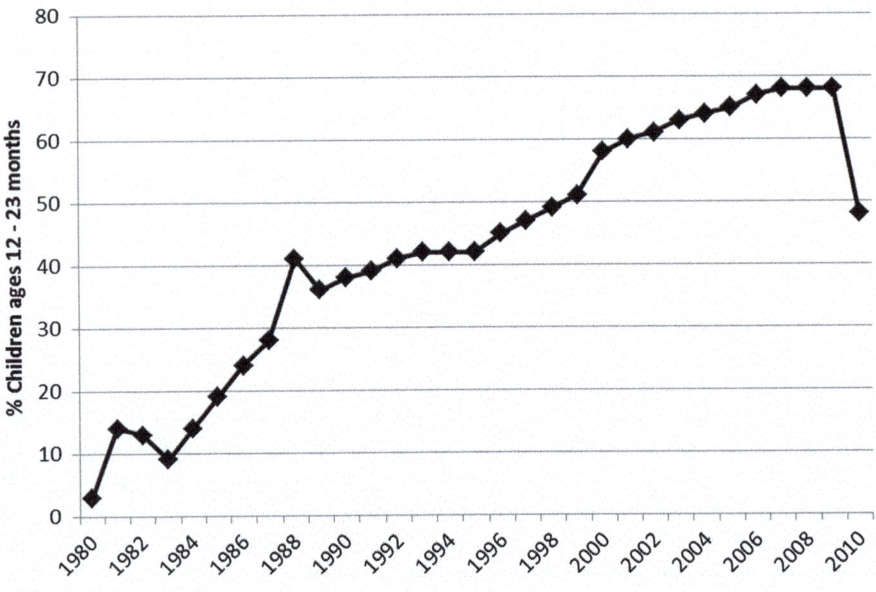

Fig. 5.2 Childhood DPT immunization rates in Haiti, 1980–2010. Data source: World Bank (2016a)

consistent increase prior to 2010, suggesting increased investment in health from both public and private actors (World Bank 2016a). The influx of medical aid following the earthquake, and proliferation of vertical health programming has contributed to improved access and outcomes for select problems. For example, the number of HIV-positive pregnant women receiving antiretroviral therapy rose from 44% in 2009 to 87% in 2014 (CDC 2015a).

HIV/AIDS is one of the most pernicious health threats in Haiti. The HIV epidemic began in the 1980s. The disease first appeared in urban areas of the country, and spread to rural communities (Farmer 1992). At the time of the disease's first manifestation, little national capacity existed to deal with health care issues in general, let alone address the challenges presented by a newly emerging and poorly

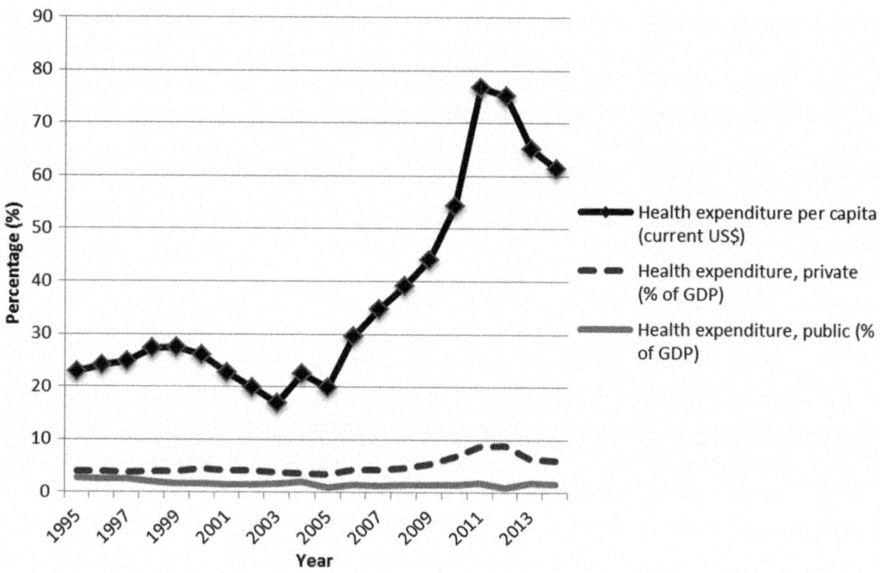

Fig. 5.3 Health expenditures in Haiti, 2002–2014. Data source: World Bank (2016a)

understood disease. The declining political and economic situation eliminated any national capacity to address the epidemic. It was in this context that the *Clinique Bon Sauveur*, a small facility located in Cange in the Central Province of Haiti, struggled to provide health care to a rural community. Included in their modest scope of services was HIV prevention (Farmer 1992; Kidder 2009; Mukherjee et al. 2003). In 1988, Partners in Health (PIH), a not-for-profit organization affiliated with Harvard Medical School, and its Haitian sister organization Zanmi Lasante (ZL) introduced voluntary HIV counseling and testing free of charge at the clinic (Walton et al. 2004; Mukherjee et al. 2003).

PIH/ZL began a concerted effort to increase the availability of HIV treatment and prevention services. In 1995, the clinic introduced zidovudine to its pre-natal care in order to prevent mother-to-child transmission of HIV. As antiretroviral drugs became available, the rate of acceptance of HIV testing increased (Walton et al. 2004; Mukherjee et al. 2003). The rates for voluntary counseling and testing for women receiving pre-natal care rose from around 30–90% over the course of a single year (Walton et al. 2004; Mukherjee et al. 2003). This change in clinical services had a positive impact on both disease-specific issues and on maternal health care in general. The rate of vertical HIV transmission from mother to child decreased while the quality of maternal care increased (Mukherjee et al. 2003). The clinic also added in-patient services. An estimated 40% of the patients who presented for in-patient services were tested and found to be seropositive (Walton et al. 2004; Mukherjee et al. 2003). Given the high HIV prevalence, and the fact that AIDS was the leading cause of adult mortality in rural Haiti, PIH/ZL prioritized the addition of HIV treatment (Walton et al. 2004). In 1998, the clinic began offering directly observed therapy with highly active antiretroviral therapy (DOT-HAART).

The DOT-HAART therapy was offered in response to locally-driven needs and observations. The delivery program was staffed largely by local residents who served as *accompagnateurs*, community health workers who deliver medication and medical assistance. The impact of this program included improvements in the quality of life and quality of health for people afflicted with HIV—some of whom, without the therapy, would not have survived for long (Walton et al. 2004; Mukherjee et al. 2003). As the number of people receiving ART increased, stigma surrounding AIDS in the area decreased. As this occurred, more individuals became willing to get tested and, if needed, receive care for HIV or other opportunistic infections (Walton et al. 2004). The clinic also became better able to identify and treat patients with other diseases such as tuberculosis and sexually transmitted infections, thereby furthering the control of specific diseases and improving public health (Walton et al. 2004). The availability of essential medications and vaccines increased as did staff morale (Walton et al. 2004).

In the early days of PIH/ZL, the program in the Central Plateau operated in a largely autonomous way. Neither resources nor political will existed at the national level to form a successful partnership, nor, one could argue, would such a partnership have been beneficial to the provision of health care services (Gastineau Campos and Farmer 2003). And yet, a goal of the center's operators was always to be able to contribute to the development of the local community and the broader nation when conditions were right. In the 1980s, the political conditions for scaling up did not exist. But this changed.

In 2002, PIH and the Haitian Ministry of Health replicated the Cange experience in the border town of LasCahobas (Walton et al. 2004). The essential components of the program at the new site included an assessment of the health and needs of the local patients as well as social conditions, training of local staff and local residents as *accompagnateurs*, prevention programs for HIV, and provision of HIV and TB treatments. The program provided for 30 essential drugs to the clinic in LasCahobas. A preliminary assessment of this project found that after 14 months, 200 TB patients had been identified and linked to DOTS (Walton et al. 2004). The data showed a preliminary surge in case detection followed by a decrease that suggested a critical mass in terms of diagnosis was reached. An AIDS clinic also opened, resulting in an increase in uptake of voluntary counseling and testing (Walton et al. 2004). As was observed in the Cange clinic, other aspects of primary care improved as a result of this program. Prenatal care, introduced as part of the HIV detection and prevention, became available, vaccination rates increased, and again, staff morale increased.

In 2002, the Global Fund to Fight AIDS, Tuberculosis, and Malaria awarded Haiti US$67 million for health care. PIH/ZL received a portion of this funding. They, in partnership with the Haitian Ministry of Health, began efforts similar to those undertaken in Cange and LasCahobas in three additional towns (Walton et al. 2004). The towns selected had public clinics that were under-funded and understaffed (Walton et al. 2004). The scaling up began when a culmination of several factors was in place, including a public-private partnership, adequate funding, and a compilation of lessons learned on the ground over the course of nearly twenty years. Among these practices, PIH/ZL identified six minimum essentials for a basic package of health services, and four ‘pillars’ that included delivery of HIV/AIDS prevention and care, TB diagnosis and case management, STI detection and treatment, and provision of women’s healthcare (Walton et al. 2004).

Assessment of the successes in Cange and LasCahobas showed that a small-scale program that began with a focus on a single disease could be up-scaled to address broader issues germane to public health, such as maternal-child care, and could be replicable when attention is paid to assessment and flexibility given to local operators so that they may best address local needs (Farmer and Garrett 2007; Mukherjee et al. 2003; Walton et al. 2004). Program assessors were adamant in highlighting reasons for the particular success of Cange. They noted that free testing for HIV as a component of a prevention program failed when no treatment for HIV was available (Walton et al. 2004; Mukherjee et al. 2003). One need not be a medical doctor or psychologist to understand why. If a positive diagnosis means only that a person becomes aware of what, barring treatment, amounts to a death sentence, why add the burden of such knowledge to daily struggles? However, when hope for a stay of execution or an improved quality of life became available via antiretroviral medication, there became reason for individuals to be tested. When expectant mothers were offered hope that they could spare their baby an infection through testing and treatment, they acted to protect their children. PIH/ZL and their partners adamantly stated that tuberculosis care had to be incorporated into HIV care as TB was the leading opportunistic infection in the service area (Walton et al. 2004). This principle is similar to the principles of the early Pholela Center in South Africa discussed in Chap. 4 in that successful health programs must identify and treat the specific agents plaguing the local population if there are to be broad-based, sustainable improvements in population health.

PIH/ZL continued to operate in Haiti in the aftermath of the quake, following through on care for HIV/AIDS and TB. Through its network of community clinics, the organization expanded services to include those critical for recovery, including working with the government and other NGOs to coordinate a cholera vaccination campaign, and opening a teaching hospital (PIH 2016a). The organization is now the largest NGO healthcare provider in the nation. The model of care PIH/ZL pioneered in Haiti has since been adopted in other countries including Rwanda, Lesotho and Malawi (PHI 2016b).

5.5 Rwanda Rising from the Ashes

Rwanda, a land-locked country in Sub-Saharan Africa, is recovering from a civil war and genocide. War broke out in 1990 between the Tutsi-led Rwandan Patriotic Front (RPF) and the largely Hutu Government of Rwanda (GoR) after decades of long-standing ethnic and political rivalries. The conflict culminated with a government-backed genocide of between 800,000 and one million Tutsis and moderate-Hutus. An estimated two million people were displaced. The war ended with RPF victory in July 2004.

The new millennium was marked by the transition from a nation recovering from war, supported by the international community and humanitarian assistance, to a country regaining control of itself and its future with a goal of sustainable development. The first post-conflict local elections were held in 1999, followed by democratic presidential and legislative elections in 2003. The GoR greeted the new millennium with Vision 2020, a comprehensive plan for sustainable human development. The main goal of this plan is to achieve high rates of economic growth that will move Rwanda from a low-income to a middle-income country by 2020. This goal requires more than doubling the per capita GDP from US$290 to US$900 (Ministry of Finance and Economic Planning 2000). Such economic development is essential to and integrated with broader national goals of poverty alleviation and human development. Economic growth would be achieved, in part, through regulatory and institutional reform favorable to free market principles and international investment. Good governance, increased competition and privatization, transformation of the agricultural sector, and development of human resources through education, health and information and communication technologies (ICT) skills are central components of the plan (Ministry of Finance and Economic Planning 2000) (Fig. 5.4).

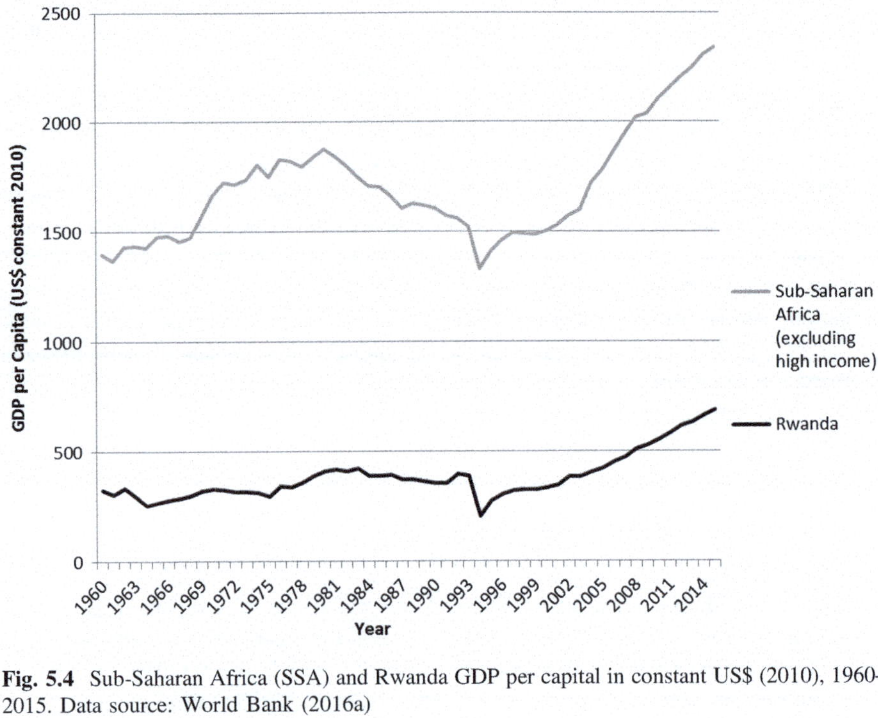

Fig. 5.4 Sub-Saharan Africa (SSA) and Rwanda GDP per capital in constant US$ (2010), 1960–2015. Data source: World Bank (2016a)

Rwanda's civil war disrupted social, economic, and political structures and progress. It interrupted moderate economic growth, and forced the country backward in terms of overall development. Between 1993 and 1994, the GDP per capita dropped from US$387 (US$ constant 2010) to US$202 (World Bank 2016a). Although Rwandan society was not highly developed or wealthy prior to the war, the conflict devastated social institutions and infrastructure, caused social contraction and deepened poverty. Between the violence and economic chaos, an estimated 80% of the population fell into poverty (Ministry of Finance and Economic Planning 2000). By 2000, the percentage of the population continuing to live on less than US$1 a day stood at 60.3% (WHO 2009b). Vaccination coverage for DTP3 fell from 83 to 23% in a single year (WHO 2009b).

Recovery from the war and genocide has been slow. The current GDP per capita of US$689 is less than half of the regional average for Sub-Saharan Africa (US$ 1650) (World Bank 2016a). Adult literacy is 68% (2012), HIV prevalence averages 4.6% (2010); respiratory disease, HIV/AIDS and malaria are the leading causes of death (World Bank 2016a; World Health Organization 2016; Institute for Health Metrics and Evaluation 2015). Malaria contributed to more than half of the deaths nationwide (World Health Organization 2016). The infant mortality rate per 1000 live births was 109 in 2000, compared to the regional average of 94. The latest data show that Rwanda achieved rates lower than the regional average. Its infant mortality rate plunged to 31 per 1000 live births, below the regional average of 56.3 (World Bank 2016a). The maternal mortality ratio per 100,000 live births in Rwanda was 1558 in 2000. The latest available data show a dramatic decrease to 210 per 100,000 (World Bank 2016a). Although still high, the decrease is a testament to improved living conditions (Fig. 5.5).

When the war and genocide ended in 1994, the GoR had to confront the challenge of not only (re)building a low income nation that was decimated by war, but also unifying a Rwandan identity and creating social and national solidarity in a context rife with fear, distrust and grief. Recreating the institutional structures and practices that would re-enforce ethnic and social division was not an option. The government received high levels of development assistance and aid, some of which could be directed to reforming and rebuilding public structures. But aid is typically short-lived and cannot serve as a substitute for domestically driven, sustainable development. The initial efforts directed towards rebuilding the health sector were modest and proved insufficient. The government implemented a district health model in which district health offices were responsible for planning, provision, regulation and allocation of health services; no centralized planning was provided (Logie et al. 2008; Soeters et al. 2006). Health care facilities in each district were owned and/or operated by the local government or churches (Soeters et al. 2006). The dearth of centrally allocated resources made it difficult for health centers to maintain staffing or adequate supplies of goods or services. Health care centers relied heavily on user fees, resulting in substandard or insufficient equipment and staffing, poor utilization of services, and inequity in access to even the most basic levels of care (Logie et al. 2008; Soeters et al. 2006). The lack of coordination led to fragmentation and poorly targeted programs. Although there were numerous donor

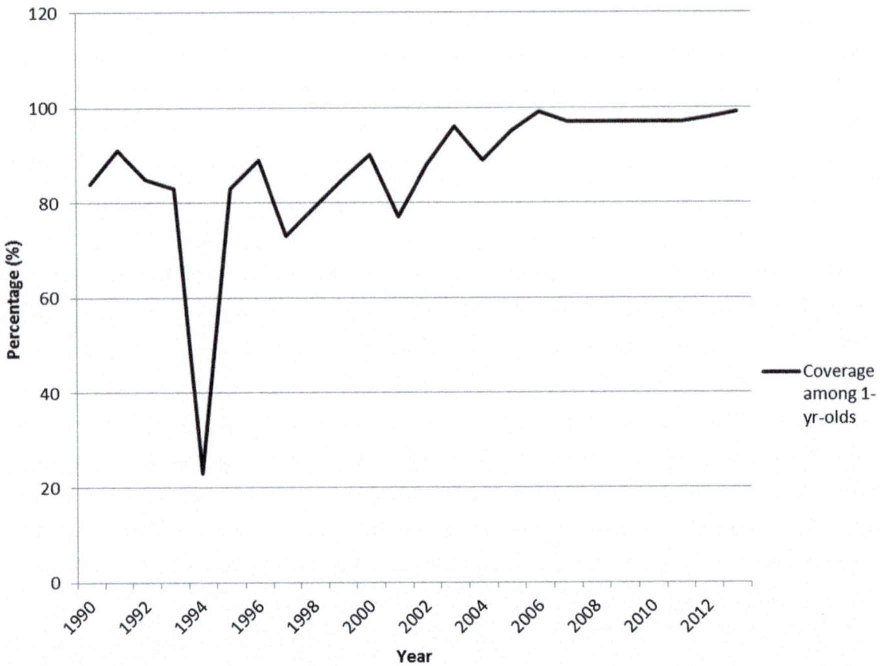

Fig. 5.5 Percentage of one-year-olds immunized with three doses of diphtheria tetanus toxoid and pertussis (DTP3), 1990–2013. Data source: WHO (2016a)

funds and NGOs operating in Rwanda, the efforts were uncoordinated, resulting in a scattershot approach that did little to address national or local priorities. By 2002 the GoR was spending 8.6% of its revenue on health care, but access and availability of care remained low (Logie et al. 2008). Two thirds of health care funding came from donor and direct payments (Logie et al. 2008) (Fig. 5.6).

With Vision 2020, the Rwandan government set forth a strategic plan to improve the health care sector. The four tenants of this strategic plan were: (a) coordinating of donor aid; (b) linking and using aid based on government goals and priorities; (c) creating a national plan of community-based health insurance; and (d) establishing performance-based pay initiatives for public sector employees. A number of heath targets improved after the implementation of Vision 2020. For example, under five mortality rates decreased from 196 per 1000 in 2000 (baseline year) to 152 in 2005 (Logie et al. 2008). IMR dropped, and MMR fell from 1071 per 100,000 live births to 750 per 100,000 live births (Logie et al. 2008). Eighty four percent of children age 11–23 months were immunized against measles during this same time (Logie et al. 2008).

Coordination of donor aid was one of the keys of the success of this health overhaul. In post-conflict/failed states, there tends to be a dearth of public resources and an abundance of donor projects and assistance, but coordination of these resources and actors is lacking. The GoR found a way to utilize the scattered but

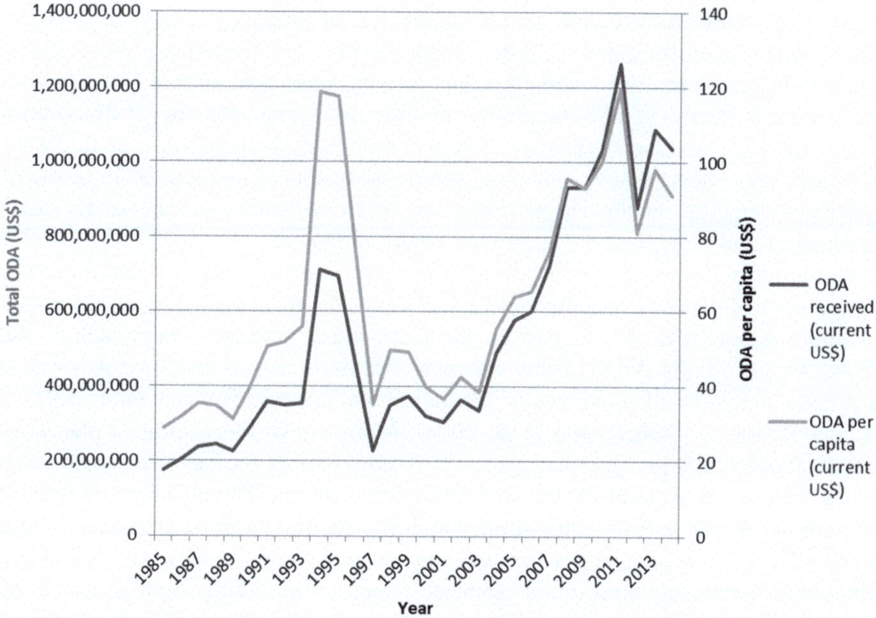

Fig. 5.6 Official development assistance and aid to Rwanda, 1985–2014. Data source: World Bank (2016a)

more plentiful resources of donors/NGOS. The GoR, with assistance from the World Bank, integrated donor funds into a single financial framework in order to better track funds and plan for medium and long-term fiscal sustainability (Logie et al. 2008). A development forum consisting of Rwandan government officials and representatives of top aid agencies meets annually to oversee the development program and compact. Some donors, such as the European Union, Sweden, and the African Development Bank, provide direct budgetary support to the GoR to utilize according to Vision 2020 (Logie et al. 2008). This type of support now accounts for 41% of international aid. In this manner, the GoR assumed ownership of the development plans and has been able to harness support and buy-in from important donors. The GoR established a transparent financial management system and monitors aid effectiveness (Logie et al. 2008). Where donors chose not to contribute directly to the centralized government budget, or where their charter prohibited them from doing so, they may still provide services but are expected to integrate their actions or funds based on sectoral aims, goals or approaches (Logie et al. 2008). The result of these actions is that NGOs and donors are beginning to align their programs with government plans, thereby building support and faith in the nascent government as well as providing for more efficient and effective utilization of resources.

But this coordination has not come easily. Twenty-seven percent of all government and donor health resources are spent on program administration (Logie et al. 2008). Government staff spends an average of three days per year servicing each NGO mission (Logie et al. 2008). With 168 missions operating in the country, this means that nearly two years of manpower days are used simply to liaise with donor organizations. In addition, many missions have one year project timeframes and so the GoR is in near constant (re)negotiation with donors (Logie et al. 2008). Although this effort is time intensive, the rewards appear to be great in terms of better coordination, better use of resources, improved public-private sector communication and planning, and improved health outcomes.

Community-based health insurance and performance-based pay are the other components of the GoR's health care vision. *Mutuelle de Sante*, a community-based insurance program funded in part by the GoR and in part by donors such as the Global Fund to Fight AIDS, Tuberculosis and Malaria, began operating in 1999. It is now available in all provinces of the nation and covered approximately 73% of the population in 2006 (Logie et al. 2008). Members of the insurance plan contribute about US$2 per year and pay a 10% co-payment for each illness episode. A reserve fund exists to cover the costs of health disasters. The plan is administered through an elected village committee, which has the authority to determine whom in the village is too poor to pay for insurance or health care. In these cases, fees are subsidized by money from donor agencies (Logie et al. 2008). As a result of the insurance program, health care utilization increased. The *Mutuelle de Sante* shows how health insurance programs evolved over time. Recall that in the late 1980s and 1990s, there were two main models of health financing put forward by the international development community. One put forward private insurance as the preferred method. This was seen as a way to diminish public costs, which was especially important where there was not fiscal balance, and as a way to reduce demand-side moral hazards. The other health financing model advocated for government provision of service, based on the ideal of health as a right, and as a way to provide for and protect an important public good. Neither model has proven to be wholly successful or sustainable. With *Mutuelle de Sante* one sees the adoption of parts of each of these models. These parts are incorporated with one of the most important lessons of community health—local control and decision-making power.

Even after implementation of these changes to the health sector, lack of adequate staffing and low levels of employee morale and motivation continued to plague the GoR. In response, the Ministry of Health implemented a pilot program on performance-based pay in conjunction with the Dutch NGO Cordaid. Data from the first pilot project suggests that the program realized cost reductions and improved availability of certain maternal and family planning services (Soeters et al. 2006). As a result of this initial success, the program is being up-scaled (Logie et al. 2008).

Although Rwanda appears to be on a positive path in terms of reconstruction and, specifically, rebuilding a stronger economy and a better health sector, much remains to be seen. Improvement in public services and the execution of a strong program for development have come at the cost of political freedoms, a growing sense of authoritarianism and a decrease in human rights (Matfess 2015; Reyntjens 2015). The administration of Paul Kagame, president since 2000, is criticized for human rights violations, suppression of civil and political rights, decreasing press freedom, movement away from rule of law, and extrajudicial violence (Freedom House 2016; Matfess 2015). Concurrently, Rwanda continues to be viewed as an important ally for donor nations such as the United States. Its relative stability positions it as an ally in regional security (Matfess 2015; Reyntjens 2015). Further, open and market-oriented economic policies, comparatively well-functioning institutions and anti-corruption programs contribute to an environment favorable for international business (Freedom House 2016; Matfess 2015; World Bank 2016b).

Whether or not Rwanda will achieve the goals stated in Vision 2020 remains to be seen, but there are positive indicators. Vision 2020 calls for Rwanda to end external aid by 2020, thus stepping away from aid dependency. Although aid levels peaked in 2011, they remain higher than they were at the inception of Vision 2020 (World Bank 2016a). As a percentage of the central government expense, ODA is decreasing but remains high. Realizing the goal of decreased dependency is partially based on achieving and maintaining high levels of economic growth. GDP has climbed and GDP growth rates averaged 7.7% over the last decade, suggesting this goal is feasible (World Bank 2016a).

The health sector, while showing improvement, remains a low performer when considering international norms. Experts suggest that the current level of government spending on healthcare, 9.5% of the budget, is insufficient and must be raised to 15% (Logie et al. 2008). As of 2014, government health spending amounted to 9.9% of government expenditures, a figure which was only moderately higher than government spending in 2000 (World Bank 2016a). Although much has been done to reign in and harness disparate donors and NGOs operating in the health care sector, the sector remains fragmented. Short term commitments are the norm, but long-term commitments are needed (Logie et al. 2008). The varied donor agendas continue to make health planning difficult, and there continues to be a mismatch between donor agendas and local needs (Logie et al. 2008). Although the merit-pay system appears promising, there remains unhealthy competition for trained employees between rural and urban areas, and between the public and private sector. Still, the achievements that Rwanda has made in terms of directing the disparate development actors and resources, and in terms of stabilizing health in the country cannot be ignored, and suggest that the aforementioned obstacles may yet be overcome.

5.6 Fragility Takes a Toll—Ebola in West Africa

In 2014, the largest Ebola epidemic ever to occur brought into stark relief the precariousness of states emerging from conflict, and the attendant fragility of regional security and human well-being. The epidemic began in December 2013 and was not declared over until June 2016 (WHO 2016a). The epidemic began in Guinea and quickly spread into Liberia and Sierra Leone. By its end, 28,616 people had been infected and 11,310 people died of the Ebola virus disease (EVD) (WHO

2016a). Although Guinea, Liberia and Sierra Leone were the epicenter of the pandemic, the virus spread to Italy, Mali, Nigeria, Senegal, Spain, the United Kingdom and the United States (WHO 2016b). At the start of the epidemic, EVD was well known disease which previously had 33 outbreaks (CDC 2015b). The earlier outbreaks were comparatively small in terms of cases and geographic extent. Despite the high virulence of the disease, the largest previous outbreak, in Uganda is 2000–2001, ended with 224 dead and 425 total cases (CDC 2015b). These outbreaks occurred in low-income, developing states and yet they were quickly contained. The global community therefore asked, how did the 2014 pandemic happen? What accounted for the dramatic difference between this and previous outbreaks? Will it happen again?

The epidemic began modestly with an outbreak in rural Guinea in December, 2013 (WHO 2015a). From its modest start, EVD spread to other rural communities and into the capital city of Conakry over the next two months. The virus entered Liberia in March 2014, and took hold of urban Monrovia in June (WHO 2015a). It also spread into Sierra Leone in January, with cases surging in April and May (WHO 2015a). Because of similarities in symptoms to other infectious diseases in the area, and a lack of laboratory testing, the early EVD deaths were attributed to unknown causes. It was not until March that EVD was officially detected (WHO 2015a). During the lag between first infection and detection by the medical system, the disease was able to spread between the three countries and become entrenched in urban areas—constituting the first outbreak of this disease in densely populated cities.

The WHO, under the Global Outbreak and Response Network (GOARN), deployed a team to Guinea in March, 2014. It did not declare a Public Health Emergency of International Concern (PHEIC) until August 9. The declaration triggered an international response under the aegis of the International Health Regulations. Fearing that the epidemic could lead to social collapse and political instability, the United Nations Security Council and the UN General Assembly created the first-ever UN health mission—the UN Mission for Ebola Emergency Response (UNMEER) in September 2014. The mission of UNMEER was to provide case management, case findings, lab and contact tracing, safe and dignified burials, and community engagement and social mobilization to combat the epidemic (UN 2016; UN Security Council 2014).

Weak public health systems and state fragility are two key factors that contributed to the lethality of this epidemic (Garrett 2015; Siedner et al. 2015; WHO 2015a). All three states at the epicenter were in the early stages of stabilizing following conflict. Guinea suffered long years of instability followed by a military coup in 2008–2009. The first free and fair elections did not occur until 2010 and 2013. World Bank and IMF aid were reinstated following the elections, and the country saw a period of economic growth. However, it continued to suffer from high food dependency, high levels of poverty, and a weak health infrastructure (World Bank 2014, 2016a; WHO 2016a). Liberia ended a civil war in 2003, and held presidential elections in 2005. Liberia's economy is largely agricultural, and the country is highly dependent on foreign aid, with high unemployment rates and poverty rates of 60% (World Bank 2014; WHO 2016a). In addition, the country has half a million refugees. Common to post-war nations, the economy was growing prior to the epidemic, although the workforce remained engaged in informal activities which proved highly vulnerable (World Bank 2014, 2016a). Two million people were displaced by the civil war in Sierra Leone which ended in 2002 (CIA 2016). The economy is driven by mining and agriculture, and is heavily dependent on foreign aid despite donors cutting back on aid due to corruption (CIA 2016; World Bank 2016a). More than half the population lives in poverty, and ¾ are under aged 35 (World Bank 2014, 2016a) (Fig. 5.7).

Despite modest improvements in economic growth and political stability, all three nations had severely neglected health care systems. Before the outbreak, Guinea had about 1 physician for every 12,500 people, Liberia had 51 physicians total, and Sierra Leone had 136 doctors (Frontline Health Workers Coalition 2015; WHO 2016a). Guinea's health infrastructure, of the three nations, was considered the strongest and most able to respond. The Ministry of Health, with the assistance of Médicins Sans Frontiéres (MSF), set up isolation wards in two of the most impacted areas comparatively quickly. Nonetheless, the disease ultimately claimed 2543 lives in that nation, and infected more than 3800 individuals (WHO 2015a, 2016b). The result of underdevelopment in the three states was that they had weak capacity to detect and manage the epidemic. The shortage of healthcare personnel grew to crisis proportions throughout the epidemic as frontline health workers were 21–32 times more likely to be infected by Ebola than was the general public (WHO

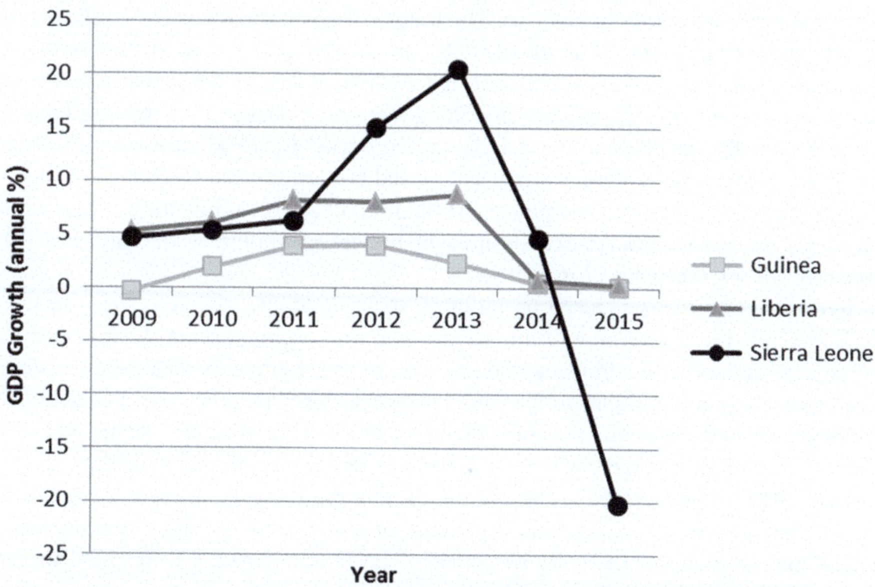

Fig. 5.7 Changes in GDP in Guinea, Liberia and Sierra Leone, 2009–2015. Data source: World Bank (2016a)

2015b). By the end of the epidemic, 881 cases were detected among medical staff, resulting in 512 deaths (Data Team 2016). Guinea lost 1% of its healthcare workers, Liberia lost 8%, and Sierra Leone lost 7% (Evansa et al. 2015). Whatever health programming may have been in place prior to the epidemic was decimated as resources were harnessed and redirected with one important mission—to stop the spread of EVD.

Following the WHO's declaration of a PHEIC, international actors entered the fray. The World Bank, the European Union, and the United States along with numerous other responders sent money, technical expertise and personnel. Although the international community was criticized for its delayed response, the response did yield results. Guinea declared an end to the initial outbreak on December 29, 2015. The epidemic ended in Sierra Leone in March, 2016, and in Liberia in June of that year (WHO 2016a).

The epidemic set these nations back years if not decades in terms of health and development. Economic development came to a halt during the epidemic as trade and international borders closed, vast areas were quarantined, and foreign investors pulled out. Domestic and international markets closed, FDI decreased, government services shut down or were diverted, wages and earnings were reduced. As a result, government revenue went down at a time when additional funds were desperately needed, and government debt increased. These nations lost between 2 and 5% of their GDP in 2014, and an estimated $1.6 billion in economic income in 2015 (World Bank 2014, 2015). Food security became and remains an issue. During the epidemic, food inflation ran between 10 and 30%, and currently ranges from 4 to 10% (World Bank 2014; Trading Economies 2016). Increased foreign aid is unlikely to address the development gap. The failure of governments in their delivery of health services and ability to respond to the health crisis exacerbated political instability. Distrust of the government and INGOs led to violence and attacks on healthcare workers in Guinea; the Liberian government declared it could not handle the response to the epidemic and U.S. military was deployed to assist; all three nations declared a state of emergency and closed borders; senate elections in Liberia were postponed due to the emergence (Al-bakri Nyei 2016). While the governments survived, the crisis exacerbated fissures in the fragile political stability and the potential for recovery remains unclear.

Recovery efforts are focused on building socio-economic security. The success, or failure, of this endeavor will impact national and regional security. Whether or not redevelopment will address social services and strengthen the healthcare system remains to be seen. Critiques of the Ebola response noted that the failure of national governments and donor states to prioritize and invest in healthcare systems was one of the key factors that contributed to the size of epidemic (Flessa and Marx 2016, Garrett 2015, WHO 2016c). The current health priorities in the Ebola-impacted nations include providing care for survivors of Ebola, and building an epidemiological surveillance for the early detection of EVD and capacity to respond to the same (WHO 2016d). While the WHO has called for strengthening health systems as an aspect of health security, there has yet to be international mobilization to this end.

5.7 Conclusion

Improving the inputs to health and improving overall human development is a difficult process in the best of circumstances. These efforts become vastly more challenging in failed states or conflict-ridden areas where fiscal and human resources are in short supply, where the physical landscape is damaged, and where social trust has been shattered. A message of this book is that context matters. Perhaps this is most true, and most important, in fragile states. A goal of development is for states to become self-sufficient in providing for and improving the needs and capabilities of its people, but at times the state may not be the main driver in development. In fact, in some cases, especially when the state is responsible for brutal repression of its people, cooperation and collaboration with state actors may go against a basic tenant of development in that human rights must be respected and leadership must prove worthy of the support of its citizens. Development actors need be cognizant of when and how to engage with state institutions and leaders. However, with the growth of INGOs and increase of profit that can be made through poverty reduction programs and the delivery of aid, one sees a proliferation of INGOs that have neither skill nor, perhaps, desire to contribute to national development. The difficult questions become how and when to scale up, with whom to partner, how to best turn local success into a broader regional or national success, or when to choose to down-scale by using centralized planning and goals to harness different actors into a unified strategy and deployment.

The achievements in Haiti were realized through long-term dedication on the part of an NGO, a belief that efforts to improve health and human development must involve the public sector, patience in building a program responsive to local needs and context, and endurance in delivering care to the community while waiting for the political situation to stabilize and working to build partnerships to support a government worthy of public trust existed. One could argue that the achievements seen in Cange, Haiti, and the program being replicated in other parts of the country were realized because of bottom-up mobilization and efforts to bring programs to scale. Such is one model to consider when addressing health and development in the most challenging of contexts. Haiti is a case study of a very fragile nation trying to build a legitimate government capable of responding to the social needs of its citizens through partnerships. The baby steps it took in terms of political and social development dissolved in the aftermath of a nature disaster.

By contrast, Rwanda presents a different model for organizing programs to improve health and human development, one which is coordinated and managed by the government, a top-down approach that attempts to merge short-and long-term public vision to myriad public and private resources scattered throughout a country that is rebuilding after war and genocide. The effort requires considerable dedication and coordination by the GoR, and considerable flexibility on the part of major donors. The result appears to be a cohesive albeit imperfect approach to national development in which the resources of state and non-state actors are harnessed towards specific goals with national (and international) mechanisms for accountability. As with Haiti, however, one of the most important elements for program success is time.

The West African Ebola epidemic highlighted the impossible circumstances of fragile states. Small steps towards improved development too easily fell apart in the face of an unpredictable epidemic. Over the course of 24 months, a singular event eroded progress in economic and political development and decimated nascent healthcare systems. The result is a decrease in human and fiscal resources and decreased institutional capacity. There is hope that increased aid and assistance from donor states and INGOs, and successful collaboration between government and community, can be harnessed to rebuild these states in a more resilient manner, but much remains to be seen.

What becomes obvious in these cases, and others presented throughout this book, is that government-driven enterprise alone is no longer proving successful in the mission of human development. Even when there is a central vision and central resources, the expertise and skills of non-governmental entities need be brought to bear. The cost of health care provision, especially in regards to new and costly diseases such as HIV/AIDS and EVD, and the growing burden of non-communicable disease, can neither be borne by the government nor by any individual alone. The private sector has thus become an important contributor to international health and development. In Chap. 6 we turn our attention to the rise of public-private partnerships.

Discussion Questions

1. How does state failure impact economic and human development in the short-term? In the long-term?
2. Discuss whether or not the advantages to having NGOs operate in a conflict or post-conflict country outweigh the problems.
3. Why do you think the utilization rates for voluntary testing and counseling for HIV increased at *Clinique Bon Sauveur* when zidovudine was introduced?
4. What are some of the program elements used by PIH/ZL in their community-based approach to health that are similar to those used by the Pholela Health Center in South Africa? Do you believe these commonalities help to explain the program's success?
5. Review the different provisions of Vision 2020 at http://www.sida.se/globalassets/global/countries-and-regions/africa/rwanda/d402331a.pdf. What parts of the plan do you believe are most important in terms of post-conflict recovery? In terms of building sustainable human development? Why?
6. Rwanda has achieved economic growth and made important gains in population health, but critics argue this has come at the cost of eroding civil and human rights. Do you believe the gains warrant the costs? Why or why not?
7. Given the cases of Guinea, Liberia and Sierra Leone, what do you believe the number one priority should be for development post-EVD?

References

Al-bakri Nyei, I. (2016). Beyond the disease: How the Ebola epidemic affected the politics and stability of the Mano River Basin. *African Centre for the constructive resolution of disputes*. http://reliefweb.int/report/liberia/beyond-disease-how-ebola-epidemic-affected-politics-and-stability-mano-river-basin. Accessed September 22, 2016.

Anderson, M. (1996). *Do no harm: Supporting local capacities for peace through aid*. MA: Collaborative for Development.

Bossert, T. J. (1984). Nicaragua health policy: The dilemma of success. *Medical Anthropology Quarterly, 15*(3), 73–74.

Brentlinger, P. (1996). Health sector response to the security threats during the civil war in El Salvador. *BMJ, 313*(7070), 1470–1474.

Centers for Disease Control and Prevention. (2015a). Update on progress in selected public health programs after the 2010 earthquake and cholera epidemic—Haiti, 2014. *Morbidity and Mortality Weekly Report, 64*(6), 137–140.

Centers for Disease Control and Prevention. (2015b). Outbreaks chronology: Ebola Virus Disease. http://www.cdc.gov/vhf/ebola/outbreaks/history/chronology.html. Accessed September 17, 2016.

Central Intelligence Agency. (2016). The World Factbook: Sierra Leone. https://www.cia.gov/library/publications/the-world-factbook/geos/sl.html. Accessed September 16, 2016.

Collier, P., Elliott, V. L., Hegre, H., Hoeffler, A., & Reynol-Querol, N. (2003). *Breaking the conflict trap: Civil war and development policy*. Washington, D.C.: World Bank and Oxford University Press.

Connolly, M. A., Gayer, M., Ryan, M., Salama, P., Spiegel, P., & Heymann, D. (2004). Communicable diseases in complex emergencies: Impact and challenges. *Lancet, 364,* 1974–1983.

Council on Foreign Relations. (2009). Global economic trends: The business of aid. Transcript document. http://www.cfr.org/publication/20553/global_economic_trends.html. Accessed June 22, 2010.

Curtis, D., & Oversees Development Institute. (2001). Politics and humanitarian aid: Debates, dilemmas, and dissension. Report of a conference organized by Oversees Development Institute, London, February 1, 2001. http://www.odi.org.uk/resources/download/244.pdf. Accessed June 22, 2010.

Data Team. (2016). Ebola in Africa: the end of the tragedy? *The* Economist. January 14, 2016.

Davis, D., & Kuritsky, J. (2002). Violent conflict and its impact on health indicators in Sub-Saharan Africa, 1980–1997. Annual Meeting of the International Studies Association. New Orleans, LA. Cited in Ghobarah et al. (2004).

Donahue, J. M. (1984). Studying the transition to socialism in the Nicaraguan health system. *Medical Anthropology Quarterly, 15*(3), 70–71.

Economist. (2000). NGOs: Sins of the secular missionaries. In R. Mansbach & E. Rhodes (Eds.), Global politics in a changing world (pp. 216–212). Boston: Houghton Mifflin Harcourt Publishing Company.

Economist. (2010). Spoonful of Ingenuity. The Economist. January 7.

Esty, D. C., Goldstone, Goldstone, J. A., Gurr, T. R., Surko, P. T., Unger, A. N., et al. (1995). Working Papers: State Failure Task Force Report. Central Intelligence Agency. http://globalpolicy.gmu.edu/pitf/SFTF%20Phase%20I%20Report.pdf. Accessed February 23, 2010.

Evansa, D. K., Goldstein, M., Popova, A. (2015). Health-care worker mortality and the legacy of the Ebola epidemic. *The Lancet Global Health* 3(8): e439–e440. doi:10.1016/S2214-109X(15)00065-0. Accessed September 13, 2016.

Farmer, P. (1992). *Aids and accusation: Haiti and the geography of blame*. Berkeley, CA: University of California Press.

Farmer, P., & Garrett, L. (2007). From "Marvelous Momentum" to health care for all: Success is possible with the right programs. Foreign Affairs. http://www.foreignaffairs.com/articles/

62458/paul-farmer-and-laurie-garrett/from-marvelous-momentum-to-health-care-for-all-success-is-possib. Accessed February 6, 2009.
Flessa, S., & Marx, M. (2016). Ebola fever epidemic 2014: A call for sustainable health and development policies. *European Journal of Health Economics 17*, 1–4.
Freedom House. (2016). Freedom in the World 2016. Washington DC: Freedom House.
Frontline Health Workers Coalition. (2015). Cost of scaling up the health workforce in Liberia, Sierra Leone, and Guinea amid the Ebola epidemic. Analysis March 2015.
Foreign Policy and Fund for Peace. (2009). The Failed States Index 2009: FAQ & Methodology—How the Failed States Index is Made. Foreign Policy. http://www.foreignpolicy.com/articles/2009/06/22/2009_failed_states_index_faq_methodology. Accessed February 23, 2010.
Fund for Peace. (2007). The fund for peace: Failed states index scores 2007. http://www.fundforpeace.org/web/index.php?option=com_content&task=view&id=229&Itemid=366. Accessed February 23, 2010.
Garfield, R. (1984). Revolution and the Nicaraguan health system. *Medical Anthropology Quarterly, 15*(3), 69–70.
Garrett, L. (2007). The challenge of global health. Foreign Affairs. http://www.foreignaffairs.com/articles/62268/laurie-garrett/the-challenge-of-global-health. Accessed January 12, 2009.
Garret, L. (2015). Can the global public health system learn from its Ebola mistakes? *Foreign Policy*. 8 October 2015.
Gastineau Campos, N., & Farmer, P. (2003). Partners: Discernment and humanitarian efforts in settings of violence. *The Journal of Law, Medicine and Ethics, 31,* 506–515.
Ghobarah, H. A., Huth, P., & Russett, B. (2004). The post-war public health effect of civil conflict. *Socical Science and Medicine, 59,* 869–884.
Goldstone, J., Bates, R., Epstein, D., Gurr, T. R., Lustik, M., Marshall, M., et al. (2010). A global model for forecasting political instability. *American Journal of Political Science, 54*(1), 190–208.
Gurr, T. R., & Harff, B. (1994). *Ethnic conflict in world politics*. Boulder, CO: Westview Press.
Hansch, S., & Burkholder, B. (1996). When chaos reigns: Responding to complex emergencies. *Harvard International Review, 18*(4), 51–54.
International Committee of the Red Cross. (1996). Annex VI: Code of Conduct for the International Red Cross and Red Crescent Movements and NGOs in Disaster Relief. http://www.icrc.org/web/eng/siteeng0.nsf/htmlall/code-of-conduct-290296. Accessed 13 January 2010.
International Committee of the Red Cross. (2010). The future of independent humanitarian action. http://www.icrc.org/Web/Eng/siteeng0.nsf/htmlall/section_debate_on_humanitarian_action?OpenDocument. Accessed January 13, 2010.
Institute for Health Metrics and Evaluation. (2015). Global Burden of Disease. Rwanda country page. http://www.healthdata.org/rwanda. Accessed September 17, 2016.
Institute of Policy Studies. (2002). *Sri Lanka National health expenditures 1990–1999*. Colombo: Institute of Policy Studies.
International Rescue Committee. (2007). Mortality in the Democratic Republic of the Congo: An ongoing crisis. International Rescue Committee New York. http://www.theirc.org/sites/default/files/resource-file/2006-7_congoMortalitySurvey.pdf. Accessed January 26, 2010.
Johnson, S., & Samarasinghe, S. (2008). *Violent conflict, health and well-being*. Paper presented at the "State security, conflict and terrorism" conference, International Centre for Ethnic Studies, Kandy, Sri Lanka, August 11–13, 2007.
Kennedy, D., Holloway, D., Weinthal, E., Falcon, W., Erhlich, P., Naylor, R., et al. (1998). Environmental quality and regional conflict. A report to the Carnegie Commission on Preventing Deadly Conflict. http://www.wilsoncenter.org/subsites/ccpdc/pubs/ken/kenfr.htm. Accessed September 3, 2009.
Kidder, T. (2009). Mountains beyond mountains: The quest of Dr. Paul Farmer, a man who would cure the world. New York: Random House Trade Paperbacks.

Lacey, M., & Thompson, G. (2010). Agreement on effort to help Haiti rebuild. The New York Times. http://www.nytimes.com/2010/01/26/world/americas/26haiti.html. Accessed January 25, 2010.

Lee, J. W., Aylward, B., Hull, H., Batson, A., Birmingham, M., & Lloyd, J. (1997). Reaping the benefits: Getting vaccines to those who need them. In M. Levine, G. Woodrow, J. Kaper, & G. Cobon (Eds.), *New Generation Vaccines* (2nd ed.). New York: Marcel Dekker Inc.

Logie, D., Rowson, M., & Ndagije, F. (2008). Innovations in Rwanda's health system: Looking to the future. *Lancet, 372,* 256–261.

Macrae, J. (1994). Dilemmas of legitimacy, sustainability, and coherence: rehabilitating the health sector. In K. Kumar (Ed.), *Rebuilding societies after civil war: Critical roles for international assistance*. Boulder, CO: Lynne Rienner Publishers.

Matfess, H. (2015). Rwanda and Ethiopia: Developmental authoritarianism and the new politics of african strong men. *African Studies Review, 58*(02), 181–204.

Matul, M., & Tsilikounas, C. (2004). Role of microfinance in the household reconstruction process in Bosnia and Herzegovina. *Journal of International Development, 16,* 429–466.

Messer, E. (1993). Food wars: Hunger as a weapon of war in 1993. In P. Uvin (Ed.), *The hunger report 1993* (pp. 43–70). Langhorne, PA: Routledge.

Ministry of Finance and Economic Planning, Republic of Rwanda. (2000). Rwanda vision 2020. Kigali, July 2000. http://www.gesci.org/assets/files/Rwanda_Vision_2020.pdf. Accessed June 22, 2010.

Mukherjee, J., Colas, M., Farmer, P., Leandre, F., Lambert, W., Raymonville, M., et al. (2003). *Access to antiretroviral treatment and care: The experience of the HIV Equity Initiative, Cange*. Haiti: World Health Organization.

Münkler, H. (2009). The new wars. In R. W. Mansbach & E. Rhodes (Eds.), *Global politics in a changing world* (pp. 38–48). Boston: Houghton Mifflin Harcourt Publishing Company.

Murshed, S. M. (2002). Conflict, civil war and underdevelopment: An introduction. *Journal of Peace Research, 39*(4), 387–393.

New York Times. (2010). Haiti. http://topics.nytimes.com/top/news/international/countriesandterritories/haiti/index.html?scp=1-spot&sq=Haiti%20earthquake&st=cse. Accessed 1 May 2010.

Partners in Health. (2015). "Haiti continues to battle cholera outbreak". http://www.pih.org/blog/haiti-continues-to-battle-cholera-outbreaks. Accessed September 16, 2016.

Partners in Health. (2016a). Haiti country page. http://www.pih.org/country/haiti. Accessed September 16, 2016.

Partners in Health. (2016b). "HIV/AIDS". http://www.pih.org/priority-programs/hiv-aids. Accessed September 16, 2016.

Reyntjens, Filip. "Rwanda: Progress or Powder Keg?" Journal of Democracy 26, no. 3 (2015): 19–33.

Rubardt, M. (1985). A glimpse of health care in turbulent Nicaragua. *American Journal of Nursing, 85*(7), 783–784.

Siedner, M., Gostin, L., Cranmer, H., & Kraemer, J. (2015). Strengthening the detection of and early response to public health emergencies: Lessons from the West Africa Ebola epidemic. *PLoSMed* 12(3), e1001804.

Soeters, R., Habineza, C., & Peerenboom, P. B. (2006). Performance-based financing and changing the district health system: Experience from Rwanda. Bulletin of the World Health Organization *84*(11), 884–889.

Toole, M. J., & Waldman, R. (1993). Refugees and displaced persons: War, hunger, and public health. *JAMA, 250*(5), 600–611.

Trading Economics. (2016). Country indicators. http://www.tradingeconomics.com/. Accessed September 20, 2016.

United Nations. (2016). Global Ebola Response. http://ebolaresponse.un.org/. Accessed September 18, 2016.

United Nations High Commissioner for Refugees. (2009). 2008 global trends: Refugees, asylum-seekers, returnees, internally displaced and stateless persons. United Nations. http://www.unhcr.org/4a375c426.html. Accessed June 22, 2010.

United Nations High Commissioner for Refugees. (2015). UNHCR statistical yearbook 2014. http://www.unhcr.org/en-us/statistics/country/566584fc9/unhcr-statistical-yearbook-2014-14th-edition.html. Accessed September 16, 2016.

United Nations Security Council. (2014). Resolution 2177. 18 September 2014.

Van Hear, N., & Harrell-Bond, B. (1991). Refugees and displaced people: Health issues. In United Nations Institute for Training and Research, *The Challenge of African Disasters* (pp. 60–76). New York: United Nations.

Walton, D. A., Farmer, P. E., Lambert, W., Leandre, F., Koenig, S., & Mukherjee, J. S. (2004). Integrated HIV prevention and care strengthens primary health care: Lessons from Rural Haiti. *Journal of Public Health Policy, 25*(2), 137–158.

Williams, H. (1984). An uncertain prognosis: some factors that may limit future progress in Nicaraguan health care system. Medical Anthropology Quarterly. *15*(3), 72–73.

World Bank. (2014). *The economic impact of the 2014 Ebola epidemic: Short and medium term estimates for Guinea, Liberia, and Sierra Leone*. New York: World Bank.

World Bank. (2015). Ebola: Most African Countries avoid major economic loss but impact on Guinea, Liberia, Sierra Leone Remains Crippling. 20 January 2015. http://www.worldbank.org/en/news/press-release/2015/01/20/ebola-most-african-countries-avoid-major-economic-loss-but-impact-on-guinea-liberia-sierra-leone-remains-crippling. Accessed September 13, 2015.

World Bank. (2016a). World Development Indicators. http://databank.worldbank.org/data/home.aspx Accessed September 15, 2016.

World Bank. (2016b). Doing business 2016: Measuring regulatory quality and efficiency. Washington, D.C.: World Bank Group.

World Health Organization. (2009a). 2009 state of the world's vaccines and immunizations (3rd ed.). http://whqlibdoc.who.int/publications/2009/9789241563864_eng.pdf. Accessed June 6, 2010.

World Health Organization. (2009b) Global health observatory. http://apps.who.int/ghodata/. Accessed March 2, 2010.

World Health Organization. (2015a). One year into the Ebola epidemic. January 2015. WHO: Geneva.

World Health Organization (2015b). Health worker Ebola infections in Guinea, Liberia and Sierra Leone. Preliminary report 21 May 2015. http://apps.who.int/iris/bitstream/10665/171823/1/WHO_EVD_SDS_REPORT_2015.1_eng.pdf?ua=1&ua=1. Accessed September 13, 2016.

World Health Organization. (2016). Global health observatory. http://apps.who.int/gho/data/view.main.80200. Accessed September 16, 2016.

World Health Organization. (2016a). *WHO situation report: Ebola Virus disease, 10 June 2016.* http://apps.who.int/iris/bitstream/10665/208883/1/ebolasitrep_10Jun2016_eng.pdf?ua=1. Accessed September 17, 2016.

World Health Organization. (2016b). *WHO situation report: Ebola Virus disease, 30 March 2016.* http://apps.who.int/ebola/current-situation/ebola-situation-report-30-march-2016. Accessed September 17, 2016.

World Health Organization. (2016c). *Ebola virus disease*. http://www.who.int/ebola/en/. Accessed September 13, 2016.

Zartman, I. W. (1995). Introduction: Posing the problem of state collapse. In Zartman (ed.), *Collapsed States: The disintegration and restoration of legitimate authority.* Boulder: Lynne Rienner Publishers.

Chapter 6
Public Private Partnerships and Health

Abstract There is an increasing amount of interaction between the public and private sectors in economic and human development. The private sector is involved in areas previously the domain of public sector actors and IGOs, through avenues that include charitable contributions and partnerships with public agencies. As a result, the number of global public-private partnerships (GPPP) operating in global health and development is growing. Such partnerships can result in innovative, multi-sectoral strategies that redress a dearth of technological and fiscal resources. Although public and private actors have tried to create common operational structures and principles, these frameworks remain fragmented. Positive outcomes of this trend towards public-private partnerships include money available to global health projects has quadrupled since 1990, and the availability of certain drugs and vaccinations in the developing world increased. But the growth of GPPPs has also given private corporations considerable power in formulating global health policy. Evaluation of the short- and long-term impacts of these partnerships is only now beginning in earnest. Much remains to be seen as to the ultimate gains and losses associated with those partnerships.

We saw in the previous chapters that improving human health and development is a process that involves multiple sectors and actors working across diverse scales. The success of the EPI program, for example, entailed a global strategy that drew together public and private actors from donor and recipient nations, and a diversity of skill sets and workers at international, national, and community levels. The failures of the EPI program came from a breakdown in local and national institutions and political will, and conflicting international pressures. A consistent idea within our case studies is that collaboration can yield better results than an effort by a singular entity, but that coordination of multiple actors is challenging. The previous chapters also showed an evolution of actors involved in development with a sea

In a technical sense, private corporations are NGOs. A common albeit erroneous perception is that NGOs all function on a not-for-profit basis. Multi-national or trans-national corporations are often classified in a separate category by development agencies. I therefore refer to NGOs and private corporations separately.

S.A. Johnson, *Challenges in Health and Development*,
DOI 10.1007/978-3-319-53204-2_6

change moving development out of the sphere of nation-states and multilateral institutions into one that includes NGOs, civil society and private corporations. The global development enterprise now consists of these multiple actors, and is witnessing a new configuration of relationships among these groups with the rise of public-private partnerships. This evolution and the challenges inherent within clearly manifest in international health. In 1990, approximately US$5.6 billion was invested in global public health; two-thirds of this came from government funds (Economist 2010). By 2015, development assistance for global health grew to $36.4 billion (Institute for Health Metrics and Evaluation 2015, pg. 9). Non-governmental actors provided $9.6 billion in funding with the Gates Foundation, Gavi and the Global Fund to Fight HIV/AIDS Malaria and Tuberculosis as major contributors (IHME 2016). The private sphere had indeed become an important player.

There is no single definitive model of a global public-private partnership (GPPP) in health. Public and private actors have different motives for involvement in each partnership. The public sector, including donor/recipient governments and IGOs such as the UN, is motivated by the desire to impact human health and development by targeting the most important causes of morbidity and mortality. The stakeholders for public endeavors are those who would potentially realize improved health either directly vis-à-vis service or indirectly through broader societal improvements in health and the impacts such improvements have on disease prevalence/incidence, epidemiological shifts, human capital, etc. The private sector ultimately exists to make a profit that will be returned to company principals, projects or shareholders. In order for there to be successful public-private partnerships, each side has to provide an incentive for the other party or players to enter into the partnership. All sides should, in theory, offer incentives and all sides should realize advantageous outcomes from the partnership.

In this chapter, we will define GPPPs as they pertain to health, examine the advantages and disadvantages associated with such arrangements, and look at the methods these partnerships use to increase access to essential drugs and spur investment in research and development that is relevant to health in the Global South. Goal 17 of the SDGS focused on building, strengthening and monitoring these partnerships. Up to this juncture, this book has addressed actions in both health and development based on the notion that each is an important factor that influences the other. The growth and impact of public-private partnerships across diverse sectors is a relatively new focus for scholarship that could easily encompass one or more books. Because of this, the remainder of this chapter will focus on public-private partnerships that target health.

6.1 Global Public-Private Partnerships

Public-private partnerships come in many forms, the most common of which is that of donor and recipient. In addition, there are a growing number of complex structured relationships, foundations, and emerging networks that serve as an interface for private sector and public sector actors (Buse and Walt 2000a). The primary component of any such relationship is that the partnership structures reciprocal rights and obligations, and entails clearly articulated objectives that will be of benefit to all of the parties involved (Buse and Walt 2000a). In health and development, many of these partnerships focus on activities to increase access to drugs to treat infectious disease and to develop vaccinations to prevent diseases. We will use the definition of GPPPs developed by Buse and Walt (2000a, pg. 550) to explore the particular form such partnerships take for global health. They define a GPPP as "… a collaborative relationship which transcends national boundaries and brings together at least three parties, among them a corporation (and/or industry association) and an intergovernmental organization, so as to achieve a shared health-creating goal on the basis of a mutually agreed division of labor."

Public-private partnerships are not a new phenomenon. However, the recent growth in the number and breadth of these partnerships and the fact that nation-states and IGOs are harnessing public-private partnerships to impact spheres that were once the sole domain of governmental actors warrants attention. Recall, for instance, that the Rockefeller Foundation was established through a public legislative act and a private endowment. The Rockefeller Foundation went on to become a leading proponent of research into and control of tropical disease, and continues to engage in global health projects to this day. But internationally, interest in tropical medicine waxed and waned. In the early days of the Rockefeller Foundation, partnerships were structured largely in terms of charitable work.

A later example of this type of GPPP is seen in the Mectizan® Donation Program that was established in 1987 as a partnership to provide treatment for onchocerciasis (River Blindness) to nations where this disease is endemic (Buse and Walt 2000a; Mectizan® Donation Program 2009). This is a partnership between Merck & Co., the WHO, the World Bank, the Task Force for Global Health, and numerous NGOs and national governments. Under this program, Merck & Co. committed to donating the drug Mectizan® to all countries in which onchocerciasis is present, for as long as necessary until the disease is controlled (Mectizan® Donation Program 2009). This is the longest continuing drug donation program operating globally. The program was expanded in 1998 to include treating lymphatic filariasis in countries where the disease co-exists with onchocerciasis. This expansion was made possible through the discovery that filariasis could be treated with the drug combination of Mectizan® and albendazole, and a donation of albendazole from GlaxoSmithKline (Mectizan® Donation Program 2009). To date, more than 300 million treatments for onchocerciasis have been made available (Mectizan® Donation Program 2009).

In the years following World War II, development was dominated by nation-states and IGOs, with openings for private sector engagement vis-à-vis encouraging capital investment to assist in the prospect of macro-economic growth. The health sector was tended to largely by donor governments and IGOs, with a modest degree of interaction with the private sector such as was seen in developing the EPI program. A renewed interest in public-private partnerships took hold in the 1980s and gained momentum during the ensuing three decades due to a confluence of socio-economic and political factors, including the influence of neoliberal economic philosophy that touted the wonders of private industry and free market (See Chap. 2). Buse and Walt (2000a) note that the World Bank issued its first Operational Policy Note on NGOs in 1981, and established an NGO-World Bank committee in 1982. By 1998, 15% of the World Bank's development assistance was administered through NGOs (Buse and Walt 2000a).

In terms of the health sector, Chap. 2 showed us that there were contradictory international forces at play during the 1980s and 1990s. One force espoused the necessity of public investment in primary health care as a public good; the other placed free-market ideals at the fore and asked for decentralization and privatization in health care financing and provision. The results of both programs were mixed. However, the failure of structural adjustment programs to protect the health of the most vulnerable populations, coupled with the inequity in health access and health outcomes associated with the health system reforms highlighted the fact that the private sphere, and market forces, could not alone address population health needs. Health care itself was often cited as a primary (and some would argue unique) realm of market failures, thereby justifying public intervention in health (Bodenheimer and Grumbach 2008).

By the late 1980s, private sector's responsibilities evolved and there was more importance placed on the triple bottom line. Social responsibility considered social and ecological impacts of corporations to be of equal import to economic growth and/or sustainability. Companies that engaged in socially-responsible actions or public philanthropy could gain a slight advantage in terms of public perception, and perhaps future sustainability, over those companies that did not engage in such actions. The importance of social responsibility grew out of the paradigm of sustainable development presented in the 1987 report from the World Commission on Environment and Development which held that economic, social and ecological spheres were of equal importance in building sustainable societies and a sustainable planet (World Commission on Environment and Development 1987).

Concurrently, actors in the public sphere were struggling to maintain legitimacy (Buse and Walt 2000a; Mathews 2009; Simmons 2009). The end of the Cold War opened up opportunities for global collaboration among IGOs that had not previously been possible due to the ideological stand-off between the West and East. But the post Cold War world was a vastly different landscape than had been envisioned when the respective charters of the UN and the WHO were written. Traditional interstate warfare had transmogrified into intrastate wars. Environmental degradation, population movement, global debt, and rapid transit complicated the various avenues to impact health and human welfare. The IGOs were strapped, and questions arose as to whether or not their institutional structures allowed for the flexibility necessary to address the new world order. There was also increasing pressure for organizational transparency and calls for democratic representation across the Global North and South (Mathews 2009; Simmons 2009). Critics of the UN and its various programs questioned these agencies' competencies to carry out their respective missions (Buse and Walt 2000a).

This state of affairs coincided with a rise in the number of INGOs and the growth of multinational corporations operating in areas both outside of the purview of nation-states and in areas once limited to the nation-state. But private sector growth was not without backlash. NGOs and private corporations were criticized for operating outside of the bounds of domestic law, usurping sovereignty and forsaking public good for private gain and profit (Mathews 2009; Simmons 2009). Even though the UN's capabilities and structures were questioned, it was still considered to have greater neutrality and moral authority than any private actor.

Together, these global forces created an environment in which the public and private sectors needed each other. The idea of social responsibility infiltrated multiple industries, including the pharmaceutical industry. The public sector had something of value to the private sector… social legitimacy as well as a venue for products and a venue to publicize both goods and actions. The private sector has greater resources and specialized expertise perceived to be lacking in the public sphere. The recognition of shared advantages, if not shared interests, helped to foster public-private partnerships in the health arena.

One of the most important foci of partnerships developed since the 1990s is the provision of drugs to lower income or less developed countries. Although there were successful efforts to direct private expertise and capital into aspects of economic and human development through such strategies as FDI, the health sector had long been at a disadvantage in terms of attracting investment through the traditional market-oriented schemes. This was, in part, due to the dominant model that placed economic development at the fore of development strategies, with health viewed as a fortunate trickle-down from economic growth. This neglect also related to market mechanisms and profit motivation. Developed countries had the economic resources to continue investing in inputs to good health and a consumer base to support such endeavors. These countries experienced both demographic and epidemiological shifts such that the illnesses that accounted for the greatest burden of disease in the high income countries were different than those of concern in the middle and low income countries.

Low income countries, on the other hand, could not cover basic necessities or meet minimal health standards, let alone pay for expensive health inputs or create a large enough market demand for these inputs such that the cost point would decrease. Only 10% of global health care expenditures are for health issues that account for 90% of the global burden of disease (Shapiro and Meslin 2001). This imbalance was created because the high global disease burden was found in the developing world and consisted of diseases largely considered controlled in the developed world (Shapiro and Meslin 2001). The problems associated with drug availability in developing countries include the following: the nations' and individual consumers' inability to pay for costly drugs, thereby rendering sales of drugs and development of the same in developing countries not profitable for drug-makers; gaps in availability of less-expensive, generic drugs to treat diseases and/or symptoms of diseases as well as side-effects of other drugs; and differences between the drugs deemed necessary in the face of new health challenges and the drugs contained in the WHO Essential Drug List (UNAIDS 1998).

HIV/AIDS, tuberculosis and malaria continue to dominate the causes of death for low and middle income countries (Lopez et al. 2006). These are conditions which need to be addressed through both prevention *and* treatment. Perinatal conditions and diarrheal disease are also prominent in the developing world, but not in the developed world. Pharmaceutical treatment for HIV, TB, malaria, and different enteric infections, as well as vaccinations for vaccine-preventable diseases are obvious interventions to address the high burden of disease. Improved environmental sanitation, nutrition, general prevention campaigns and increased access to primary care are also important, but without medications to arrest the development of the negative sequelae of the aforementioned diseases, or cure TB and malaria, the health toll will continue to be high. Access to vaccinations and medications are therefore of pre-eminent concern. And the dominant actors in supplying these goods are private pharmaceutical corporations, corporations that had little economic incentive to invest in treatments for a low-return market. When the public sector recognized that the private sector was extremely important in terms of drug and vaccine development, the global community's strategies for improving health changed (Buse and Walt 2000a). The private sector had something that the public sector wanted and so the public sector needed to better motivate and involve the private sector in global health.

In terms of collaboration in the health arena, the notion that population health resulted from multiple inputs across a variety of sectors presented ample cause and opportunities for actors from public and private spheres to come together. The private sector, specifically pharmaceutical companies, recognized that partnership opportunities could be beneficial in that such partnerships could improve the corporation's public image at a relatively low cost.

At the end of the 1990s, there was a call for reform across public and private agencies. UN Secretary-General Kofi Annan undertook institutional reform within the United Nations and tried to act upon the ideals of integrating economic, social and ecological sectors (Buse and Walt 2000a). Mr. Annan approached the International Chamber of Commerce (ICC) to encourage greater partnering between UN agencies and the private sector through a global compact (Buse and Walt 2000a). The ICC agreed in principle so long as any compact addressed the need of the private sector to realize a profit (Buse and Walt 2000a). The initiative became a reality in July 2000, with the launch of the UN Global Compact. The compact called upon the private sector to act in a socially and environmentally responsible way, offered a policy framework to harness public and private actors to work together for global sustainable development, and provided ten operating principles (UN Global Compact Office 2008). The compact encapsulated the ideal of corporations operating with the triple-bottom line of economic, social and environmental goods. Participation in and compliance with the compact were and remain voluntary. Incentives for private sector participation included access to UN networks, knowledge-sharing networks and strategic/technical toolkits (UN Global Compact 0ffice 2008). The Global Compact established an operating framework for public-private engagement at the global level, with its mission focused on the broad ideals of sustainable human development. Both the MDGs and SDGs call for action from public and private actors in order to address the global development agenda.

The WHO put together a Working Group to define principles and an operating framework for public-private partnerships. The core ethical principles included beneficence, non-maleficence, autonomy, and equity (Buse and Walt 2000a). These are the same ethical principles which underpin the field of medicine. In terms of the framework for WHO partnerships, the Working Group identified the need to maintain WHO's reputation as an impartial health authority and to evaluate the appropriateness of partnership activities as important concerns, and proposed procedures to help mitigate potential conflicts of interest (Buse and Walt 2000a). The WHO draft guidelines for collaboration included the provision that public-private partnerships be subject to review by the WHO Ethics Committee and a Committee on Public Sector Collaboration (WHO 1999).

The growth of GPPPs addressing health covered numerous issues and problems. Partnerships coalesced around the topics of HIV/AIDS, malaria, tuberculosis, and **neglected tropical diseases**. This latter topic included a diverse array of illnesses that affect an estimated one billion people, primarily those living in poverty in the most isolated or unempowered pockets of the world (WHO 2010). The partnerships sought to address both access to drug therapy, and to instill interest in investment in research and development targeting tropical disease. Such activity entailed clinical trials to develop more effective, efficient and/or cost effective therapies, in the hope of making such therapies accessible to low income countries.

6.1.1 GPPPs, Global Research and Clinical Trials

Attendant to the rise of GPPPs has been a dramatic increase in research studies conducted in developing countries during the past decade. Between 1998 and 2008, pharmaceutical companies moved approximately half of their clinical trials to developing countries (Loewenberg 2008). Concurrently, there was a rise in out-sourcing of clinical trials to middlemen in countries such as Indonesia, Thailand, and India (Loewenberg 2008). The causes of the shift in the former are uncertain, but may include a decrease in governmental funding for medical research. Costs for conducting research and development in developing countries can be as much as 60% lower than the costs in developed countries thereby providing economic motivation for the move (Nundy and Gulhati 2005). Rising concern for emerging infections such as HIV/AIDS that impact the health of both the developed and developing world, may also have contributed to the growing interest and investment in clinical research in the Global South (Loewenberg 2008). One could also argue that the success of GPPPs contributed to this shift. The increase in middlemen involved in research were due to market forces; a growing demand for research in developing countries and shifting price points for the services provided greater cost efficiencies and motivation for out-sourcing.

It is difficult to ascertain whether the globalization of clinical trials is bringing about more harm than good in economic and social terms (Dept. of Health and Human Services 2001; Glickman et al. 2009; Loewenberg 2008; Lurie and Wolfe 1997; Shapiro and Meslin 2001). The conduct of clinical trials is guided by the ethical principles contained within the Declaration of Helsinki.[1] Adherence to these principles is mandatory in countries with regulatory agencies that have adopted this code, and voluntary where such regulation does not exist.

The increase of health studies in developing countries raised important issues for GPPPs to address, including ethical obligations associated with such research. The main concerns surrounding such trials are that the benefits may not accrue to the population from which test subjects are drawn, that there are double standards in terms of ethics and accountability for trials in the developed versus developing world, and that subjects in low income countries may be exploited because of their poverty (Dept. of Health and Human Services 2001; Glickman et al. 2009; Loewenberg 2008; Lurie and Wolfe 1997; Shapiro and Meslin 2001).

Concern about the dual standard of trials conducted in developed and developing countries includes disquiet over differential standards of review. While it is common practice, indeed a legal requirement, in developed countries for proposed clinical trials to undergo one (or several) ethical reviews, the *Journal of Medical Ethics* found that one quarter of the clinical trials in developing countries received no form of local review (Loewenberg 2008). Other trials operate without any regulatory approval (Nundy and Gulhati 2005). Further, trials in countries overseas may be understaffed or may utilize staff who are not appropriately trained to monitor the trials adequately or to uphold human subject protections (Dept. of Health and Human Services 2001; Nundy and Gulhati 2005).

The dual standard is especially visible in debates surrounding standards related to the use of **placebo-**versus **equivalency-studies**. A placebo is an inert medication. In a placebo study, a portion of the study subjects would receive the medication under investigation and the other portion would receive a placebo in order to determine the effectiveness of the new drug. An equivalency study tests the experimental medication against the existing standard of care. In other words, if a new antiretroviral agent is being tested, it should be tested against the existing available drug or drug regimen. In clinical trials, the ethical obligation of those conducting research is to test the effectiveness of the new drug/regimen against the available standard of care. Some argue that the standard of care in a developing country is no care at all, justifying use of a placebo, even though medication for the disease of interest is used as a standard in the developed world (Dept. of Health and Human Services 2001; Lurie and Wolfe 1997; Shapiro and Meslin 2001). The cost incentive for placebo studies is high in that they are more cost-efficient, are generally of shorter duration, and typically require fewer subjects than do equivalency studies (Dept. of Health and Human Services 2001; Lurie and Wolfe 1997). Revisions to the Declaration of Helsinki state that new methods should be treated against the best current available methods, regardless of whether or not that method is typically available in the country where the study is being conducted. There may

[1]The Declaration of Helsiki is available on-line at http://www.wma.net/en/30publications/10policies/b3/index.html.

be special circumstances that warrant exceptions to this ideal, specifically if the condition being studied is not life threatening (Shapiro and Meslin 2001).

Other ethical concerns with the globalization of clinical trials include issues of trial transparency and of informed consent, such as whether or not written informed consent is viable where functional literacy is low. The trials themselves may introduce economic distortion by providing financial incentives to participants. In some trials, the medications provided to study subjects are worth more than the study subject's annual salary (Nundy and Gulhati 2005). While this may be financially beneficial to the study subject, such actions may exploit those living in poverty and distort the idea of informed consent.

Ethical considerations associated with clinical trials extend into the post-trial period. One issue is whether or not the medication supplied during the trial will continue to be available to study subjects or to the general population at the conclusion of the trial (Nundy and Gulhati 2005; Shapiro and Meslin 2001). Should a medication in a trial prove successful, a further ethical consideration is whether or not that medication will be available at an affordable price within the study country (Buse and Walt 2000a; Nundy and Gulhati 2005). Public and private debate of these ethical concerns will likely continue.

6.2 Methods of the GPPPs

The GPPPs employ a variety of methods to increase access to, affordability of, and innovation in drug regimens, vaccinations and treatment. These methods include utilizing charitable donations, pricing and regulatory mechanisms, and market-based initiatives. Of the aforementioned methods, charitable donations are the most traditional and straightforward method. Such donations include funding for partnership activities, donations for research, drug procurement and distribution, and funding for programming. The Bill & Melinda Gates Foundation is an example of a private philanthropic organization that donates for all of the aforementioned purposes. Drug donations are another example of this method. We saw, for instance, that Merck & Co. committed to donating Mectizan® until onchoceriasis is eliminated in endemic nations. Critics of this method argue that charitable contributions provide positive outcomes to private donor companies in terms of public relations but at the public's expense. For example, some pharmaceutical companies are located in nations that provide tax write-offs for a portion of the drugs donated to international campaigns (Buse and Walt 2000b). Thus, the donation may partially be underwritten by public revenues.

Tiered pricing, loosening patent restrictions and forced licensing are examples of pricing and regulatory mechanisms utilized to increase access to necessary drugs, with varying degrees of success. One example of partnerships utilizing tiered-pricing is seen in the Accelerating Access Initiative (AAI). In the 1990s, UNAIDS and the WHO, among other IGOs, began pressuring the private sphere for differential pricing of essential drugs and those used in the treatment of HIV and its related complications (UNAIDS 2008). Differential pricing entails a floating fee scale, so that lower income countries pay a lower price for medications than do those in higher income countries that are perceived to be better able to afford higher prices. Such pricing results in a cross-subsidy. These efforts yielded results in 2000 with a commitment to tiered-pricing from five pharmaceutical companies. Recipient governments would reciprocate for the tiered-pricing by absorbing the purchasing cost (pricing to be negotiated between each recipient country and company) and (re) enforcing industry patent protection (UNAIDS 2008). As a result of this agreement, drug prices in the 39 targeted nations dropped by approximately two-thirds, but the reception to AAI was mixed with several ministries of health accusing UNAIDS of closed-door negotiations (UNAIDS 2008). UN agencies continued to negotiate with the pharmaceutical industry for accelerated price reduction and inclusion of 'qualified' NGOs and private companies as beneficiaries of the tiered-pricing in countries where these institutions would be able to expand access to care in targeted communities (UNAIDS 2008). The manufacture of generic drugs to further reduce costs, and the loosening of patent restrictions were also subjects of negotiation.

Generic drugs posed a special promise to the health sector, and a special challenge to the private sector. Domestic and international law provides a period of exclusivity for the developer of a new drug—a temporary monopoly—in order to allow the manufacturer to recoup the high costs of research and development. Once the patent expires, the laws of free market take over and other drug manufacturers can recreate the formulation, which can be sold at a much lower cost since the new manufacturer need not cover the costs of initial research and development. Developing nations with domestic drug-manufacturing capabilities and other advocates argued that the needs of public health outweighed the needs of drug makers to protect their patents, and argued that international patents should be broken when the health need was great. This would allow countries to either produce generic versions in violation of patents, or to import generic versions manufactured in other countries. The private industry acted to protect its interests in maintaining patent exclusivity while health and social justice advocates pushed for loosening patent restrictions to provide medicines to save lives. The World Trade Organization's (WTO's) Trade-Related Aspects of Intellectual Property Rights (TRIPS), signed in 1994, protected the international patent rights of the private sector in countries that were members of the WTO, and international law appeared to side with the pharmaceutical industry.

The price difference between generic drugs and non-generic drugs can be quite large. For example, when legal generic antiretrovirals for HIV treatment became available in 2000, the price of treatment dropped from around US$1200 per person per year to about US$350 (UNAIDS 2008). The implications for public health and affordability are clear. In May 2001 the World Health Assembly resolved to increase the availability of generic drugs and to evaluate the impact of TRIPS on access to drugs and, by extension, health. The result of this, and mounting international pressure, was that the WTO passed the Doha Declaration in November, 2001, at the Fourth Ministerial Conference in Doha, Qatar. The Doha Declaration stated that members of the WTO could issue compulsory licensing for the manufacture of certain medications, including those used for HIV/AIDS, tuberculosis and malaria, should a public health emergency exist. In other words, countries with a public health crisis could override international patent protection and authorize the manufacture of medications.

There are numerous reasons for the successful passage of the Doha concession, including actions taken by South Africa, Brazil and Thailand to manufacture generics leading up to the Doha conference (UNAIDS 2008; Wilson et al. 1999). All three nation-states possessed domestic drug-manufacturing capabilities and had begun to manufacture generic versions of patent-protected antiretrovirals in order to provide/increase access to these life-saving drugs through price reduction. Domestic manufacturing of generic antiretrovirals in Brazil cut prices by 70% over the course of four years. During that same time, hospital admissions for HIV-related complications dropped by 80%, creating a strong argument for the benefit of public health over guarantees of high profits (UNAIDS 2008). Although implementation of the Doha provision remains contentious, the threat of forced licensing now enshrined in WTO doctrine, might give pharmaceutical companies additional motivation to participate in pricing structures and other arrangements in which they maintain a locus of control, as well as to loosen patent restrictions or share patents (Associated Press 2007; Avert 2010).

Market-based mechanisms seek to manipulate supply and demand in such a way as to decrease price-points for medications, increase spending efficiencies, and offset risks involved in R&D in order to decrease price points for new therapies. Many of the aforementioned methods intersect with market and the idea of manipulating supply and demand. For example, associations such as GAVI, the Global Fund and various other partnerships/NGOs attempt to make spending on medication more efficient by aggregating demand. In so doing, suppliers are encouraged to cut costs through the promise of a secure, larger-scale market than could be guaranteed through any single purchase by an institution or low-income nation-state. Further, the aggregation of demand incentivizes suppliers to develop new formulations that are as efficient in terms of health impacts, but that can be delivered at a lower cost vis-à-vis the formulation itself, a regimen that requires smaller doses/fewer medications, or a regimen with fewer side effects that will thereby decrease the amount of money a purchaser needs to spend on medications to manage a disease in its entirety. At the same time, such increased efficiencies and lower costs can drive up demand so suppliers can realize higher income, albeit through lower price point, because of increased demand and sales.

Advanced market commitments are another avenue to manipulate market forces in order to incentivize the development of medications and vaccines. In these operations, funding organizations subsidize the initial purchase of a new vaccine/drug for neglected diseases with a proviso that the developing company agrees to continue selling the vaccines at a low cost in the future (Economist 2010). Thus, drug developers gain assurance that they will recoup development costs and potentially make a profit. Similar incentives are found in product development partnerships between the public and private spheres. The idea is that the partners share the costs and risks of developing new products. This is especially important when one considers the high failure rate of drug and vaccine development, and the long period of time necessary to bring a new agent from the lab, to animal trials and lastly, to human trials. Public sector investment helps offset not only financial costs but also opportunity costs with the expected gain being new tools to combat disease at potentially more affordable prices than would otherwise be available (Buse and Walt 2000a).

6.3 Examples of Recent GPPPs

The Joint United Nations Program on HIV/AIDS (UNAIDS) was one of the early proponents of public-private partnerships. UNAIDS itself represented a unique arrangement of envoys across diverse UN bodies organized to address a singular threat to global health and development: HIV/AIDS. The UN Economic and Social Council formed UNAIDS in 1994 because the global response to HIV/AIDS necessitated coordinated response across multiple sectors— a response that could not be achieved with compartmentalized activities and strategies. UNAIDS was formed to coordinate responses across the UNDP, UNICEF, United Nations Population Fund (UNFPA), WHO, UNESCO, and the World Bank (UNAIDS 2010). The organization and Program Coordinating Board (PCB) include representatives from member states, from multiple UN agencies, and from non-governmental organizations representing individuals impacted by the disease (UNAIDS 2009).

Textbox 6.1 UNAIDS Objectives (ECOSOC Resolution 1994/24):

*To provide global leadership in response to the epidemic.

*To achieve and promote global consensus on policy and program approaches.

*To strengthen the capacity to monitor trends and ensure that appropriate and effective policies and strategies are implemented at country level.

*To strengthen the capacity of national governments to develop comprehensive national strategies and implement effective HIV/AIDS activities.

*To promote broad-based political and social mobilization to prevent and respond to HIV/AIDS.

*To advocate greater political commitment at global and country levels including the mobilization and allocation of adequate resources.

Source: UNAIDS. (2010). *The Governance Handbook*. pg. 2.

UNAIDS sought corporate funding and partners for involvement in UNAIDS activities. An early UNAIDS partnership was the HIV Drug Access Initiative (Bridging the Gap) initiated in November, 1997 in order to make HIV/AIDS treatment-related drugs more accessible and affordable to developing countries (Buse and Walt 2000a; UNAIDS 1998). This initiative entailed a two year pilot project in four developing countries (Chile, Côte d'Ivoire, Uganda and Vietnam) with dual goals of improving health infrastructure to ensure successful distribution of HIV/AIDS drugs and improving availability of drugs for HIV/AIDS through discounting and subsidizing drug purchases (UNAIDS 1998). The initial partners included five pharmaceutical companies and the participating nation-states. Each participating nation formed an advisory board under the Ministry of Health (UNAIDS 1998). The pharmaceutical company partners established and funded a non-profit company to act as a clearing house for drug orders (Buse and Walt 2000a). UNAIDS provided US$1 million for oversight, and further asked each partner company to donate $25,000 in each pilot country to subsidize the purchase of AIDS drugs (Buse and Walt 2000a).

Another important partnership, the Global Fund to Fight AIDS, Tuberculosis, and Malaria Tuberculosis and Malaria (Global Fund), formed in 2002. The impetus for this partnership included growing awareness of the interaction of unresolved health crises and economic growth, the challenges HIV/AIDS presented to worldwide development, the commonality of constraints the developing world faced in any effort to improve population health, and the recognition that detriments to health and development in one geographic area could not easily be contained to one area in the highly globalized society of the 21st century. While the Global Fund was officially established in 2002, the seeds of its creation began several years earlier. We saw in Chapter Two that in January, 2000, the UN Security Council for the first time addressed a disease, HIV/AIDS, as a primary threat to global development and security. This led to a follow-up UN Security Council session that focused on prevention of HIV among peacekeepers and those in military services, a concern with the growing deployment of both around the world (UNAIDS 2008). The United States designated AIDS a threat to national security in 2000, and President Bill Clinton signed an executive order to help make AIDS-related drugs and technologies more accessible and affordable in Africa (UNAIDS 2008). In June, 2001, the United Nations General Assembly Special Session (UNGASS) was held to address HIV/AIDS and to obtain international agreement on the significance of this health threat. A number of international goals targeting health, specifically maternal-child care, HIV/AIDS and malaria, were also incorporated into the Millennium Development Goals.

The stage was set for expanding global resources and collaboration directed toward health and, through health, improving human and economic development and global security. At the 13th International AIDS Conference in Durban in 2000, Dr. Peter Piot, executive director of UNAIDS, called for a massive expansion of international funding to combat AIDS in Africa, and called for wealthy nations to cancel the debt of the hardest hit African nations. He stated that US$3 billion was necessary for this effort—an amount more than ten times larger than the funding that was then being directed towards all of Africa (UNAIDS 2008). Dr. Piot said,

"We need billions, not millions, to fight AIDS in this world. We can't fight an epidemic of this magnitude with peanuts." (UNAIDS 2008: 111) That same year, the G8 acknowledged that disease was linked to poverty and played a central role in economic development, and announced a plan to combat infectious disease (UNAIDS 2008). With the commitment of several donor nations to move forward, participants agreed that efforts would target HIV/AIDS, malaria and tuberculosis due to the high health burden these diseases posed to the developing world. In April, 2001, parties agreed that there would become a single global fund to fight HIV and other diseases. So important was the task at hand that donations did not only come from the high income nations; a number of developing countries also pledged to contribute money to the fund. Further, a number of developing nations pledged to dedicate 15% of their budget to the health sector (UNAIDS 2008). In March, 2002, this became the Global Fund.

The Global Fund's membership consists of representatives from donor and recipient governments, international financial organizations, civil society and the private corporate sector. The Global Fund sponsors various health programs and harnesses public-partnerships in a multiplicity of settings. As of 2010, the Global Fund had awarded more than US$19 billion in grants (Global Fund 2010). One of the Global Fund's programs is the Affordable Medicines Facility—Malaria (AMFm) that seeks to roll-out anti-malarial medication in 2010 (Economist 2010). Under this facility, the Global Fund will spend US$216 million over the course of two years to subsidize a bulk purchase of Artemisinin Combination Therapy (ACT) for wholesale buyers who will then resell the medication at a reduced cost to ten countries most in need (Economist 2010). The idea is to reduce the cost of ACT treatment from US$10 to between 20 and 50 cents while utilizing market mechanisms to increase demand of this treatment such that economies of scale are achieved and prices drop (Economist 2010). The Global Fund will spend an additional US$127 million on training and marketing to support this effort.

Another example of public-private partnerships is the Global Alliance for Vaccines and Immunization (GAVI). This GPPP includes members from nations in the developed and developing world, the WHO, UNICEF, World Bank, the Bill & Melinda Gates Foundation, representatives of civil society, vaccine manufactures, and public health and research institutions (GAVI Secretariat 2006). The objectives of this alliance include strengthening national health systems to deliver vaccinations and health care, expanding access to vaccinations, and building sustainability of systems and programs (GAVI Secretariat 2006). In an innovative strategy, GAVI raised US$1 billion in short-term financing by issuing bonds backed by donor pledges of future aid (GAVI Secretariat 2006). The financial instruments were attractive to investors because in some cases they offered higher earnings on bond than regular interest rates and were backed by donor nations' aid pledges (GAVI Alliance 2010; Samarasinghe 2010). The monies raised will be used for bulk purchasing of vaccines, again with an idea to impact economies of scale.

6.4 Pros and Cons of GPPPs

Numerous benefits derive from GPPPs for population health, the clearest of which is that there are increased resources available for global public health activities. In terms of funding, nearly four times the amount of money that was available in 1990 is now directed towards global health endeavors (Economist 2010). The number of people in need of medical treatment who are able to access such care is rising, although a large gap between need and provision remains. An estimated ¾ of the children who are taking AIDS-related medications are able to access this supply because of the GAVI and Global Fund initiatives (Economist 2010). In 2003, an estimated 5,700,000 people needed access to antiretroviral therapy in Sub-Saharan Africa, but such therapy was available to only 2%, with a mere 100,000 people receiving the drug regimen. By 2007, the number of people in need had risen to 7,000,000, but coverage was estimated to have increased to 30% with approximately 2,000,000 people on ART (WHO 2010).

In addition to increasing access to care, the GPPPs have also helped build national capacity. In 2000, the Bill & Melinda Gates Foundation, Merck & Co., Bristol-Myers Squibb and the Harvard AIDS Institution launched an HIV treatment initiative in collaboration with the Ministry of Health in Botswana. The goal of this initiative was to improve access to anti-retroviral therapies and treatment for opportunistic infections. To this end, Merck & Co agreed to donate ART, Bristol-Myers Squibb agreed to discount drugs used in HIV management, the Gates Foundation agreed to subsidize the purchase of medication, and Harvard would design a health care program, including disease management, drug distribution and monitoring (Garrett 2007). While conducting the baseline needs assessment, it became evident to the partnering agencies that there was both insufficient health infrastructure and an insufficient number of skilled health workers to effectively roll-out the program (Garrett 2007). The collaboration, with support from additional donors, delayed the roll-out of the program and, first invested in building laboratories and clinics, and recruiting and training health care staff. The ART initiative was finally launched in 2005. By 2006, it made ART available to an estimated 55,000 HIV + individuals in Botswana (Garrett 2007). Although the long-term sustainability of this program will be tied to the ability of Botswana's government to sustain the health care network and continue purchasing medications, this example shows that carefully considered collaborations can contribute to the broad mission of public health.

Another obvious advantage of public-private partnerships is that the risks and benefits associated with drug development are shared. Consider that only one percent of the new drugs discovered in the past 25 years targeted tropical disease (Nundy and Gulhati 2005). Global public-private partnerships provided mechanisms to encourage growth in R&D to target neglected diseases and the illnesses of the developing world. Such partnerships have indeed increased interest in drugs for the developing world. Along with such interest have come an increasing number of clinical trials being conducted in the developing world. Such trials allow for a more diverse study population, which more accurately represents the vulnerabilities that can contribute to differential impacts of various drug regiments, and can contribute to increased generalizability of clinical trial outcomes to potential beneficiaries in the developing world. Of course, not all trials are conducted in the developing world solely for such philanthropic purposes. The decreased expenses associated with carrying out clinical trials in developing countries provide a clear benefit to drug developers.

GPPPs can increase the credibility and authority of both public and private actors. Alliances with the public sector and with IGOs have increased the perceived legitimacy of private industry (Buse and Walt 2000b). They have also granted private sector actors a type of moral 'white-washing' in which their actions can be viewed as being based in social responsibility and philanthropy. By comparison, IGOs and government agencies have been seen to improve their own technical capacity through collaboration with private partners who specialize in specific areas. Also, the resources that were brought to bear for the improvement of public health through such partnerships were greater than any individual government or agency could muster on its own. As citizens see resources being made available to address their health needs and concerns, their trust can be built in the governing authority and national governance can be (re)legitimized so long as the public sector's involvement is communicated. Of course, these partnerships also increase the private sector's access to policy makers, and this sector's ability to influence the political decision-making (Buse and Walt 2000b). To the extent that the access provides two-way communication and that policy-makers benefit by developing a network of actors with diverse expertise, benefits may also accrue to the public sector. Where such access permits technical or scientifically-informed expertise to guide policy so that decisions are not merely political, such can be viewed as a pro.

Clearly, however, this access has a down-side. The access given to the private sector can indeed influence policy, and not necessarily in a positive or representative manner. One could argue that the political power gained by the private sector is much more valuable than the access to private networks gained by the public sector (Buse and Walth 2000b). In fact, the public-private relationships may threaten the perceived integrity and independence of public actors, IGOs and multilateral organizations (Buse and Walt 2000b). Much depends upon whom specifically is given access to the policy makers, and what such access provides. In the case of GPPPs, industry representatives draw from pharmaceutical companies largely based in the developed world. As such, representation from the developing world, and of developing world concerns is limited (Buse and Walt 2000b). The question of accountability remains, and has yet to be adequately addressed. A common normative framework could better guide relationships and appropriate actions on the part of both public and private actors. Although efforts have been made to establish such a framework for GPPPs, these efforts remain fragmented and adherence is voluntary.

The diseases and health issues that are targeted by the GPPPs are highly selective and may not address the most urgent issues within any single national context (Buse and Walt 2000b; Garrett 2007). A critique of GPPPs is that programs and goals are driven by donors; this can divert global and national resources from the main health issues of a particular context to issues of lower priority (Buse and Walt 2000b; Garrett 2007). Consider, for instance, the ramifications of a GPPP partnering with a MoH to address disease A. In order to participate, the MoH must commit a certain percentage of its fiscal resources to the disease. But in a context of scarce resources, little may be left to cover other programming costs, thereby leaving disease B, C and D uncontrolled. One must therefore be conscious of opportunity costs at national and international scales in addressing one health problem rather than another. Economic strength versus moral authority can create tensions within any partnership, and can also distort power relations, especially if economic strength carries more weight in determining program direction. One could argue that the balance of power in the partnership most favors the party which is least desperate. Those who represent regions where people are poor and dying may, perforce, rarely have negotiating power equal to that of those with money who are not facing imminent death or disability. They may therefore make compromises based on immediate needs and desperation rather than on the ideal of equal but different gains.

The risks and benefits of the GPPPs may not accrue equally to all partners. Fiscal stakes may be much greater for the public sector than the private sector (Buse and Walt 2000b). Public investment may be higher, especially in terms of initial costs, and more reliable than private sector commitments (Buse and Walt 2000b). The initial public investment helps to subsidize new innovations that the private industry will ultimately own. Although public investment may spur the research, the future profits may be controlled by the private entity (Buse and Walt 2000b). Further, the partnerships can strain public resources, and can build rather than decrease dependency (Buse and Walt 2000b).

6.5 Conclusion

GPPPs continue to evolve. They have unquestionably leveraged greater resources to address global issues of health, with the explicit and implicit inter-relation with development, than would have been harnessed without these partnerships. And yet, the mechanisms of such partnerships continue to change and the impacts of such partnerships, both for the better and for the worse, remain to be seen. The actors involved in each partnership have different motives and different goals. The partnership mandate is secondary to the mandates of each partner's individual organization and the motive of each partner may never be fully clear. This has been a topic of considerable debate especially as regards the motivation of private actors in global partnerships. Do the motives behind Merck & Co. donating ART to Botswana matter to those whose quality of life, indeed longevity, have improved because of the access? Probably not. Do they matter to other actors in the partnership? To the extent that such understanding can be helpful in negotiating division of labor and responsibilities in each partnership, perhaps. The utility depends upon the mandate with which each party is operating, which in turn will inform and be informed by the actors/sectors involved, the degree of integration necessary to achieve the goals of each partnership, and how these goals feed into broader national and international goals of improving health and development.

Questions of power relationships, financing and appropriate targeting of global public-private resources remain. In terms of financing, GPPPs are using multiple creative mechanisms to raise money from private individuals, charitable organizations, and larger donors. Yet the target of the funds is determined by the flow of information between poor and wealthy governments, firms and individuals, which is suggestive of an unequal playing field. The ability of disease-specific projects to be up-scaled, not geographically, but systematically, in a way that promotes overall health improvements and contributes to the cycle of economic growth and improved well-being, remains uncertain.

In terms of the achievements of these partnerships, much monitoring and evaluation remains. There is a moderate amount of data available in terms of short-term impacts of partnerships, such as the amount of money raised and the number of vaccinations/specific drugs distributed, all of which suggest positive achievements. To the extent that the GPPPs draw upon the integrated ideals of the MDGs to build sustainable human development, there is cause for optimism about what will be achieved in the long-term. And yet, the mid- and long-term impacts of such partnerships remain unknown. There are two avenues of inquiry—one of which looks at the impacts of specific partnerships, and the other which tries to understand the confluence of multiple programs and their impact on the global project of human development. But so many questions remain. Will the health program changes and increases in drug availability be sustainable? Will host governments be able to assume responsibility for the purchase and procurement of medications such as those used in ART once the subsidies and bulk purchasing efforts of GPPPs end? Will donor commitment to the programs be sustainable enough to transition lead authority from the GPPPs to the national governments? Will the attempts at changing price point of drugs through bulk purchasing successfully lower costs to the point where developing countries can afford to buy the drugs for an indefinite period of time? Will the partnerships targeting R&D for neglected diseases yield effective therapies, and will these therapies be available to low-income countries? Will the power relationships and decision-making authority of nation-states, IGOs and multilateral agencies be forever altered? And will such change contribute to a decrease in global poverty and an increase in human well-being? We simply do not yet know.

Discussion Questions

1. What are some of the reasons for the rise of global public-private partnerships in the late 20th and early 21st century?
2. What are the most important ethical considerations for conducting clinical trials in developing countries?
3. Describe two of the market-based mechanisms used by GPPPs to increase the availability of essential drugs in low income countries.

4. What actions will the Affordable Medicines Facility—Malaria (AMFm) use to try to increase access to anti-malarial medication?
5. What are the arguments against forced licensing of drug patents?
6. What are the arguments in favor of forced licensing?

References

Associated Press. (2007). Brazil to break Merck AIDS drug patent: Government wants lower price on anti-retroviral medication. MSNBC. http://www.msnbc.msn.com/id/18490388/. Accessed May 2, 2010.

Avert. (2010). AIDS, drug prices and generic drugs http://www.avert.org/generic.htm. Accessed on May 2, 2010.

Bodenheimer, T., & Grumbach, K. (2008). *Understanding health policy: A clinical approach* (5th ed.). New York: McGraw-Hill Medical.

Buse, K., & Walt, G. (2000a). Global public-private partnerships: Part I—A new development in Health. *Bull. W.H.O.*, 78(4), 549–561.

Buse, K., & Walt, G. (2000b). Global public-private partnerships: Part II—what are the health issues for global governance? *Bull. W.H.O.*, 78(5), 699–709.

Department of Health and Human Services. (2001). The globalization of clinical trials: A growing challenge in protecting human subjects. http://oig.hhs.gov/oei/reports/oei-01-00-00190.pdf. Accessed April 25, 2010.

The Economist. (2010). Spoonful of Ingenuity. *The Economist*. January 7.

Garrett, L. (2007). The Challenge of Global Health. *Foreign Affairs*. http://www.foreignaffairs.com/articles/62268/laurie-garrett/the-challenge-of-global-health. Accessed January 9, 2010.

GAVI Alliance. (2010) http://www.gavialliance.org/. Accessed April 19, 2010.

GAVI Secretariat. (2006). GAVI Alliance Strategy (2007–10). http://www.gavialliance.org/resources/GAVI_Alliance_Strategy__2007_2010_.pdf. Accessed April 3, 2010.

Glickman, S., McHutchison, J., Peterson, E., Cairns, C., Harrington, R., Califf, R., et al. (2009). Ethical and scientific implications of the globalization of clinical research. *The New England Journal of Medicine, 360*(8), 816–823.

Global Fund. (2010). The global fund: To fight AIDS, tuberculosis and malaria. http://portfolio.theglobalfund.org/?lang=en. Accessed May 21, 2010.

Institute for Health Metrics and Evaluation (IHME). Financing Global Health. (2015). *Development assistance steady on the path to new Global Goals* (p. 2016). Seattle, WA: IHME.

Joint United Nations Programme on HIV/AIDS (UNAIDS). (1998). Access to drugs: UNAIDS technical update. United Nations. http://data.unaids.org/Publications/IRC-pub01/jc111-accesstodrugs-tu01_en.pdf. Accessed April 2, 2010.

Joint United Nations Programme on HIV/AIDS (UNAIDS). (2008). UNAIDS: the first 10 years, 1996–2007. UNAIDS/07.20E/JC126E. Geneva: UNAIDS.

Joint United Nations Programme on HIV/AIDS (UNAIDS). (2009). Composition of the programme coordinating board. United Nations. http://data.unaids.org/pub/InformationNote/2009/pcb_members_updated_en.pdf. Accessed April 23, 2010.

Joint United Nations Programme on HIV/AIDS (UNAIDS). (2010). *The governance handbook*. Geneva: UNAIDS.

Loewenberg, S. (2008). Drug company trials come under increasing scrutiny. *Lancet, 371,* 191–192.

Lopez, A., Mathers, C., Ezzati, M., Jamison, D., & Murray, C. (Eds.). (2006). *Global burden of disease and risk factors*. New York: Oxford University Press.

Lurie, P., & Wolfe, S. M. (1997). Unethical trials of interventions to reduce perinatal transmission of the human immunodeficiency virus in developing countries. *The New England Journal of Medicine, 337*(12), 853–856.

Mathews, J. (2009). Power Shift. In R. W. Mansbach & E. Rhodes (Eds.), *Global politics in a changing world* (pp. 200–209). Boston: Houghton Mifflin Harcourt Publishing Company.

Mectizan® Donation Program. (2009). http://www.mectizan.org/history. Accessed April 20, 2010.

Unit, N. G. O., & Development, Social. (1998). *The bank's relations with NGOs: Issues and directions*. Washington, D.C.: The Social Development Family of the World Bank.

Nundy, S., & Gulhati, C. M. (2005). A new colonialism?—conducting clinical trials in India. *The New England Journal of Medicine, 352*(16), 1633–1636.

Samarasinghe, SWR. (2010). Personal communication. April 19, 2010.

Shapiro, H. T., & Meslin, E. M. (2001). Ethical issues in the design and conduct of clinical trials in developing countries. *The New England Journal of Medicine, 345*(2), 139–142.

Simmons, P. J. (2009). Learning to live with NGOs. In R. W. Mansbach & E. Rhodes (Eds.), *Global politics in a changing world* (pp. 210–215). Boston: Houghton Mifflin Harcourt Publishing Company.

UNAIDS—See Joint United Nations Programme on HIV/AIDS.

UN Global Compact Office. (2008). United Nations global compact: corporate citizenship in the world economy. United Nations. http://www.unglobalcompact.org/docs/news_events/8.1/GC_brochure_FINAL.pdf. Accessed April 20, 2010.

Wilson, D., Cawthorne, P., Ford, N., & Aongsonwang, S. (1999). Global trade and access to medicine: AIDS treatment in Thailand. *Lancet, 354,* 1893–1895.

World Commission on Environment and Development. (1987). Report of the world commission on environment and development: Our common future. http://www.un-documents.net/wced-ocf.htm. Accessed May 18, 2010.

World Health Organization. (1998). Selected topics in health reform and drug financing—health economics and drugs. WHO/DAP/98.3. Geneva: World Health Organization.

World Health Organization. (1999). WHO guidelines on collaboration and partnerships with commercial enterprises. Draft discussion document. Geneva: World Health Organization. Cited by Buse & Walt, (2000a), pg. 555.

World Health Organization. (2010). Control of Neglected Tropical Diseases. World Health Organization. http://www.who.int/neglected_diseases/en/. February 21, 2010.

World Health Organization, United Nations Children's Fund, and UNAIDS. (2010). Towards universal access: scaling up priority HIV/AIDS interventions in the health sector: Progress report 2008. http://www.who.int/hiv/topics/treatment/data/en/index.html. Accessed June 23, 2010.

Chapter 7
Conclusion

Abstract We have seen that health and development have multiple definitions and there are multiple approaches to obtaining them. No single perspective or approach is correct or can address every desirable aspect of the development enterprise. While in the past, health took a secondary position to economic development, that changed in the 21st century. We now see that sustainable development entails economic, social and environmental sectors and the concept of human development stresses the importance of human health and education as a constituent of economic growth. The Millennium Development Goals and Sustainable Development Goals approach health as being critical to the development process. Global collaborations now focus on development as a holistic process that entails economic and social aspects, with more resources are directed specifically towards health. The promise of the 21st century is to see new directions and new developments in the global endeavor of development. The challenge is to sustain these efforts.

7.1 Conclusion

Health, economic development and human development are inextricably linked. They are linked through the panoply of institutions and organizations whose actions, be they directed towards economic growth, building livelihoods, delivering medications or providing services at community clinics, are enabled only through a convergence of social and economic forces. They are linked because of the diverse sectors which create inputs to health conditions, to social conditions, to environmental conditions and to economic conditions that drive the greater endeavor of improving capabilities and choices for people and the societies they create. They are linked through a cycle in which human capabilities feed into avenues of economic growth. Likewise, the economic growth and the magnitude of national and household income create opportunities and resources to invest in the goods that enhance human capital and quality of life. Health, economic and human development are also connected across geographic and institutional scales. Policies and actions initiated at the global scale, and resources made available through networks

S.A. Johnson, *Challenges in Health and Development*,
DOI 10.1007/978-3-319-53204-2_7

of international actors, influence the reality of development and health experienced by large populations, by communities, by households and by individuals. Careful consideration of the impact global actions will have across these levels, and across the diversity of abilities and vulnerabilities contained within each, is therefore warranted. But the trajectory of health and development experienced in any one setting is not dictated solely through top-down policies or resource allocation. The actions of communities and individual enterprises contained therein can also resonate upward.

The macro perspective is the domain of policy concerns for of nation-states, IGOs and institutions that focus on national or supranational trends, forces and policies. This is the realm of national governments, of the United Nations, the World Bank, the WHO, and a growing number of public-private partnerships. The priorities and methods employed by the actors at this level create forces that shape and re-shape the global political economy. Changes in the global political economy and socio-cultural forces in turn create feedbacks to these macro actors. Consider, for instance, the policy re-alignment that took place in the global financial crisis in 2008 and 2009 which saw decrease of spending from developed countries, and dialogue about more restrictive rather than less restrictive regulation for transnational financial actions. Consider too, the dramatic uptick in global development funding for health as a result of the Ebola epidemic that began in 2014.

New policies continue to emerge in response to the ever changing global landscape. In the preceding chapters, we saw that macroeconomic theory guided much of the discussion about both health and development at this aggregated national and global level where considerable importance was placed on growing national income from which, it was believed, all good things would flow. The interest in income growth as a defining trait of development expanded to include a concern for poverty alleviation and building equity in the distribution of the economic goods. Although a small but persistent voice was given to the need for social stability and betterment of human health as factor in economic prosperity and global peace, it has only been in the last twenty years that more consistent, unified actions to address health as an input to development, economic and otherwise, has become a consistent operating principle for the global actors. It is only with the SDGs that explicit connections are made between development goals and preserving/protecting environmental quality.

As the macro views shift more inward, to conditions within the nation-state, comparisons are made between states and between diverse groupings within a state. Attention is paid to distribution of resources and of disease. Inequalities become more closely linked to manifestations of social systems, institutions, culture and the experience of inequality in suffering begins to take on a narrative. In our exploration of nation-states, we saw that national government differentially prioritize investment in economic development or investment in human development. In the case of Sri Lanka, human development took precedence whereas Chile focused on economic growth. Neither Sri Lanka, nor Chile, proved to be islands unto themselves. Global economic pressures co-mingled with domestic movements that created unsustainable fiscal demands upon each state. As a result, the governments of both states had to revise social and economic policy or go bankrupt. Both undertook economic liberalization. Both revised their health systems and continued these efforts today. Whereas the changes within the Sri Lankan health care system were initiated largely in response to internal calls for reform, the Chilean reforms were driven by neo-liberal economic principles and external pressures as well as internal need for change because of insolvency in the public welfare system. Although Chile achieved higher levels of economic growth than did Sri Lanka, both have comparable health outcomes. In terms of equity, Sri Lank is held to have greater equity than Chile although erosion in equity and quality of care threatens the system. We see in these cases that when we have a national level perspective, we gain details in the picture of health and development as compared to the global view, but much is still obscured.

It is at the local, community of 'sub-population' level where assessment goes beyond quantified measures of health and economic outcomes and seeks to incorporate unique community, cultural and individual experiences which inform the web of causation of well-being. Cultural context, world view, and differential vulnerabilities inform and shape the experience of health and human development. Individuals who make up the community translate numbers into a lived experience. Concern at the local level is focused not only on that which is 'health' but on the material, physical, mental and emotional resources which are necessary to heal, to survive or to thrive.

The local sphere is where one sees innovation and adaptation of health care and development that accounts for the unique strengths, challenges and opportunities of any specific context. Our local case studies are where we saw the seed of good ideas that used local evaluation of resources and challenges to inform program design. The local evaluation and programming incorporated the skills and priorities of local people into the creation of community health care and micro-enterprises that could successfully tackle problems in resource-efficient ways and, in so doing, contributed to the development process. The examples we reviewed a micro-credit program, community-based health care, and the multi-sectoral approach of the MDVs in terms of the ability of these programs to impact economic and human development at local and national levels. The small scale operations that proved successful offered lesson learned that can be employed when scaling up a program from its local base or when up-scaling a program to include a greater number of outcomes such as moving from disease-specific health care to improving primary health care. We saw in the MDVS, however, that local success does not always translate into dramatic change in national programming and that political commitment and shared responsibility across actors is critical.

There can, however, be a dangerous disconnect between local needs and the ability of any one government to meet these needs. This is especially evident in the context of failed, conflict-ridden or post-conflict states. In such a context, we saw that national and local actors were not always enough to restart the engines of human development. NGOs, both domestic and international, stepped into the void and provided the basic necessities for survival with an eye towards stabilization and eventual improvement in economic and social well-being. The largest challenge associated with such endeavors was integrating the resources and programs of disparate actors towards unified goals that would more effectively contribute to national prospects for development and ensure that such endeavors would become sustainable. No one approach proved to be the best. In Haiti, we saw Partners-in-Health/Zanmi LaSante build health capacity at a local clinic and eventually tie delivery of HIV-therapies to broader health goals of improved primary care, and broader national goals of improving human development. A grassroots approach proved both appropriate and successful. In Rwanda, however, it took a centralized, national plan for economic growth to prioritize health and to create an administrative structure that could bind together the resources of multiple donors and NGOs into a cohesive program to address national health priorities. We also learned that the incredibly fragility of these states means they are highly vulnerable to internal and external shocks. When Ebola emerged in three Western African nations, these countries were unable to contain the threat without external assistance. The epidemic had high costs in terms of human health, economic growth and political stability. Even as these countries enter the recovery phase, they have lost progress in economic and human development. These cases, perhaps more than any other, demonstrated how local, national and international actors benefit from relationships that cut across geographic and institutional scales. They also demonstrate that change takes time to realize and gains are indeed very fragile.

The recognition that by working together across sectors and institutions can achieve greater outcomes than can be gained by any one agency working alone, encouraged global public-private partnerships. Diverse configurations of public and private actors harness international resources and target them to national and local programs. We explored this trend in terms of GPPPs addressing issues of global health. What we saw is that there are numerous IGOs working with INGOs, NGOs, charities and pharmaceutical manufacturers to develop health interventions for diseases concentrated in the developing world, and increase global access to drug therapies for diseases such as HIV. The tools of these partnerships are varied ranging from donations to manipulating market forces, from helping strengthen public health infrastructure to subsidizing drug purchases for wholesalers. These initiatives transcend geographic and institutional scales, and draw together economic and health interests to provide for better health. While there are important criticism and concerns surrounding biases perceived to favor the private actors, it cannot be denied that these partnerships improved the health of thousands if not hundreds of thousands of individuals whose suffering would otherwise have gone unabated. The ultimate impact of these partnerships, in terms of human health, development, domestic and international policy, remains to be seen.

In summary, as we approach the enterprise of obtaining health and improving human and economic development, we need to be aware that health and development have multiple definitions and there are multiple approaches to obtaining them. There is not a single perspective or approach which is correct or can address every desirable aspect of the development enterprise. Recent history demonstrated that health often took a secondary position to economic development. But this is changing. The Brundtland Commission report posited that sustainable development entailed economic, social and environmental sectors. The concept of human development stresses the importance of human health and education as a constituent of economic growth. The Millennium Development Goals positioned multiple health outcomes as being critical to the development process. The Sustainable Development Goals fully realize the inextricable links between the economy, human well being, society and the environment.

Global collaborations are beginning to focus on development as a holistic process that entails economic and social aspects, with more resources directed specifically towards health. But the challenge of fully incorporating investment in human health into development efforts, and placing equal import on human development as that given economic development remains. The recent global financial downturn raised important questions about dominant economic theory and practice, questions that may inform a major shift in development practice. The global community is acting against persistent and pernicious infectious diseases such as HIV/AIDS, malaria and tuberculosis. However, there is a growing burden of chronic disease in the developed and developing world, the care of which has yet to be adequately addressed. There continues to be a critical shortage of supplies, human, fiscal and medical, to address the main causes of death and disability around the world, and poverty and inequity in well-being persist, but there is greater momentum now to address this gap than has been evident in the last 60 years. The 21st century promises to see new directions in the global endeavor of development.

Chapter 8
Discussion Question Answers

Abstract This chapter provides answers to the discussion questions in Chapters One to Seven.

8.1 Chapter One Questions

1. State security is concerned with the institutions and instruments necessary to preserve a nation-state whereas human security focuses on individuals living within a state.
2. Industrialization brought about environmental and social change. Factories and the mechanisms of industrialization were associated with high levels of air and water pollution, and were blamed for causing various types of disease. The working conditions in factories were criticized for being unsanitary, and the long working hours were considered exploitive, all of which raised public concern for inhumane treatment of factory workers. Also, many of the industries were located in or around cities. Laborers migrated from rural areas to the urban areas, causing rapid growth in the urban population and overcrowding. Conditions associated with urban squalor proliferated. In many places, there were overcrowding and a lack of sanitary facilities, both conditions that contributed to the rapid spread of infectious diseases.
3. In terms of state security, the political power of the colonizer was maintained through the presences of troops and administrative personnel. The health of the military was therefore an important area for investment in health. The preservation of health of civil administration, colonizers, and labor were also important in order to maintain political stability and fuel commercial activity. In some cases, the colonizers were operating in environments with completely alien ecosystems and therefore had to confront novel health challenges. This spurred investment in research and treatment of the indigenous illness and is one of the reasons why western powers invested in tropical medicine.
4. Maintaining a healthy workforce, is an example of where health becomes a concern for economic policy. Or, investing the income earned from economic growth into better living conditions, improved food, or the provision of health

S.A. Johnson, *Challenges in Health and Development*,
DOI 10.1007/978-3-319-53204-2_8

care shows how economic growth at the macro level can be used to invest in human capital. Examples from the text include the Panama Canal. In the case of the Panama Canal, investment in health decreased the death rates in the laborers building the canal. The high death rates due to infectious disease was one of the reasons for the failure of the earlier French attempt to build a canal.

5. Answers will vary.
6. Answers will vary.
7. Answers will vary. However, where data do not match, this may be due to slightly different indicators being employed, for example using GDP as opposed to GNI, or because of different methodology was used to gather or calculate the data.
8. Answers will vary.
9. Answers will vary.
10. Answers will vary. However, for the demographic transition, you should discuss changes in birth rates, or fertility rates, and infant mortality rates through time. You may also want to look at levels of urbanization and contribution of agricultural sector to the economy. In terms of the epidemiological transition, you should look at the main causes of death and disability in the country and whether or not these have changed over time. The time frames used should be at least twenty years.
11. The standard of living theory understands increased economic wealth leading to improved nutrition as being a central reason why life expectancy improved during the Industrial Revolution. Thus, the idea of economic growth is central to improved living conditions and provides a trickledown effect. By contrast, some argue that medical innovations, and improved access to the same, revolutionized health care in both prevention and treatment. Innovations includes not only the availability of medications, but the methods to impact public health, such as through water chlorination. One could argue that there is some overlap in that increased wealth and increased specialization allowed for greater investment in medical research. The imperative to maintain a healthy population, for economic reasons and due to the visibility of health problems in an urban context, may have greater public will to invest in health care.

8.2 Chapter Two Questions

1. Health can be considered a human right, with intrinsic value. It can also be viewed as an input to different outcomes such as economic growth or political stability. Lastly, it is viewed as an outcome of societal forces and factors such as public investment in health care, availability of food, etc.
2. Social medicine is concerned with social, political and economic factors that increase or decrease the individual's ability to procure inputs to good health, or mitigate risk factors for poor health. By couching health in a broader social

environment, social medicine accepts that health is not merely a product of individual status but rather, is influence by political, social, and economic forces outside of individual control. In other words, health is a product of the political economy. This difference suggests that improving health is not simply a matter of providing access to healthcare. Rather, it entails changing broad social aspects.

3. The inclusion of social insurance would have potentially ceded political and economic authority, a traditional realm of sovereignty, to an international body. The second argument is that biomedicine was only recently becoming professionalized in certain western countries. The newly organized professional bodies were becoming politically active and politically powerful. Professional societies were invested in maintaining domestic accreditation. It could also be argued that biomedicine was only one approach to health care and there was reticence to give this approach preference of place in the new international organization.
4. Maternal health outcomes include maternal death and disability associated with giving birth, and complications that occur during pregnancy and in the recovery period, usually 42 days after delivery, following the end of the pregnancy. One out of every four maternal deaths is due to complications related to pregnancy rather than to childbirth. Technocratic routes to decreasing maternal deaths include increasing the access to prenatal and antenatal care, as well as increasing access to trained birth attendants. Social routes may entail changing social norms to heighten the value of women independent of their reproductive abilities, increase recognition of risks associated with pregnancy, and/or increase knowledge and information about pre- and post-birthing care for the woman.
5. Although the obstacles to each vary, important differences include: some vaccinations require one to three administrations to confer (presumed) life-long immunity whereas maternal health requires continual access to services over the reproductive life of a woman; vaccinations are technological intervention which require only modest social changes whereas changes to maternal health interventions may require dramatic social change (e.g. consider access to abortion) and/or legal changes; vaccinations are comparatively low cost interventions whereas maternal care requires on-going funding. A final difference has to do with global political will—the control of infectious disease through vaccination would theoretically provide benefits not just to the geographic location in which vaccines were administered but rather to other states where people, and disease could spread. Even without 100% vaccination, herd immunity could be confirmed. Maternal mortality and morbidity are not contagious so the global public good associated with a decrease in maternal deaths is not as clearly visible as the global public good associated with immunization.
6. When first created in 1944, the World Bank's main mission was to finance the reconstruction of the post-war Europe and parts of Asia. Today, it is the leading development agency providing loans, grants and technical expertise. It is also highly involved in debt management. By comparison, the IMF was initially established to promote international monetary cooperation, to encourage the expansion of global trade and to facilitate exchange rate stability. The IMF

changed its direction with the end of the Bretton-Woods system in the early 1970s when the U.S. moved from the gold standard and, subsequently, international exchange rates were no longer pegged to the US dollar/gold standard. The IMF further adapted to the oil and debt crises of the 1970s and 1980s when it began trying to address long-term balance of payment issues and began focusing on long-term debt issues and macro-economic restructuring through intensive loan operations and structural adjustment programs.

7. Structural adjustment programs are tools used by the World Bank and IMF to try to instill macro-economic stability in debt-ridden nations or nations struggling with balance of payment deficits. Recipients of loans under the SAPs agreed to adopt specific policies, the loan conditionalities. These included reducing fiscal deficits by reducing public expenditures, free-floating the country's currency—an action that often causes currency devaluation, privatizing government holdings, and liberalizing the market through such actions as trade barrier reduction.
8. The purpose of decentralizing health care was to allow for the delivery of more effective and cost efficient health care by allowing local authorities to determine what goods and services would be supplied based on locally defined needs. While shifting authority to local areas had positive benefits, among them local empowerment and increased resources from primary and secondary care, not all program aspects were successful. In some cases, the local human capacity was not sufficient in terms of management skills or in terms of the availability of trained medical personnel, who tended to migrate to urban areas. There continued to be a shortage of both essential medicines and medical equipment in some regions. Another problem was that market conditions were such that in some rural areas, the cost of providing care actually increased with decentralization. Some efforts to privatize health care financing and provision failed because of a lack of competition, and because of the small size of the (isolated) markets which failed to create an economy of scale.
9. Answers will vary.
10. The peace dividend allowed nations to focus on freedom from want as a route to preserve peace. At the same time, the HIV/AIDS epidemic is/way taking a toll on human development, economic and state security.
11. Several of the SDGs speak to similar issues as did the MDGs, and incorporate targets. One of the main differences is that many of the MDGs had clear numerical goals and deadlines whereas the SDGs are more open-ended without absolute targets.

8.3 Chapter Three Questions

1. Although answers to this will vary, it can be argued that nation-states are not human and so cannot feel pain. Further, they are made up of many individuals

and the actions of individuals and institutions, and so can absorb a larger degree of ill-health, poverty, etc. than can any one individual or even household without suffering negative consequences. The two, however, are linked because a state can only function so long as its citizens support the institutions of state and contribute labor to the engines necessary to maintain a state… such as labor through which income can be generated, service in the military through which borders and institutions are protected, and so forth.

2. Answers will vary.
3. In the case of Chile, early investment in health created a costly system riddled with inequity. Funds set up in the early part of the 20th century became financially unsustainable for the government by the 1970s, and were also not able to provide adequate income or support for some of those covered by the welfare system. The financial insolvency was due in part to the size of the program and in part because of changes in national revenues. There were large disparities in terms of access to health care even for those with public insurance. Sri Lanka's health care system provided greater equity in coverage, but was also financially unsustainable over time because the demand for coverage grew with an increase in population concurrent to a contraction of foreign earnings due to a collapse in international prices for agriculture.
4. Chile engaged in neoliberal reforms that included fiscal restraint that included cutting the amount of public money invested in social programs, market liberalization and privatization, and decentralization of public services including health care. Public and private health financing mechanisms and providers were established, with employed individuals given a choice as to which fund they preferred to pay into. Because of the lack of government regulation, the private funds tended to attracted healthier and wealthier individuals whereas the public fund became responsible for more of the elderly, more women, and the poorer segment of the population, thereby skewing the risk pool such that public revenues would likely not cover the costs for care.
5. Answers will vary.
6. The most important difference in the Sri Lanka's health care system was that coverage was universal prior to market liberalization, and that access was equally strong in rural and urban areas. The market liberalization helped to stabilize the balance of payment deficit, thus avoiding absolute failure of public healthcare. However, the amount of money dedicated to the health sector decreased following the reforms. The decrease in financing is linked to a deterioration in perceived quality of some services, and growth in private delivery of ambulatory care. Likewise, following market liberalization, the food subsidies decreased—a move that improved the financial sustainability of the program.
7. Answers will vary.

8.4 Chapter Four Questions

1. Answers will vary.
2. Positive aspects of community-based health care include better targeting of services to match medical needs of the local population, improved ability to design programs that are culturally-appropriate and acceptable, therefore potentially contributing to increased buy-in of the program, increased local hiring and increased program legitimacy, potential to improve costs for health care personnel and program delivery, and, in some causes. Such programs may also contribute to improving human development by providing medical and management training to local residents.
3. The death meetings provide a forum for medical staff, family, neighbors, and others to discuss the processes that may have contributed to preventable early death. In so doing, there is open dialogue surrounding the immediate cause(s) of death, as well as the cumulative events that led to the death… such as delays in seeking medical care, recognizing risky pregnancies, prolonged under nutrition, and so forth. The open dialogue allows for members of the social network to learn about appropriate health care and about supports necessary for pregnant or recently-delivered women and neonatal. It also allows for collective problem solving, and communal education. The messages about prevention and good health may be better (re)enforced through the social network. That network can also foster the ideal of mutual responsibility and accountability.
4. The use of solidarity groups is similar in many ways to the death meetings in that each member of the group becomes invested in the success of other group member's entrepreneurial activity. There is social support and a social network that is invested in each project succeeding. This may result in increasing resources for each of the entrepreneurial activities and so a network for poverty alleviation is formed. Solidarity group members also learn from one another, and have mutual accountability.
5. The initial agricultural subsidy, with the expectation of decreasing subsidy and further investment, is one example. As a farmer raises a larger crop yield, s/he will be able to purchase inputs without the subsidy and will continue to invest in improved seed and agricultural practice. This will allow for continued accumulation of wealth which can be reinvested in diverse crops, crops for market. Also, raising household income will improve opportunities for household members. Other examples include positive cycles from stabilizing health by elimination of malaria, or improvement of child survival.
6. Answers will vary.
7. Answers will vary.

8.5 Chapter Five Questions

1. In the short term, state failure and conflict causes a loss of public revenue, a loss of private investment, human and capital flight, and diversion of public resources to military endeavors or to a small sector of society (through

corruption and political patronage). If failure becomes conflict, there may be an immediate loss of human life and infrastructure. In the long term, health continues to suffer and public health problems that may have been controlled before conflict may no longer be controlled. Public revenues that could have been invested in human development end up being used to rebuild shattered infrastructure. Economic growth that stagnated under the war may not come back quickly because the inputs to such growth were destroyed. These inputs can include physical structures as well as social and psychological necessities such as faith in the governing institutions and social stability. With little investment or economic growth, few public goods can be provided. Further, the disruption of social life, and destruction of physical goods, can set a society back to pre-conflict stages in terms of health needs and economic achievements. In the long term, psychological issues may also plague the population.

2. Answers will vary.
3. Prior to the introduction of zidovudine, there was no anti-retroviral therapy available to the clientele of the clinic. Thus, testing for HIV meant that one could learn they had a death sentence but there was nothing to be done to delay that sentence. Psychologically, one could say there was little incentive for individuals to be tested. With the availability of zidovudine, two changes occurred. First, pregnant women who tested positive for HIV now had access to a medical means to prevent transmission of HIV to their unborn children. Second, there was hope that the ravages of the disease for the individual could be staved off.
4. The programs had several elements in common. These include hiring and training local staff, targeting the diseases which accounted for the greatest amount of morbidity and mortality at the local level for prevention and treatment, providing maternal-child health care, maintaining staff in the local clinic, and providing in-patient and out-patient services and community education. Both programs used cyclical planning and, while targeting specific health problems, address health in terms of a 'community syndrome' in which socio-economic conditions interact with physical and mental health.
5. Answers will vary.
6. Answers will vary.
7. Answers will vary.
8. Answers will vary.

8.6 Chapter Six Questions

1. Reasons for the rise of GPPPs include globalization that allowed for increased exchange of goods, people, and ideas; the realization that in the globalized world, health and economic problems in one country cannot easily be isolated and that solving these problems requires coordinated action across public and

private sectors; reaffirmation that infectious disease spreads rapidly and impacts both the developed and developing world; changes in the perceived role, capabilities and legitimacy of IGOs; changes in the perception of a nation-state's ability to address health issues; a rising number of INGOs; acknowledgement of the special skills and resources available to the private sector, especially private companies involved in drug research and development; visible successes in terms of public-private partnerships such as EPI; movement in the development paradigm to include sustainable human development and social responsibility; increased credence given to transnational issues such as global climate change, pollution, and the health-security nexus, to name a few.

2. Although the answers to this question will vary, the chapter focused considerable discussion on the idea of standard of care in clinical trials, especially equivalency trials, and what type of care will be available to test subjects at the conclusion of the trial. Other considerations include what constitutes informed consent and coercion, especially within the context of conducting research in poor populations that may not otherwise be able to access medical care, or who may receive medication in a trial that are worth more than the individual's annual income. There are also ethical considerations regarding whether or not the drug or therapy being tested will be available or affordable in the nation/community of the trial pending successful completion of the research.
3. The answers to this question will vary but may include aggregating demand (such as employed by the GAVI alliance) that seeks to lower price points through bulk purchasing. Advanced market commitments operate in a similar manner, by drawing together current and future demand for certain medications, the purchaser increased the demand and may force down the cost. Such mechanism also alleviates the drug developer of some financial risk so can spur investment in drug development.
4. The Affordable Medicines Facility—Malaria (AMFm) is using money from the Global Fund to subsidize a bulk purchase of anti-malarial medication. This medication will be resold, through wholesalers, at lower than market prices to countries most heavily impacted by resistant strains of malaria.
5. Those who argue against forced licensing say that it is in both corporate interest and in the interest of public good to protect the financial operations of drug manufacturers. Developing new drugs is a time consuming and costly process. In order for there to be R&D, drug manufacturers must have some small assurance that they will be able to recoup their investment costs through pricing mechanisms of developed drugs. The price points generally include costs to cover the development of the specific drug as well as costs of R&D on the numerous products that never make it to market. Without such guarantee, drug manufacturers risk huge financial loses and may not be willing to invest in R&D of drugs needed in markets/countries that ignore patent protections.
6. Arguments in favor of forced licensing are couched in terms of health as a human right and human security. If a drug exists to prolong life, or cure a patient of a disease, it is a moral imperative to provide that drug to the patient regardless of intellectual property rights designed to protect corporate profit. Governments

have an obligation to protect the health of its citizens. When the magnitude of the health is great, the government has a greater obligation to take action to protect its people that it does to protect non-corporeal entities and financial security of any corporation. If drugs to alleviate the public health threat exist, but are priced too high for purchase, a government should therefore seek out a manufacturer to reproduce the drug at a lower cost. Further, untreated health problems may create problems of both human and state security and so addressing the issue serves national and international interests.

Index

S.A. Johnson, *Challenges in Health and Development*,
DOI 10.1007/978-3-319-53204-2

The manufacturer's authorised representative in the EU is Springer Nature Customer Service Centre GmbH, Europaplatz 3, 69115 Heidelberg, Germany. If you have any concerns regarding our products, please contact ProductSafety@springernature.com

Printed and bound by CPI Group (UK) Ltd, Croydon, CR0 4YY
30/09/2026
02225236-0001